ALTERNATIVE SCHOOLS

Ideologies, Realities, Guidelines

ALTERNATIVE SCHOOLS

Ideologies, Realities, Guidelines

Terrence E. Deal
Robert R. Nolan
Editors

NELSON-HALL
CHICAGO

Library of Congress Cataloging in Publication Data
Main entry under title:

Alternative schools.

    1. Free schools—Addresses, essays, lectures.
2. Education—Experimental methods—Addresses,
essays, lectures. I. Deal, Terrence E. II. Nolan,
Robert R.
LB1029.F7A44   371   78–18505
ISBN 0–88229–383–4 (*cloth*)
ISBN 0–88229–613–2 (*paper*)

Manufactured in the United States of America

10   9   8   7   6   5   4   3   2   1

To all those risk-takers—students, teachers, parents, and administrators—who have the courage to experiment with new approaches to learning

CONTENTS

ACKNOWLEDGMENTS

The task of preparing this book began in 1975 when the two of us compared our experiences in alternative schools. We agreed that a selective compilation of some of the current literature in this area would indeed be helpful to people planning and operating alternative schools and to those who simply want to know more about these new educational institutions.

As we moved from this initial agreement to the final stages of preparing this book, we have been assisted by a number of people.

First, without the cooperation of contributors, this book would not exist. As we surveyed the alternative school literature, we noted a good deal of what we considered to be exemplary work. At the same time, we felt that the work in print could be usefully augmented by ideas and experiences that had not yet been published. We are especially grateful to our many colleagues who were able to take time away from other pressing activities to write original articles for this book.

Second, we are grateful for the helpful criticism provided by colleagues at various points in our task of compiling and editing this material. Prominent among these critics have been: Sandra N. Deal, Sue Simmons, Pat Fitzgerald, Pauline Zemaitis, Jean Rosaler, Polly Hildebrand, and Dan Duke. Pauline Zemaitis made substantial editorial suggestions.

Third, we would have been lost without the assistance of people who typed manuscripts, obtained permissions, performed countless other tasks, and contended with our various trials and tribulations. Chief among these was Shirley Weitz, who carried an immense share of this burden. Larry Brillson, Barbara Wigton, Beth Ziegler, and Sue Simmons also contributed more than their fair share. Bruce Harlow, Director of Publication and Dissemination, Center for Educational Research at Stanford, provided initial guidance as we approached the publishing world.

CONTRIBUTORS

JEFF AMORY is with the National Alternative Schools Program, School of Education, University of Massachusetts.

RONALD BARNDT is a mathematics teacher, Murray Road School, West Newton, Massachusetts.

HELEN CAREY teaches at Torrens College of Advanced Education, South Australia.

CENTER FOR NEW SCHOOLS, Chicago, is a nonprofit organization whose purpose is to improve the quality of urban public education.

JOAN CHESLER, formerly a Research Associate with the Educational Change Team at the University of Michigan, is now teaching and consulting on a volunteer basis.

LAWRENCE A. CREMIN is President of Teachers College, Columbia University.

TERRENCE E. DEAL is Associate Professor, Harvard Graudate School of Education.

JOHN DEWEY (1859-1952) was one of America's leading educational philosophers.

SANFORD M. DORNBUSCH is Professor of Sociology, Stanford University.

DANIEL LINDEN DUKE is Assistant Professor of Education, Stanford University.

MARIO D. FANTINI is Professor and Dean of the Faculty of Education, State University College, New Paltz, New York.

MARYFRANCES CRABTREE teaches at Francis W. Parker School, Chicago.

KATHY GROSS is an undergraduate at Stanford University.

FRANCISCO HERNANDEZ teaches in the Chicano Studies Program, University of California (Berkeley).

KATHY HUGUENIN is a research assistant at the Center for Educational Research at Stanford and a Ph.D. candidate, School of Education, Stanford University.

DAVID L. JOHNSON is Codirector of Walden III, Racine, Wisconsin.

BRIAN McCAULEY is with the American School, Lima, Peru.

DAVID MURPHY is Coordinator of the Alternative School in Cubberly, Palo Alto, California.

GARY NATRIELLO is a research assistant at the Center for Educational Research at Stanford and a Ph.D. candidate, School of Education, Stanford University.

A. S. NEILL (1883-1973) was the founder and Headmaster of Summerhill, Leiston, England.

ROBERT R. NOLAN is Principal of Mar Vista Continuation High School and Opportunity School, Ventura Unified School District, Ventura, California.

JACKSON V. PARKER is Codirector of Walden III, Racine, Wisconsin.

MORTIMER SMITH is a Director of the Council for Basic Education, Washington, D.C.

JOHN THEROUX is with the National Alternative Schools Program, School of Education, University of Massachusetts.

J. KELLY TONSMEIRE is the Director of the Charles County/University of Maryland Teacher Corps Project.

TOM WOLF is with the National Alternative Schools Program, School of Education, University of Massachusetts.

BARRY WOOD is a former junior high school teacher.

1
An Overview of Alternative Schools
by Terrence E. Deal and Robert R. Nolan

The Landscape and a New Perspective

The middle 1960s saw the beginnings of a new movement in American education. Large numbers of new institutions, developing first outside and then increasingly within the public system, were established as alternatives to regular public schools.

In some respects alternative schools are merely old wine in new skins— alternatives to the "official" state schools have existed since the beginning of public education in this country. But historically, these alternatives have been largely limited in access (private schools) and/or scope (parochial schools). Moreover, most of these schools have often prided themselves in covering essentially the same territory as public schools, but doing it better and with more "style."

In other respects, however, the new generation of "free," or alternative, schools, is different. Such schools are "almost always the results of voluntary grass-roots efforts to build schools where children and young people are not oppressed by arbitrary discipline and total power characteristic of most public schools and where the possibilities for experimenting and searching for new and better ways for children to live and learn can be explored" (Graubard 1972, p. x).

In addition to their grass-roots character and novel curricular and instructional patterns these new alternative schools depart significantly from traditional patterns of school organization. Students, teachers, and often parents in alternative schools are given more access to decision making and have more influence than they do in regular public schools. Some think that this departure from bureaucratic patterns is the distinguishing feature of modern alternative schools (Duke 1975).

Although alternative schools are having and will continue to have a marked impact on the field of education, we actually know little about them. There is a voluminous amount of literature which either extols the virtues or denigrates the basic character of alternative schools. But there simply is not much in the growing literature of alternative schools which approaches these new institutions theoretically, describes them empirically, or provides operational guidelines based on thoughtful analysis or case studies. Filling that gap is the main goal of this book.

This introductory chapter has three sections:

The first section sketches the alternative school landscape. We demographically explore the terrain by (1) looking briefly into the historical roots of alternative schools; (2) exploring the proliferation of alternative schools; (3) noting the expansion of alternative school ideas into state educational policies; and (4) probing the apparent instability of many alternative schools.

The second section constructs a conceptual map intended to help people find their way in the rough, relatively unexplored, alternative school terrain. We do this by developing a perspective which views alternative schools as complex, dynamic organizations based on existing educational ideologies. In developing this perspective we (1) note the importance of ideologies; (2) identify four predominant educational ideologies; (3) identify the essential features of school organizations, and how they interact with the four ideologies to produce four types of schools; and (4) suggest some implications of this perspective for organizing and operating alternative schools.

The third section provides an orientation to the rest of the book, describing how subsequent parts are laid out to provide detailed information for those who wish to design and implement a new alternative school or to improve an existing school which may have begun without the benefit of existing knowledge or some lessons of the past.

SECTION ONE
The Alternative School Landscape

Historical Roots

The historical roots of the alternative school movement are diverse. While these schools have not, consciously at least, built on the experiences of the past, they seem to espouse a number of themes comparable to those of the progressive education movement (Dewey 1915; Cremin 1961). These themes include:

a. the individual student's needs and experiences as a beginning point (personalization of education)

b. the teacher as advisor

c. the school as a social community—education is seen as a social activity

d. active rather than passive learning

e. a variety of learning resources, especially using those of the local community

f. skills as a means, not an end

g. student participation in at least some of the major decision making of the school

h. the individuality of both students and teachers.

Undoubtedly, the current alternative school movement drew much of its energy from the broad social critiques of the 1960s. Among the prominent social targets of this criticism were educational institutions. While much of this criticism focused on the multiple failings of America's public schools (Graubard 1972), some went beyond polemics to develop positive models of how they thought schools should be reformed.

Many of the new schools which developed under the social critique umbrella followed the nondirective model described by A. S. Neill in his widely read book—*Summerhill—A Radical Approach to Child Rearing.* Many of the early reformers seized upon this model claiming to have found the best and only way to educate children. Hence, the spread of "free" schools. But actually implementing Summerhillian ideas proved difficult. Most educators failed in their attempts to apply this model outside the isolated estate of Summerhill, in settings stocked with "regular" students, and run by personnel less exceptional than Neill.

Moving beyond these early failures (and some hard-won successes), some educators began to experiment with different models. With this experimentation, the one best approach idea died. Instead of claiming to have found the *best* way to educate *all* children, many members of the alternative school movement advanced more modest claims of having developed *better* ways to educate *some* children. The newer image was based on the belief that "different students learn best in different ways" (Roslyn Public Schools 1974, p. 1). The "free" schools were thus replaced by "alternative" schools—a label which includes many diverse educational approaches and practices. Some alternative schools are organized within the public sector while others, following the lead of the early free schools, continue to operate as private schools.

The Spread of Public Alternative Schools

According to many sources, the number of public alternative schools is rapidly increasing. While there is no definitive catalog of public alternative schools, the International Consortium on Options in Public Education (ICOPE) at Indiana University estimates that "the number of public alternative schools in operation by September, 1975, may well be as high as 5,000" (Barr 1975, p. 3). Significantly, "this vast experimentation is occurring during one of the most difficult periods that public education has ever faced. School districts throughout the country are currently confronted with declining enrollments, escalating inflationary costs, and shrinking tax dollars. While school districts are eliminating high school athletic programs, reducing music and art programs, terminating support services and personnel, enlarging average class size, and closing schools; communities continue to initiate new alternative schools in increasing numbers" (Barr 1975, pp. 3–4). While ICOPE's typology provides few hints about basic organizational or instructional characteristics, it does provide a breakdown of the 1,250 known public alternative schools.

Types of Public Alternative Schools*
(percentage of 1975 total)

Continuation Schools	20
Learning Centers	18
School-Within-Schools	17
Open Schools	15
Schools Without Walls	6
Alternative School Clusters	5
Multi-Cultural Schools	4
Free Schools	3
Others (too difficult to type)	12

*Source: Robert D. Barr, "The Growth of Alternative Public Schools, The 1975 ICOPE Report," *Changing Schools* XII (1975):9.

In 1974 the National Alternative Schools Program (NASP) of the University of Massachusetts conducted a survey of over 300 alternative schools (Wolf et. al., 1975). This survey revealed that over 60 percent of the programs were begun during the previous three years and that over 80 percent were less than five years old. On the average, six months were spent in planning before their doors opened for the first time. Most of the programs were small (less than 200 students); only 12.6 percent had over 500 students. Over 60 percent of the students enrolled came from urban areas. "The fact that only one third of the students are from suburban areas tends to dismiss the impression, still prevalent among many school administrators, that alternative schools are synonomous with suburban free schools. The overall student population within alternative schools breaks down as 64 percent white and 36 percent nonwhite. (These figures, incidentally, are consistent with the percentages for the total school populations within the systems surveyed)." (Wolf et al. 1975, p. 4.)

Although the quantitative increase of alternative schools is documented by these figures, their essential characteristics and *modus operandi* remain obscure. Some empirical work sheds light on such patterns and processes. McCauley, Dornbusch, and Scott (1971) have shown that evaluation systems and task emphases in nonpublic alternative schools are different from those in regular public schools. Duke (1975) has shown that decision-making processes in alternative schools differ from those in conventional schools. But essentially the operational world of alternative schools remains a mystery shrouded, in part, by the diversity of alternatives and the lack of unifying conceptual schemes to assist in classification and evaluation. What one educator may see as a strength, another may consider a critical problem; what one researcher singles out for special attention may be ignored by another.

Some tentative conclusions, however, can be made about the role of public alternative schools. Such schools *have* provided options to thousands of students. Their presence has been the impetus for many reforms in the traditional schools. On some indicators they seem to outperform traditional schools. For example, many alternative schools claim to experience little or no vandalism, less absenteeism, and fewer dropouts than traditional schools. This is treated by many as concrete evidence that students who attend alternative schools have a more positive attitude toward their education. This concrete evidence is bolstered by "testimonials" of many parents, students, and teachers who claim that alternative schools are decidedly superior to their traditional counterparts.

Extension of Ideas into State Policies

The alternative school movement is having an increasing impact on state legislation and educational policy. California, for example, has recently passed a bill (California Senate Bill 445, 1975), authored by state senator John F. Dunlap, which requires that a school district inform parents of their right to request the establishment of an alternative school within the district. Moreover, this bill requires that boards of education actually consider such requests. Alternative schools, as defined by the bill, are schools which (1) address a wide range of student needs—including the development of affective characteristics; (2) emphasize student interests and self-motivation; (3) provide opportunities for parents, students, and teachers to cooperatively determine the course of the school; and (4) encourage a constant reassessment of the program in response to a rapidly changing world. The bill stipulates that alternative schools can request waivers of any provision of California's Education Code (except earthquake provisions), which would hamper their design and operation.

The California State Department of Education was also engaged in a major effort to reform intermediate and secondary education in the state (RISE). Although vetoed, the proposed RISE legislation provided general guidelines for reform including personalized learning, parent and student participation in school governance, competency-based instruction, interpersonal and vocational as well as cognitive goals, and the use of the community as a learning environment. These characteristics can be found in many alternative schools. Although the proposed legislation gave school sites considerable latitude in developing the specifics of reform, many alternative school ideas can be easily identified in California's RISE framework.

The Instability of Alternative Schools

Despite the proliferation of alternative schools and the adaptation of many alternative ideas by state departments of education, the other side of the coin reveals some problems and instabilities.

The proselytizing, messianic zeal of many alternative school participants often not only blinds them to serious problems within their programs but alienates school board members and administrators who ultimately decide the life or death of most alternative schools. As noted earlier, the movement suffers from a shortage of well-designed, systematic studies of different programs. Internal difficulties usually plague typical alternative schools at one time or another and, unless effectively dealt with, they are a key factor in the demise of many alternative schools (Deal 1975). Many alternative schools lack a systematic guiding philosophy and, overall, the movement is decidedly ahistorical. Many of the problems alternative schools face are encapsulated by Wolf et al. (1975):

> The early romance with the notion of 'freeing the children" [has been] replaced by hard ideological and economic struggles. School superintendents [have] lost their jobs over the issue, Teacher Unions [are beginning] to mobilize against non-traditional personnel practices. If the fad is over, what remain[s] as viable education reform . . .?

As alternative schools continue to proliferate and as alternative school ideas are increasingly legitimized and extended by state agencies, it is critical that those charged with their organization and operation have the knowledge and tools to confront and resolve the unavoidable problems. Many of these problems are unpredictable. Consequently, it is difficult to plan, implement, and maintain an alternative school following a cookbook recipe. Alternative school participants need to add a pinch of this, a dash of that, taste, and reevaluate as the school evolves. But to do this, they need to think systematically about the complex task they have undertaken.

SECTION TWO
A Conceptual Map for Alternative Schools

One of the weaknesses of the alternative school movement is its heretofore tenuous link to history, philosophy, or the social sciences. The absence of such linkages has made it difficult to look systematically at alternative schools and has undoubtedly created some operational problems for alternative school participants.

We believe that alternative school participants need a framework for analyzing educational philosophies, identifying aspects of social organization, and seeing how the two are linked to produce a setting which will, positively or negatively, influence the behavior of all the participants. Such a framework may help provide teachers, administrators, students, and parents ways to define problems and develop alternative courses of action. Our assumption is that melding alternative school ideas with philosophical and organizational concepts (something the existing alternative school literature by and large does not do) will provide participants ways of thinking about the problems that implementing such ideas will inevitably entail. We don't think a recipe approach will work. Rather we think each alternative school will need to develop or "tailor make" its own unique plan of organization and action based on the local availability of ingredients and tools as well as a continuing assessment of desired outcomes.

We don't believe our framework is the only way to view alternative schools. We do think it may be useful to those who wish to create a new institution or to make an existing institution into an alternative school.

The Importance of Ideologies

Ideologies are the intellectual patterns of any culture or movement. An ideology conditions what individuals believe and value, and generally how they view the world. Ideologies influence how people relate to one another, how they behave, and what they expect. Ideologies are transmitted by music, literature, the media, and word of mouth. Ideologies are reflected in institutions and affect institutional goals and norms, and they help define important structural, and even technical, patterns within organizations.

For example, the counterculture revolution of the 1960s can be viewed as a challenge to the then predominant ideology—"Big is bad," "If it feels good, do it," and "Do your own thing" were slogans which reflected the emphasis of the counterculture ideology (Roszak 1969). However, the revolution was never entirely successful in replacing the prevailing ideology. The end result was a set of mutually incompatible, but peacefully coexistent, ideologies. Consequently, social institutions in the 1970s are confronted with and influenced by at least two ideologies or a curious synthesis of the two. Organizations are often staffed with people who hold different ideologies. Ideological wars—the battle between Archie Bunker and the "meathead"—are common features of most modern institutions. Ideological inconsistencies often give organizations mixed messages about their mission or the means through which that misson will be achieved.

Four Existing Educational Ideologies

We have identified four existing educational ideologies which, we think, influence educational organizations (Kohlberg and Mayer 1972). These patterns of thinking influence instructional approaches, student-teacher interaction, curriculum content, organizational structure, and all other facets of life in schools. Each of these ideologies has different sources, metaphors, conceptions of students, ideas about learning, and emphases. These four ideologies are summarized in Figure 1.

The first ideology represents the traditional pattern of educational thinking. In the "school as filling station," new students are empty vessels

Figure 1
Four Educational Ideologies*

	School as a Filling Station	School as a Garden	School as a Tool	School as a Market Place
Sources	The "classicists." Traditional academics	The "romanticists." Rousseau; Neill	The "revolutionists."	The "progressives." Dewey
Metaphor	Kids as empty vessels	Kids as plants	Kids as agents of social change	Kids as philosophers, bargaining agents, and problem solvers
Source of Knowledge	Outside	Inside	The new regime	Interaction between inside and outside
Main task of schools	Transmit to present generation bodies of information, rules, and values of the past	Create a permissive environment in which innate qualities can unfold	Change the society. Create individuals for a new social order	Create an environment that will nourish a natural conflict or negotiation between students and society
Emphasis	Traditional; established	Unique, novel, and personal	Using the school as a lever for effecting social change	Resolvable but genuine problems or conflicts between the established and the emerging

*This figure is based, in part, on the conceptualization of Kohlberg and Mayer (1972).

9

to be filled by the wisdom of the ages. The next three ideologies represent patterns of thought which have more commonly influenced alternative schools. The "school as a garden" ideology reflects many of the ideas and values of the countercultural revolution of the 1960s. From this vantage point students are viewed as "flowers" who, if left alone, will blossom forth. As a variation of this theme, the "school as a tool" ideology emphasized the potential of schools as an instrument for bringing about social change. Schools are seen as a means to a more just social order; students are seen as change-agents.

The "school as a market place" ideology came out of the progressive movement of the 1930s and, although itself an alternative ideology, represents in many respects a synthesis of the "school as a filling station" and "school as a garden" perspectives. Schools are seen as a market place in which students engage in a continual transaction with social beliefs, values, and information.

In practice, of course, those ideologies are rarely found in pure form. Some schools, run by "true believers," probably come close. Generally, however, the ideologies are combined in diverse ways yielding eclectic approaches. Inconsistencies, conflict, and indecision may characterize individuals or organizations who strongly espouse more than one.

The Organizational Setting of Schooling

Educational ideologies become embodied, intentionally or unintentionally, in educational organizations. Like all organizations (Udy 1957), schools have five major components or subsystems: goals, technologies, formal structures, informal patterns and norms, and an environment. Goals are generally statements of purpose which give a school a direction; technologies are the instructional practices, approaches, and programs which are employed to reach these goals; formal structures define the roles of students, administrators, and teachers, and help determine how these roles relate to one another; informal patterns and norms interact with the formal structure to keep determined what "really goes on" in a school, and the environment consists of everything external to a school—parents, community people, and other organizations—to which a school must relate in carrying out its principal tasks. Educational ideologies potentially have an impact on each of the organizational components in schools.

Paralleling the four educational ideologies described previously there are four basic models of educational organizations. Each model is produced by applying the values, beliefs, and ideas of a particular ideology to the five parts of a school's organization. In reality, of course, one would probably not find these models in their pure form. As organizations, schools are loose collectives (Meyer and Rowan 1975) and thus may contain individuals who operate from different ideological perspectives. It is also possible that one aspect of school organization may be unaffected by another. A school, for example, could have a "tight" formal structure and a "loose" instructional program. As with individuals, however, schools probably lean toward one ideology or another. But some schools may contain smaller departments, pods, or units each of which operates from a radically different ideological base.

The first organizational model represents the application of the classical or "school as a filling station" ideology. This is the traditional school organization which processes age-graded batches of students through a fairly regimented set of activities. Within a classroom the teacher makes instructional decisions and the student follows them. Within a school the principal makes decisions which teachers are expected to carry out. Informal patterns, separated from the formal structure, emphasize autonomy and competition. The school's internal workings by and large are buffered from the community. See Figures 2 and 3.

The "do your own thing" school organization is typical of many schools which were begun in the early 1960s. Following the "school as a garden" ideology such schools exist primarily to provide a protected place for students to grow on their own. What students learn as well as how, when, and where they learn it varies according to individual wants and whims. Within the classroom, students make instructional decisions with little input or interference from teachers. Teachers, in fact, are defined as "fellow learners." Schoolwide decisions are normally made by consensus within the "innercommunity." Because of the "loose" formal structure informal norms become exceedingly important. Such norms emphasize freedom, harmony, and "if it feels right, do it."

The "revolutionary" school, based on the "school as a tool" ideology, emphasizes the role of school in changing society. The program emphasizes the acquisition of the doctrine, tools, and techniques for accomplishing social change. Students are expected to become change-agents. The teacher's role is highly autocratic. And the school, itself, is usually run by a single individual or small group which is responsible for interpreting the revolutionary doctrine around which the school is intimately structured. The informal norms like the formal structure are infused with the revolutionary

Figure 2

Figure 2
The ''Traditional'' School Organization

GOALS:

Transmit Knowledge and Traditional Cultural Values and Norms

PROGRAM:

—Age-graded ''batches'' of students move through discipline-based courses.

—The teacher lectures, students recite and are tested on their ''knowledge.''

—Emphasis is on existing knowledge.

FORMAL STRUCTURE

—Schoolwide: Decisions are made and conflicts resolved by hierarchical superiors. Evaluations occur at the end of a program or performance. Roles divided by age or subject areas.

—Classroom: Teacher makes instructional decisions (objectives, activities, evaluation). Teacher active, student passive

ENVIRONMENT:

Learning and the central decisions of the school ''buffered'' from immediate environment

INFORMAL PROCESSES AND NORMS:

—Separated from the formal structure of the school

—Autonomy of the individual teacher

—Competition

Figure 3
The ''Do Your Own Thing School'' Organization

GOALS:

Remove barriers to ''natural'' acquisition of knowledge and personal growth

PROGRAM:

—Students individually learn whatever captures their interest at that moment

FORMAL STRUCTURE

Schoolwide:

—Little or no formal authority

—Decisions made by consensus

—Conflicts resolved in similar manner

—No formal evaluation

Classroom:

—Students choose objectives and activities

—Students initiate, teachers respond

ENVIRONMENT:

—Used as site for learning

—Either totally interpenetrates decision-making aspects of school

or

—Buffered from school

INFORMAL PROCESSES AND NORMS:

—Since there is little formalization, informal norms are extremely important

—''If it feels right, do it.''

—Freedom

—Harmony

doctrine. The community environment is seen as a thing to be acted upon. Having the environment eventually conform to the basic philosophy and structure of the school is the primary aim.

The "negotiation school," fostered by the beliefs and values of the "school as a market place" ideology, exists to provide an environment which produces "real-life" problems which students ultimately solve. The school often resembles the "do your own thing school"; but in the negotiation school, what is learned is determined by a tension between what a student "wants" and what he "needs." Structurally, the negotiation school is a mixture of authority, autonomy, and consensus. Some schoolwide decisions are made in a hierarchical fashion; others are made by consensus. In the classroom teachers and students make some decisions jointly; others are made by the students individually. See Figures 4 and 5.

Figure 4
The "Revolutionary" School Organization

GOALS:	PROGRAM:
Use the school to change society; shape students into change-agents	Students learn the doctrine and techniques to bring about major social change.
	Emphasis on doctrine and proper social consciousness

FORMAL STRUCTURE

Schoolwide: Authority wielded by a single individual or small group which interprets the revolutionary doctrine.

Classroom: Teachers are responsible for developing the students as change-agents, imparting to them relevant doctrine and technique.

ENVIRONMENT:	INFORMAL PROCESSES AND NORMS:
Viewed as the target of the school's central activities	Influenced heavily by revolutionary doctrine; "The end justifies the means."

The teacher expands options although the student ultimately decides objectives, activities, and evaluation criteria. The tension between the teacher and student roles represents the heart of the negotiation school approach. Informal norms are integrated with the formal structure and emphasize cooperation, interdependence, and conflict as a natural process. The community environment is intimately connected with the school. It is

Figure 5
The Negotiation School Organization

GOALS:	PROGRAM:
Provide an environment where students can interact with and solve problems	—Students individually participate in a variety of activities worked out jointly between teachers and students
	—Competency-based contracts
	—Learning takes place at diverse times and in a variety of locations
	—Emphasis on a tension between what kids want and what they need

FORMAL STRUCTURE

Schoolwide:
—Some decisions made by consensus, others by hierarchical superiors
—Various strategies for resolving conflicts. Clear-cut distinctions between who makes which decisions and how various kinds of conflicts are resolved
—Emphasis on continuous evaluation to improve programs or performance

Classroom:
—Teachers and students make decisions jointly—objectives, activities, and evaluation criteria. Students active in making individual decisions.
—Teachers active in developing options.
—Negotiation.

ENVIRONMENT:	INFORMAL PROCESSES AND NORMS:
—Used as a site for learning	—Cooperation
—Formal channels for bringing community and parents into decision making	—Interdependence
—Specific roles and responsibilities for community and parent ''teachers''	—Conflict as natural process
	—Integration of informal and formal

used as a site for learning to increase the market-place-of-educational-transactions atmosphere of the school.

Implications

The four educational ideologies and their derived models of school organization have several implications for designing and implementing alternative schools.

1. Educational ideologies will influence the organizational character of an alternative school either intentionally or unintentionally. Many problems can be avoided if a systematically developed ideology is used to guide the planning of a school's organization.

2. All individuals—administrators, students, teachers, and parents—have definite ideological leanings. Moreover, since most people are eclectic, ideological inconsistencies within the same individual are common. Many teachers will charge off with "do your own thing" goals, later becoming confused and depressed as they evaluate their

role behavior by the more traditional criteria of the "school as a filling station" ideology. In beginning a school it may be helpful to confront these differences and inconsistencies head-on.

3. Each model of school organization has certain benefits, but also certain costs. When designing an alternative school, participants should weigh the costs and benefits, ultimately choosing a pattern of school organization that best fits the needs of a particular situation —and meshes with existing ideologies.

4. When designing an alternative school, each aspect of the organization should be considered initially as a separate entity. What goals do we want to pursue? What should the instructional program look like? How, or in what ways, should the community be involved? What formal and informal patterns of roles and relationships will make the best use of our human resources?

5. Once the different parts of the school organization have been developed separately, they should be considered as a whole. Will the instructional technology achieve the desired goals? Does the formal structure provide ample support for the instructional activities? Will the direct involvement of parents in the classroom violate any informal norms? Will the presence of students in the community cause problems and conflict?

6. When a new school moves from the planning board to reality, it is important to keep in mind the relationship between ideologies and the organization as well as the interrelationships between the various organizational aspects of the school.

When the school becomes tangible, it may run afoul of other ideologies—either within or external to the school. When a "do your own thing" school becomes a reality, for example, it often produces a negative reaction from parents and community members who are accustomed to the "rigid factory" patterns.

7. When any aspect of the school organization changes, it has implications for all the rest. Increasing the level of student influence in making instructional decisions has an impact on the instructional program and often broadens the scope of educational goals.

8. Some organizational models are stable; others are not. Within our culture, for example, the "traditional" school and the "negotiation" school have the benefit of tradition. And in some respects they represent a more coherent package from an organizational standpoint. The "do your own thing" model, on the other hand, may be highly

unstable in our culture. Previous speculation has suggested that such schools, once implemented, pass through distinct stages ultimately (1) closing, (2) becoming "traditional," or (3) developing the characteristics of "negotiation" schools (Deal 1975).

9. The critical question for those wishing to design an alternative school is: which model—or mixture thereof—do we want our school to become? The subsidiary question is: Can we pull it off given our skills, resources, and the prevailing educational ideologies?

SECTION THREE
How This Book Is Organized

Part I: "Ideologies" presents five articles. Four discuss the educational ideologies noted above and the fifth provides a plan for all to peacefully coexist. After reading these selections, readers will hopefully be able to identify the major elements of each ideology and fit their own some place into the overall ideological scheme.

Part II: "Realities" is a series of case studies of different kinds of alternative schools. The cases cover some examples of what to do and what to avoid in starting and operating an alternative school. Upon completing this section, we would expect readers to have acquired both an appreciation for the difficulties involved in making an alternative school work and some concrete ideas for avoiding some of the common pitfalls.

Part III: "Guidelines for the Future" contains a series of articles that cover the various aspects of organizing and operating an alternative school. Suggestions are provided for planning, problem solving, evaluation, in-service training, decision making, and other activities which are crucial in successfully implementing or changing an alternative school.

References

Barr, Robert D. "The Growth of Alternative Public Schools: The 1975 ICOPE Report." *Changing Schools* XII (1975):3. Bloomington, Indiana: International Consortium for Options in Public Education.

Cremin, Lawrence A. *The Transformation of the School.* New York: Vintage Books, 1961.

Deal, Terrence E. "An Organizational Explanation of the Failure of Alternative Schools." Stanford Center for Research and Development in Teaching. Stanford, Calif.: Stanford University, 1975.

Dewey, John, and Evelyn Dewey. *Schools of Tomorrow.* New York: E. P. Dutton, 1915.

Duke, Daniel Linden. "Challenge to Bureaucracy: The Contemporary Alternative School." *The Journal of Educational Thought* X, 1 (April 1976): 34–48.

Graubard, Allen. *Free the Children.* New York: Vintage Books, 1972.

Kohlberg, Lawrence, and Rochelle Mayer. "Development as the Aim of Education," *Harvard Educational Review* XXXXII, 4 (November 1972): 449–96.

McCauley, B. L., S. M. Dornbusch, and W. R. Scott. "Evaluation and Authority in Alternative Schools and Public Schools." Stanford Center for Research and Development in Teaching. Stanford, Calif.: Stanford University, 1972.

Meyer, John W., and Brian Rowan. "Notes on the Structure of Educational Organizations: Revised Version." Paper presented at the Annual Meeting of the American Sociological Association, San Francisco, August 1975. Stanford, Calif.: Stanford Center for Research and Development in Teaching.

Neill, A. S. *Summerhill—A Radical Approach to Child Rearing.* New York: Hart, 1960.

Rosak, Theodore. *The Making of a Counter Culture.* New York: Doubleday, 1969.

Roslyn Public Schools. *Progress Report on the School-Within-A-School Program.* Roslyn, New York. January 21, 1974.

Udy, Stanley H., Jr. "The Comparative Analysis of Organizations," in James G. March, ed., *The Handbook of Organizations.* Chicago: Rand McNally, 1965.

Wolf, Thomas E., Michael Walker, and Robert A. Mackin. *Summary of the NASP Survey, 1974.* Amherst, Mass.: University of Massachusetts, 1975.

Part 1
IDEOLOGIES

Educational ideologies or philosophies play a central role in educational debates. From the perspective of one ideology or another, educational practices are praised or criticized. In recent years ideological conflict has been particularly sharp. This conflict has been essentially among four competing ideologies, each of which is represented in Part I by a selected reading. The fifth selection outlines a plan by which all ideologies could find expression in the public schools.

The first selection, "Traditional vs. Progressive Education," is by John Dewey, who developed the "school as a market place" ideology. Dewey criticizes the rigid *either-or* character of the debate between progressive and traditional educators and develops his own ideology of the "middle." In Dewey's mind, education is an active transaction between students and the society. The key to learning is experience, but experience which leads somewhere. Many activities of traditional or progressive schools are "miseducative" because they are disconnected—either from the learner or from man's cumulative experience.

The second selection is by A. S. Neill, the most influential proponent of the "school as a garden" ideology. No work has had a greater impact on the alternative school movement than Neill's *Summerhill: A Radical Approach to Child Rearing*. Neill not only advocated a radical approach to schooling, but also described how one school had embodied such practices and functioned for almost forty years. In "The Idea of Summerhill," taken from *Summerhill,* Neill emphasizes that schools must be fashioned to fit

19

the child rather than vice versa. He takes this position because of his belief that schools have traditionally been reflections of an oppressive, hateful society whereas children are basically good. Schools should thus let students develop their natural talents and interests rather than attempt to direct and regiment them.

While Neill was aware that schools like Summerhill could lead to social change, others made social change or even revolution the cornerstone of their educational ideologies. Barry Wood in the third reading, "Free Schools and The Revolution," presents a somewhat strident example of the "school as a tool for social change" ideology. (Wood wrote during a period when alternative schools were known by many as "free" schools, a term since largely abandoned for the less value-ladened, more encompassing label "alternative" schools.)

The Council for Basic Education has been an influential advocate of the "school as a filling station"—the fourth main educational ideology. From this perspective, schools have a clearly limited function: the teaching of certain basic intellectual skills and the transmission of our cultural heritage. Mortimer Smith, in "CBE Views the Alternatives," argues that most alternative schools depart from this basic function. Recently, however, an increasing number of public alternative schools have been established to implement the educational ideology which Smith articulates (see "The Hoover Structured School" in Part II: Realities).

Moving beyond particular ideologies, Mario Fantini in the final selection, "Alternatives in the Public Schools," outlines a plan for a system of public schools which would incorporate a variety of educational ideologies. Fantini's argument is based on the assumption that *no one* ideology will be appropriate for *all* parents and students. In Fantini's system, parents and students choose the school whose ideology and methods best meet their needs. Fantini suggests a set of guidelines to implement and run such a system of choice. These guidelines are those which most in the alternative school movement are now working to have adopted by local school districts.

2

Traditional v. Progressive Education
by John Dewey

Mankind likes to think in terms of extreme opposites. It is given to formulating its beliefs in terms of *Either-Ors,* between which it recognizes no intermediate possibilities. When forced to recognize that the extremes cannot be acted upon, it is still inclined to hold that they are all right in theory but that when it comes to practical matters circumstances compel us to compromise. Educational philosophy is no exception. The history of educational theory is marked by opposition between the idea that education is development from within and that it is formation from without; that it is based upon natural endowments and that education is a process of overcoming natural inclination and substituting in its place habits acquired under external pressure.

At present, the opposition, so far as practical affairs of the school are concerned, tends to take the form of contrast between traditional and progressive education. If the underlying ideas of the former are formulated broadly, without the qualifications required for accurate statement, they are found to be about as follows: The subject-matter of education consists of bodies of information and of skills that have been worked out in the past; therefore, the chief business of the school is to transmit them to the new generation. In the past, there have also been developed standards and rules of conduct; moral training consists in forming habits of action in

*From *Experience and Education* (New York: Macmillan Co., 1939). Reprinted by permission of the copyright owner, Kappa Delta Pi, An Honor Society in Education, Box A, West Lafayette, Indiana 47906.

conformity with these rules and standards. Finally, the general pattern of school organization (by which I mean the relations of pupils to one another and to the teachers) constitutes the school a kind of institution sharply marked off from other social institutions. Call up in imagination the ordinary schoolroom, its time-schedules, schemes of classification, of examination and promotion, of rules of order, and I think you will grasp what is meant by "pattern of organization." If then you contrast this scene with what goes on in the family, for example, you will appreciate what is meant by the school being a kind of institution sharply marked off from any other form of social organization.

The three characteristics just mentioned fix the aims and methods of instruction and discipline. The main purpose or objective is to prepare the young for future responsibilities and for success in life, by means of acquisition of the organized bodies of information and prepared forms of skill which comprehend the material of instruction. Since the subject-matter as well as standards of proper conduct are handed down from the past, the attitude of pupils must, upon the whole, be one of docility, receptivity, and obedience. Books, especially textbooks, are the chief representatives of the lore and wisdom of the past, while teachers are the organs through which pupils are brought into effective connection with the material. Teachers are the agents through which knowledge and skills are communicated and rules of conduct enforced.

I have not made this brief summary for the purpose of criticizing the underlying philosophy. The rise of what is called new education and progressive schools is of itself a product of discontent with traditional education. In effect it is a criticism of the latter. When the implied criticism is made explicit it reads somewhat as follows: The traditional scheme is, in essence, one of imposition from above and from outside. It imposes adult standards, subject-matter, and methods upon those who are only growing slowly toward maturity. The gap is so great that the required subject-matter, the methods of learning and of behaving are foreign to the existing capacities of the young. They are beyond the reach of the experience the young learners already possess. Consequently, they will use devices of art to cover up the imposition so as to relieve it of obviously brutal features.

But the gulf between the mature or adult products and the experience and abilities of the young is so wide that the very situation forbids much active participation by pupils in the development of what is taught. Theirs is to do and learn, as it was the part of the six hundred to do and die. Learning here means acquisition of what already is incorporated in books and in the heads of the elders. Moreover, that which is taught is thought of as essentially static. It is taught as a finished product, with little regard either to the ways in which it was originally built up or to changes that will surely occur in the future. It is to a large extent the cultural product of societies that assumed the future would be much like the past, and yet it is used as educational food in a society where change is the rule, not the exception.

If one attempts to formulate the philosophy of education implicit in the practices of the newer education, we may, I think, discover certain common principles amid the variety of progressive schools now existing. To imposition from above is opposed expression and cultivation of individuality; to external discipline is opposed free activity; to learning from texts and teachers, learning through experience; to acquisition of isolated skills and techniques by drill, is opposed acquisition of them as means of attaining ends which make direct vital appeal; to preparation for a more or less remote future is opposed making the most of the opportunities of present life; to static aims and materials is opposed acquaintance with a changing world.

Now, all principles by themselves are abstract. They become concrete only in the consequences which result from their application. Just because the principles set forth are so fundamental and far-reaching, everything depends upon the interpretation given them as they are put into practice in the school and the home. It is at this point that the reference made earlier to *Either-Or* philosophies becomes peculiarly pertinent. The general philosophy of the new education may be sound, and yet the difference in abstract principles will not decide the way in which the moral and intellectual preference involved shall be worked out in practice. There is always the danger in a new movement that in rejecting the aims and methods of that which it would supplant, it may develop its principles negatively rather than positively and constructively. Then it takes its clue in practice from that which is rejected instead of from the constructive development of its own philosophy.

I take it that the fundamental unity of the newer philosophy is found in the idea that there is an intimate and necessary relation between the process of actual experience and education. If this be true, then a positive and constructive development of its own basic idea depends upon having a correct idea of experience. Take, for example, the question of organized subject-matter—which will be discussed in some detail later. The problem for progressive education is: What are the place and meaning of subject-matter and of organization *within* experience? How does subject-matter function? Is there anything inherent in experience which tends toward progressive organization of its contents? What results follow when the materials of experience are not progressively organized? A philosophy which proceeds on the basis of rejection, of sheer opposition, will neglect these questions. It will tend to suppose that because the old education was based on ready-made organization, therefore it suffices to reject the principle of organization *in toto,* instead of striving to discover what it means and how it is to be attained on the basis of experience. We might go through all the points of difference between the new and the old education and reach similar conclusions. When external control is rejected, the problem becomes that of finding the factors of control that are inherent within experience. When external authority is rejected, it does not follow that all authority should be rejected, but rather that there is need to search for a more effective source of authority. Because the older education imposed the knowledge, methods, and the rules of conduct of the mature person upon the young, it does not follow, except upon the basis of the extreme *Either-Or* philosophy, that the knowledge and skill of the mature person has no directive value for the experience of the immature. On the contrary, basing education upon personal experience may mean more multiplied and more intimate contacts between the mature and the immature than ever existed in the traditional school, and consequently more, rather than less, guidance by others. The problem, then, is: how these contacts can be established without violating the principle of learning through personal experience. The solution of this problem requires a well-thought-out philosophy of the social factors that operate in the constitution of individual experience.

What is indicated in the foregoing remarks is that the general principles of the new education do not of themselves solve any of the problems of the actual or practical conduct and management of progressive schools. Rather, they set new problems which have to be worked out on the basis of a new philosophy of experience. The problems are not even recognized, to say nothing of being solved, when it is assumed that it suffices to reject the ideas and practices of the old education and then go to the opposite extreme. Yet I am sure that you will appreciate what is meant when I say that many of the newer schools tend to make little or nothing of organized subject-matter of study; to proceed as if any form of direction and guidance by adults were an invasion of individual freedom, and as if the idea that education should be concerned with the present and future meant that acquaintance with the past has little or no role to play in education. Without pressing these defects to the point of exaggeration, they at least illustrate what is meant by a theory and practice of education which proceeds negatively or by reaction against what has been current in education rather than by a positive and constructive development of purposes, methods, and subject-matter on the foundation of a theory of experience and its educational potentialities.

It is not too much to say that an educational philosophy which professes to be based on the idea of freedom may become as dogmatic as ever was the traditional education which is reacted against. For any theory and set of practices is dogmatic which is not based upon critical examination of its own underlying principles. Let us say that the new education emphasizes the freedom of the learner. Very well. A problem is now set. What does freedom mean and what are the conditions under which it is capable of realization? Let us say that the kind of external imposition which was so common in the traditional school limited rather than promoted the intellectual and moral development of the young. Again, very well. Recognition of this serious defect sets a problem. Just what is the role of the teacher and of books in promoting the educational development of the immature? Admit that traditional education employed as the subject-matter for study facts and ideas so bound up with the past as to give little help in dealing with the issues of the present and future. Very well. Now we have the problem of discovering the connection which actually exists *within* experience between the achievements of the past and the issues of the present. We have the problem of ascertaining how acquaintance with the past may be translated into a potent instrumentality for dealing effectively with the future. We may reject knowledge of the past as the end of education and thereby only emphasize its importance as a *means*. When we do that we have a problem that is new in the story of education: How shall the young become acquainted with the past in such a way that the acquaintance is a potent agent in appreciation of the living present?

... In short, the point I am making is that rejection of the philosophy and practice of traditional education sets a new type of difficult educational problem for those who believe in the new type of education. We shall operate blindly and in confusion until we recognize this fact; until we thoroughly appreciate that departure from the old solves no problems. What is said in the following pages is, accordingly, intended to indicate some of the main problems with which the newer education is confronted and to suggest the main lines along which their solution is to be sought. I assume that amid all uncertainties there is one permanent frame of reference: namely, the organic connection between education and personal experience; or, that the new philosophy of education is committed to some kind of empirical and experimental philosophy. But experience and experiment are not self-explantory ideas. Rather, their meaning is part of the problem to be explored. To know the meaning of empiricism we need to understand what experience is.

The belief that all genuine education comes about through experience does not mean that all experiences are genuinely or equally educative. Experience and education cannot be directly equated to each other. For some experiences are miseducative. Any experience is miseducative that has the effect of arresting or distorting the growth of further experience. An experience may be such as to engender callousness; it may produce lack of sensitivity and of responsiveness. Then the possibilities of having richer experience in the future are restricted. Again, a given experience may increase a person's automatic skill in a particular direction and yet tend to land him in a groove or rut; the effect again is to narrow the field of further experience. An experience may be immediately enjoyable and yet promote the formation of a slack and careless attitude; this attitude then operates to modify the quality of subsequent experiences so as to prevent a person from getting out of them what they have to give. Again, experiences may be so disconnected from one another that, while each is agreeable or even exciting in itself, they are not linked cumulatively to one another. Energy is then dissipated and a person becomes scatterbrained. Each experience may be lively, vivid, and "interesting," and yet their disconnectedness may artificially generate dispersive, disintegrated, centrifugal habits. The consequence of formation of such habits is inability to control future experiences. They are then taken, either by way of enjoyment or of discontent and revolt, just as they come. Under such circumstances, it is idle to talk of self-control.

Traditional education offers a plethora of examples of experiences of the kinds just mentioned. It is a great mistake to suppose, even tacitly, that the traditional schoolroom was not a place in which pupils had experiences. Yet this is tacitly assumed when progressive education as a plan of learning by experience is placed in sharp opposition to the old. The proper line of attack is that the experiences which were had, by pupils and teachers alike, were largely of a wrong kind. How many students, for example, were rendered callous to ideas, and how many lost the impetus to learn because of the way in which learning was experienced by them?

How many acquired special skills by means of automatic drill so that their power of judgment and capacity to act intelligently in new situations was limited? How many came to associate the learning process with ennui and boredom? How many found what they did learn so foreign to the situations of life outside the school as to give them no power of control over the latter? How many came to associate books with dull drudgery, so that they were "conditioned" to all but flashy reading matter?

If I ask these questions, it is not for the sake of wholesale condemnation of the old education. It is for quite another purpose. It is to emphasize the fact, first, that young people in traditional schools do have experiences; and, secondly, that the trouble is not the absence of experiences, but their defective and wrong character—wrong and defective from the standpoint of connection with further experience. The positive side of this point is even more important in connection with progressive education. It is not enough to insist upon the necessity of experience, nor even of activity in experience. Everything depends upon the *quality* of the experience which is had. The quality of any experience has two aspects. There is an immediate aspect of agreeableness or disagreeableness, and there is its influence upon later experiences. The first is obvious and easy to judge. The *effect* of an experience is not born on its face. It sets a problem to the educator. It is his business to arrange for the kind of experiences which, while they do not repel the student, but rather engage his activities and nevertheless, more than immediately enjoyable since they promote having desirable future experiences. Just as no man lives or dies to himself, so no experience lives and dies to itself. Wholly independent of desire or intent, every experience lives on in further experiences. Hence the central problem of an education based upon experience is to select the kind of present experiences that live fruitfully and creatively in subsequent experiences.

Later [in the book *Experience and Education*] I shall discuss in more detail the principle of the continuity of experience or what may be called the *experimental continuum*. Here I wish simply to emphasize the importance of this principle for the philosophy of educative experience. A philosophy of education, like any theory, has to be stated in words, in symbols. But so far as it is more verbal it is a plan for conducting education. Like any plan, it must be framed with reference to what is to be done and how it is to be done. The more definitely and sincerely it is held that education is a development within, by, and for experience, the more important it is that there shall be clear conceptions of what experience is. Unless experience is so conceived that the result is a plan for deciding upon subject-matter, upon methods of instruction and discipline, and upon material equipment and social organization of the school, it is wholly in the air. It is reduced to a form of words which may be emotionally stirring but for which any other set of words might equally well be substituted unless they indicate operations to be initiated and executed. Just because traditional education was a matter of routine in which the plans and programs were handed down from the past, it does not follow that progressive education is a matter of planless improvisation.

The traditional school could get along without any consistently developed philosophy of education. About all it required in that line was a set of abstract words like culture, discipline, our great cultural heritage, etc., actual guidance being derived not from them but from custom and established routines. Just because progressive schools cannot rely upon established tradition and institutional habits, they must either proceed more or less haphazardly or be directed by ideas which, when they are made articulate and coherent, form a philosophy of education. Revolt against the kind of organization characteristic of the traditional school constitutes a demand for a kind of organization based upon ideas. I think that only slight acquaintance with the history of education is needed to prove that educational reformers and innovators alone have felt the need for a philosophy of education. Those who adhered to the established system needed merely a few fine-sounding words to justify existing practices. The real work was done by habits which were so fixed as to be institutional. The lesson for progressive education is that it requires in an urgent degree, a degree more pressing than was incumbent upon former innovators, a philosophy of education based upon a philosophy of experience.

I remarked incidentally that the philosophy in question is, to paraphrase the saying of Lincoln about democracy, one of education of, by, and for experience. No one of these words, *of, by,* or *for,* names anything which is self-evident. Each of them is a challenge to discover and put into operation a principle of order and organization which follows from understanding what educative experience signifies.

It is, accordingly, a much more difficult task to work out the kinds of materials, of methods, and of social relationships that are appropriate to the new education than is the case with traditional education. I think many of the difficulties experienced in the conduct of progressive schools and many of the criticisms leveled against them arise from this source. The difficulties are aggravated and the criticisms are increased when it is supposed that the new education is somehow easier than the old. This belief is, I imagine, more or less current. Perhaps it illustrates again the *Either-Or* philosophy, springing from the idea that about all which is required is *not* to do what is done in traditional schools.

I admit gladly that the new education is *simpler* in principle than the old. It is in harmony with principles of growth, while there is very much which is artificial in the old selection and arrangement of subjects and methods, and artificiality always leads to unnecessary complexity. But the easy and the simple are not identical. To discover what is really simple and to act upon the discovery is an exceedingly difficult task. After the artificial and complex are once institutionally established and ingrained in custom and routine, it is easier to walk in the paths that have been beaten than it is, after taking a new point of view, to work out what is practically involved in the new point of view. The old Ptolemaic astronomical system was more complicated with its cycles and epicycles than the Copernican system. But until organization of actual astronomical phenomena on the ground to the latter principle had been effected the easiest course was to follow the line of least resistance provided by the old intellectual habit. So we come back to the idea that a coherent *theory* of experience, affording positive direction to selection and organization of appropriate educational methods and materials, is required by the attempt to give new direction to the work of the schools. The process is a slow and arduous one. It is a matter of growth, and there are many obstacles which tend to obstruct growth and to deflect it into wrong lines.

3

The Idea of Summerhill
by A. S. Neill

This is a story of a modern school—Summerhill.

Summerhill was founded in the year 1921. The school is situated within the village of Leiston, in Suffolk, England, and is about one hundred miles from London.

Just a word about Summerhill pupils. Some children come to Summerhill at the age of five years, and others as late as fifteen. The children generally remain at the school until they are sixteen years old. We generally have about twenty-five boys and twenty girls.

The children are divided into three age groups: The youngest range from five to seven, the intermediates from eight to ten, and the oldest from eleven to fifteen.

Generally we have a fairly large sprinkling of children from foreign countries. At the present time (1960) we have five Scandinavians, one Hollander, one German, and one American.

The children are housed by age groups with a house mother for each group. The intermediates sleep in a stone building, the seniors sleep in huts. Only one or two older pupils have rooms for themselves. The boys live two or three or four to a room, and so do the girls. The pupils do not have to stand room inspection and no one picks up after them. They are left free. No one tells them what to wear: they put on any kind of costume they want to at any time.

---

*From *Summerhill—a Radical Approach to Child Rearing* by A. S. Neill (New York: Hart Publishing Co., copyright 1960). Reprinted by permission of the publisher.

Newspapers call it a "Go-as-you-please School" and imply that it is a gathering of wild primitives who know no law and have no manners.

It seems necessary, therefore, for me to write the story of Summerhill as honestly as I can. That I write with a bias is natural; yet I shall try to show the demerits of Summerhill as well as its merits. Its merits will be the merits of healthy, free children whose lives are unspoiled by fear and hate.

Obviously, a school that makes active children sit at desks studying mostly useless subjects is a bad school. It is a good school only for those who believe in *such* a school, for those uncreative citizens who want docile, uncreative children who will fit into a civilization whose standard of success is money.

Summerhill began as experimental school. It is no longer such; it is now a demonstration school, for it demonstrates that freedom works.

When my first wife and I began the school, we had one main idea: *to make the school fit the child*—instead of making the child fit the school.

I had taught in ordinary schools for many years. I knew the other way well. It was wrong because it was based on an adult conception of what a child should be and of how a child should learn. The other way dated from the days when psychology was still an unknown science.

Well, we set out to make a school in which we should allow children freedom to be themselves. In order to do this, we had to renounce all discipline, all direction, all suggestion, all moral training, all religious instruction. We have been called brave, but it did not require courage. All it required was what we had—a complete belief in the child as a good, not an evil, being. For almost forty years, this belief in the goodness of the child has never wavered; it rather has become a final faith.

My view is that a child is innately wise and realistic. If left to himself without adult suggestion of any kind, he will develop as far as he is capable of developing. Logically, Summerhill is a place in which people who have the innate ability and wish to be scholars will be scholars; while those who are only fit to sweep the streets will sweep the streets. But we have not produced a street cleaner so far. Nor do I write this snobbishly, for I would rather see a school produce a happy street cleaner than a neurotic scholar.

What is Summerhill like? Well, for one thing, lessons are optional.

Children can go to them or stay away from them—for years if they want to. There *is* a timetable—but only for the teachers.

The children have classes usually according to their age, but sometimes according to their interests. We have no new methods of teaching, because we do not consider that teaching in itself matters very much. Whether a school has or has not a special method for teaching long division is of no significance, for long division is of no importance except to those who *want* to learn it. And the child who *wants* to learn long division *will* learn it no matter how it is taught.

Children who come to Summerhill as kindergarteners attend lessons from the beginning of their stay; but pupils from other schools vow that they will never attend any beastly lessons again at any time. They play and cycle and get in people's way, but they fight shy of lessons. This sometimes goes on for months. The recovery time is proportionate to the hatred their last school gave them. Our record case was a girl from a convent. She loafed for three years. The average period of recovery from lesson aversion is three months.

Strangers to this idea of freedom will be wondering what sort of madhouse it is where children play all day if they want to. Many an adult says, "If I had been sent to a school like that, I'd never have done a thing." Others say, "Such children will feel themselves heavily handicapped when they have to compete against children who have been made to learn."

I think of Jack who left us at the age of seventeen to go into an engineering factory. One day, the managing director sent for him.

"You are the lad from Summerhill," he said. "I'm curious to know how such an education appears to you now that you are mixing with lads from the old schools. Suppose you had to choose again, would you go to Eton or Summerhill?"

"Oh, Summerhill, of course," replied Jack.

"But what does it offer that the other schools don't offer?"

Jack scratched his head. "I dunno," he said slowly; "I think it gives you a feeling of complete self-confidence."

"Yes," said the manager dryly, "I noticed it when you came into the room."

"Lord," laughed Jack, "I'm sorry if I gave you that impression."

"I liked it," said the director. "Most men when I call them into the office fidget about and look uncomfortable. You came in as my equal. By the way, what department did you say you would like to transfer to?"

This story shows that learning in itself is not as important as personality and character. Jack failed in his university exams because he hated book learning. But his lack of knowledge about *Lamb's Essays* or the French language did not handicap him in life. He is now a successful engineer.

All the same, there is a lot of learning in Summerhill. Perhaps a group of our twelve-year-olds could not compete with a class of equal age in handwriting or spelling or fractions. But in an examination requiring originality, our lot would beat the others hollow.

We have no class examination in the school, but sometimes I set an exam for fun. The following questions appeared in one such paper:

"Where are the following:—Madrid, Thursday Island, yesterday, love, democracy, hate, my pocket screwdriver (alas, there was no helpful answer to that one)."

"Give meanings for the following: (the number shows how many are expected for each)—Hand (3) ... only two got the third right—the standard of measure for a horse. Brass (4) ... metal, cheek, top army officers, department of an orchastra. Translate Hamlet's To-be-or-not-to-be speech into Summerhillese."

These questions are obviously not intended to be serious, and the children enjoy them thoroughly. Newcomers, on the whole, do not rise to the answering standard of pupils who have become acclimatized to the school. Not that they have less brain power, but rather because they have become so accustomed to work in a serious groove that any light touch puzzles them.

This is the play side of our teaching. In all classes much work is done. If, for some reason, a teacher cannot take his class on the appointed day, there is usually much disappointment for the pupils.

David, aged nine, had to be isolated for whooping cough. He cried bitterly. "I'll miss Roger's lesson in geography," he protested. David had been in the school practically from birth, and he had definite and final ideas about the necessity of having his lessons given to him. David is now a lecturer in mathematics at London University.

A few years ago someone at a General School Meeting (at which all school rules are voted by the entire school, each pupil and each staff member having one vote) proposed that a certain culprit should be punished by being banished from lessons for a week. The other children protested on the ground that the punishment was too severe.

My staff and I have a hearty hatred of all examinations. To us, the university exams are anathema. But we cannot refuse to teach children the required subjects. Obviously, as long as the exams are in existence, they are our master. Hence, the Summerhill staff is always qualified to teach to the set standard.

Not that many children want to take these exams; only those going to the university do so. And such children do not seem to find it especially hard to tackle these exams. They generally begin to work for them seriously at the age of fourteen, and they do the work in about three years. Of course they don't always pass at the first try. The more important fact is that they try again.

Summerhill is possibly the happiest school in the world. We have no truants and seldom a case of homesickness. We very rarely have fights— quarrels, of course, but seldom have I seen a stand-up fight like the ones we used to have as boys. I seldom hear a child cry, because children when free have much less hate to express than children who are downtrodden. Hate breeds hate, and love breeds love. Love means approving of children, and that is essential in any school. You can't be on the side of children if you punish them and storm at them. Summerhill is a school in which the child knows that he is approved of.

Mind you, we are not above and beyond human foibles. I spent weeks planting potatoes one spring, and when I found eight plants pulled up in June, I made a big fuss. Yet there was a difference between my fuss and that of an authoritarian. My fuss was about potatoes, but the fuss an authoritarian would have made would have dragged in the question of morality —right and wrong. I did not say that it was wrong to steal my spuds; I did not make it a matter of good and evil—I made it a matter of *my spuds*. They were *my* spuds and they should have been left alone. I hope I am making the distinction clear.

Let me put it another way. To the children, I am no authority to be feared. I am their equal, and the row I kick about my spuds has no more significance to them than the row a boy may kick up about his punctured bicycle tire. It is quite safe to have a row with a child when you are equals.

Now some will say: "That's all bunk. There can't be equality. Neill is the boss; he is bigger and wiser." That is indeed true. I am the boss, and if the house caught fire the children would run to me. They know that I am bigger and more knowledgeable, but that does not matter when I meet them on their own ground, the potato patch, so to speak.

When Billy, aged five, told me to get out of his birthday party because I hadn't been invited, I went at once without hesitation—just as Billy gets out of my room when I don't want his company. It is not easy to describe this relationship between teacher and child, but every visitor to Summerhill knows what I mean when I say that the relationship is ideal. One sees it in the attitude to the staff in general. Rudd, the chemistry man, is Derek. Other members of the staff are known as Harry, and Ulla, and Pam. I am Neill, and the cook is Esther.

In Summerhill, everyone has equal rights. No one is allowed to walk on my grand piano, and I am not allowed to borrow a boy's cycle without his permission. At a General School Meeting, the vote of a child of six counts for as much as my vote does.

But, says the knowing one, in practice of course the voices of the grownups count. Doesn't the child of six wait to see how you vote before he raises his hand? I wish he sometimes would, for too many of my proposals are beaten. Free children are not easily influenced; the absence of fear accounts for this phenomenon. Indeed, the absence of fear is the finest thing that can happen to a child.

Our children do not fear our staff. One of the school rules is that after ten o'clock at night there shall be quietness on the upper corridor. One night, about eleven, a pillow fight was going on, and I left my desk, where I was writing, to protest against the row. As I got upstairs, there was a scurrying of feet and the corridor was empty and quiet. Suddenly I heard a disappointed voice say, "Humph, it's only Neill," and the fun began at once. When I explained that I was trying to write a book downstairs, they showed concern and at once agreed to chuck the noise. Their scurrying came from the suspicion that their bedtime officer (one of their own age) was on their track.

I emphasize the importance of this absence of fear of adults. A child of nine will come and tell me he has broken a window with a ball. He tells me, because he isn't afraid of arousing wrath or moral indignation. He may have to pay for the window, but he doesn't have to fear being lectured or being punished.

There was a time some years back when the School Government resigned, and no one would stand for election. I seized the opportunity of putting up a notice: "In the absence of a government, I herewith declare myself Dictator. Heil Neill!" Soon there were mutterings. In the afternoon Vivien, aged six, came to me and said, "Neill, I've broken a window in the gym."

I waved him away. "Don't bother me with little things like that," I said, and he went.

A little later he came back and said he had broken two windows. By this time I was curious, and asked what the great idea was.

"I don't like dictators," he said, "and I don't like going without my grub." (I discovered later that the opposition to dictatorship had tried to take itself out on the cook, who promptly shut up the kitchen and went home.)

"Well," I asked, "what are you going to do about it?"

"Break more windows," he said doggedly.

"Carry on," I said, and he carried on.

When he returned, he announced that he had broken seventeen windows. 'But mind," he said earnestly, "I'm going to pay for them."

'How?"

"Out of my pocket money. How long will it take me?"

I did a rapid calculation. "About ten years," I said.

He looked glum for a minute; then I saw his face light up. "Gee," he cried, "I don't have to pay for them at all."

"But what about the private property rule?" I asked. "The windows are my private property."

"I know that but there isn't any private property rule now. There isn't any government, and the government makes the rules."

It may have been my expression that made him add, "But all the same I'll pay for them."

But he didn't have to pay for them. Lecturing in London shortly afterward, I told the story; and at the end of my tale, a young man came up and handed me a pound note "to pay for the young devil's windows." Two years later, Vivien was still telling people of his windows and of the man who paid for them. "He must have been a terrible fool, because he never even saw me."

Children make contact with strangers more easily when fear is unknown to them. English reserve is, at bottom, really fear; and that is why the most reserved are those who have the most wealth. The fact that Summerhill children are so exceptionally friendly to visitors and strangers is a source of pride to me and my staff.

We must confess, however, that many of our visitors are people of interest to the children. The kind of visitor most unwelcome to them is the teacher, especially the earnest teacher, who wants to see their drawing and written work. The most welcome visitor is the one who has good tales to tell—of adventure and travel or, best of all, of aviation. A boxer or a good tennis player is surrounded at once, but visitors who spout theory are left severely alone.

The most frequent remark that visitors make is that they cannot tell who is staff and who is pupil. It is true: the feeling of unity is that strong when children are approved of. There is no deference to a teacher as a teacher. Staff and pupils have the same food and have to obey the same community laws. The children would resent any special privileges given to the staff.

When I used to give the staff a talk on psychology every week, there was a muttering that it wasn't fair. I changed the plan and made the talks open to everyone over twelve. Every Tuesday night, my room is filled with eager youngsters who not only listen but give their opinions freely. Among the subjects the children have asked me to talk about have been these: The Inferiority Complex, The Psychology of Stealing, The Psychology of the Gangster, The Psychology of Humor, Why Did Man Become a Moralist?, Masturbation, Crowd Psychology. It is obvious that such children will go out into life with a broad clear knowledge of themselves and others.

The most frequent question asked by Summerhill visitors is, "Won't the child turn round and blame the school for not making him learn arithmetic or music?" The answer is that young Freddy Beethoven and young Tommy Einstein will refuse to be kept away from their respective spheres.

The function of the child is to live his own life—not the life that his anxious parents think he should live, nor a life according to the purpose of the educator who thinks he knows what is best. All this interference and guidance on the part of adults only produces a generation of robots.

You cannot *make* children learn music or anything else without to some degree converting them into will-less adults. You fashion them into accepters of the *status quo*—a good thing for a society that needs obedient sitters at dreary desks, standers in shops, mechanical catchers of the 8:30 suburban train—a society, in short, that is carried on the shabby shoulders of the scared little man—the scared-to-death conformist.

4

Free Schools and the Revolution
by Barry Wood

There's a hard rain a gonna fall. And if it's true that the repression will start to come down now that the elections are over, a good share of that rain is going to fall all over the education reform, or the free schools movement (FSM). The politicians' battle cry, led by Nixon/Agnew, has been ... "Stop permissiveness." Attacks on the "radiclibs" in the university administrations and in the news media have been second only to the assaults on blacks and youth. We can only assume that those of us in the FSM (who really do favor permissiveness and freedom in the schools!) will bear some of the brunt of the Establishment's new offensive.

What we are going to increasingly see is the forced radicalization of the educational reformers. This is to be welcomed and is in a sense overdue. John Holt, by calling for fundamental changes in our schools, will at last be seen for what he is—a very radical reformer.

For too long the free schools movement has operated in a political vacuum. Not only has there been a lack of awareness that we were/are radical, but there has been a disdain of any attempt to even mildly suggest a linkage of the FSM into the greater Movement to humanize Amerika. (I remember the extremely negative reaction when two revolutionary films were shown at the Santa Barbara conference last spring.)

But as a statement of fact, the free schools movement has, whether we knew it or not, been radical since its inception. One could even say that

---

its being included in the spiraling web of repression is some indication that the movement has had an effect and that the ideas underpinning it have some validity. In the tolerant/repressive society of Amerika, movements are seldom suppressed until they pose some threat to the smooth working of the system. In that sense, we've made it!

What we haven't generally recognized, up to now, is that by calling for basic changes in the nature of schooling, we have challenged not just the school system, but the larger system of which the schools are only a part. Beatrice and Ronald Gross make reference to this reality in their introduction to *Radical School Reform*:

> The radical critics (of the schools) all start with some kind of radical criticism of America as a sick society. They come at it from many angles: its competitive ethos, its cultural vulgarity, its neglect or suppression of minority groups, its inherent racism and imperialism, its failures in compassion. . . . Their critique of the schools derives from this questioning of society, for they see the schools as mere agents of the society.

Schools are indeed "mere agents of the society," but beyond that, and more importantly, they are the primary institution for transferring values from the old generation to the new. School is the great enculturator. It is from the schools that we "learn" to be good Amerikans, to believe that God is on our side, that blacks are lazy, that boys become breadwinners and girls housewives, that commies are bad and yanks good, that the war in Vietnam is just, and that the American past is great and glorious!

By starting our own schools or by seeking changes in the public schools we have not *just* challenged what has traditionally happened in the classroom. We haven't *just* pointed out that schools have failed to accomplish what they set out to do. On the contrary, all too often they have "succeeded" . . . miserably! We are not *just* rebelling from the boredom, coercion, stultification, and irrelevance of the American classroom. Rather, WE ARE CHALLENGING THE VERY RIGHT OF THE SCHOOLS AND THE SOCIETY TO LAY A FALSE VALUES TRIP ON OUR KIDS! We righteously say that's not learning; it's brainwashing! And we don't want it any more!

The free schools movement is saying that we have a better idea of what learning is all about. The FSM is echoing what John Holt, in *The Underachieving School*, suggests should be the shape of the schools:

... let every child be the planner, director, and assessor of his own education, allow and encourage him ... to decide what he is to learn, when he is to learn it, how he is to learn it, and how well he is learning it. Make our schools, instead of what they are, which is jails for children, into a resource for free and independent learning. . . .

We are saying that the nature of the child is curiosity. Real learning and growth emerges from indulging that curiosity to ask questions and then proceeding to find answers. The school system, however, suppresses questions and substitutes regimentation. The process of the Amerikan educational system causes the child to cease defining his own world as the definitions are imposed from the Establishment. ("Don't ask why we say the pledge of allegiance, just say it!") Each succeeding year of schooling suppresses a little more creativity and curiosity, until finally, the student emerges from the assembly line, is stamped "graduate," and proclaimed "good citizen." Having swallowed the myths, convinced that his own ideas are inferior to those in authority, and convinced he really isn't worth much, the new graduate presumably goes off to Vietnam or assumes his place as an obedient consumer in the suburban death culture. Amerika thus devours its children.

Clearly, free learning serves to derail the student from this deadly process. But what we must understand is that this derailment, whether it results from school reforms or by dropping out due to the increasingly obvious internal illogic of the system itself, is dangerous to the Establishment. There is a heavy price to be paid for asking the basic questions. Mr. Nixon himself knows that the system cannot sustain a critical analysis that results from questioning the heretofore sacrosanct values of authority, individualism, free enterprise, competition, Christianity, ad nauseam. Therefore, as the system is increasingly questioned, the Establishment responds in the only way it knows how. It falls back on the values that are already under attack, and with increased tenacity defends the legitimacy of the status quo while trying doubly hard to indoctrinate the people with the "holy writ." The old bugaboo of permissiveness is resurrected from the closet. Those who question are attacked not so much because of what they question, but rather because they had the audacity to raise questions in the first place. The logic here is that had there not been people in the system who encouraged questions, the question would not have been raised. Thus—the attack on the liberal educators.

It would appear that the liberals in the educational establishment will find themselves in a particularly tight bind. They know full well that there is a nationwide school crisis. This crisis knows no geographical or ethnic bounds and is characterized by wholesale rejection of traditional education by a growing number of the nation's youth. The irony seems to be that this near collapse of the public schools, while certainly not caused by education reforms, would nonetheless be exacerbated and accelerated by eleventh hour and piecemeal reforms. These educators know full well that the schools are in crisis. The literature of educational reform from John Holt to Ivan Illich is now gobbled up voraciously by would-be reformers who struggle to keep their administrative and teaching jobs in the wake of parent and taxpayer disgust.

There are fundamentally two choices for the public schools. One, they can follow the national mood as laid down from Washington, and shape up. They must force the kids into line through stiff application of police state measures in the schools (this is already being done in many universities and urban high schools). The problem with this alternative, in the liberal educator's context, is that he knows that it will not work. The relationship between repression and rebellion is too well known. Plus, in light of the new literature on learning, even these educators know that learning cannot take place in a police state atmosphere.

The second alternative is to move toward more freedom in the schools. This is probably what many liberal educators would like to do, but they know that this would bring strong opposition from many parents and local authorities. And more importantly, if the educator is tuned in, he would know that this approach would allow students to begin to realize their own self worth and potential, thus leading them to press for more fundamental and structural reforms that the educational establishment is unable to deliver. (Questions like why do we pay principals $25,000 to police the hallways might be only one example.)

The educators are caught in a bind. They are vulnerable merely because many of their most cherished assumptions on learning (and control!) have been blown out the window since the onset of student protest. The educational establishment is thus in a very vulnerable position. It may well be the softest, hard-line institution to crack. The educational reformers must seize this opportunity and push harder than ever for curriculum changes, experimental colleges, and in short for student initiated programs. There is a great opportunity here, and all reforms that may be possible should be encouraged unconditionally. (Let the school administrators defend the changes to the school board or the trustees.)

Ultimately, a strong attempt will be made to bring the educational system around to more closely match the pattern of repression that must take place throughout all institutions in the society. The seeds of the educational establishment's demise are now sown and built into the logic of the system, no matter in which direction short-run education policies go.

We must begin to see ourselves for what we are. We are tampering with one of the basic institutional forces in the country. As our ideas proliferate and our numbers increase, we become more of a threat, first to the system of education, and then, to Amerika itself. And as we become a threat, we invite repression. (I am reminded of the Jefferson Airplane's line, "Everything they say we are, we are!") Freedom and questioning are becoming dangerous and impossible in Amerika. (Postman and Weingarten's kind of teaching *is* subversive.) And that reality in itself should force us to become political. The time when "our free school" or "our experimental college" can be our political cop-out is approaching an end. No longer can free schoolers say "politics is not my bag." It is your bag by definition! Too often free schools have been analogous to communal land trips in the country. In point of fact, there can be no escape. It has always been a myth to assume that a free school in the country could be an island of growth and joy in an ocean of repression. We can't escape the reality of Amerika 1970. We can't escape the reality of Angela Davis and Bobby Seale being ripped off, or that the war in Asia is being intensified, or that McDonald's hamburgers will follow us into the hills. It's impossible to be self-actualized in a repressive society.

In closing, I would point out that as repression becomes the watchword of our society, we would do great damage to youth if we were to hide them for as long as possible from the bitter realities of Amerika. On the contrary, revolutionary education must relate to the needs of the people. Those needs become survival skills. Knowledge of the trial of Bobby Seale becomes as important as almost anything else we can learn.

The free schools movement must see itself as part of a larger revolutionary movement. The forces of repression do not just signal out bombers for attack, but rather they go after all who deviate from the cultural norm. The concept of free learning is incompatible with the Amerikan system.

5

CBE Views the Alternatives
by Mortimer Smith

In any discussion of alternative schools we must begin by defining what we mean by schools. Dr. Johnson said that definitions are hazardous, and he might have added, especially those definitions which attempt to state the purposes of social institutions. In a fragmented society such as ours, where to a large degree we have lost a sense of community and shared purpose, we cannot assume that everyone means the same thing when the talk is about the use of any of our institutions. To make my own position clear at once, my view of the purpose of schools is that proclaimed by the Council for Basic Education when it was founded more than 16 years ago: "They exist to provide the essential skills of language, numbers, and orderly thought, and to transmit in a reasoned pattern the intellectual, moral, and aesthetic heritage of civilized man." Although such a definition of purpose is in some circles considered quaint, if not actually antediluvian, perhaps a majority of Americans are still able to accept it, are still willing to say that while schools may have peripheral purposes their chief purpose is to make young people literate in word and number and in historical knowledge.

Now to accept this traditional idea of the function of schools does not mean that one accepts as sacrosanct their present structure and organization. Schools don't have to be run on a 10-month, 9-to-3 schedule. Reading, the social studies, and English don't have to be taught by methods devised by educationists in the 1940s and 1950s. The road to teaching does not have to be only through certification based on a training that is long on education courses and short on academic preparation. More lay par-

*From *Phi Delta Kappan* LIV, 7 (March 1973): 441–43. Reprinted by permission.

ticipation in the conduct of schools, performance contracting, even voucher plans, should not make educators blanch, nor should programs that combine part-time work and part-time study. The site for learning does not have to be an either-or matter—old-fashioned egg-crate building or the new open type which resembles an air terminal with wall-to-wall carpeting.

In schools particular programs or arrangements or organizational patterns are not important. The important thing is the human element— teachers who combine a sense of humanity and justice in dealing with young people with the requisite knowledge and teaching skills. My point was summed up a few years ago by William H. Cornog of New Trier High School: "We think our school's central task is to train youth in the use of the mind. We assume that this can still be done in box-like classrooms, if the right people are put in the right boxes and get their minds agitated by subjects, or the ideas in them."

The view of the Council for Basic Education is that the more alternatives we have the merrier, as long as they are alternatives to conventional arrangements and not to the historic function of schools. Unfortunately, I see very little in the present leadership of the movement for alternative schools that encourages me to think that the new arrangements will foster rather than discourage the old purposes. Some of these leaders are cultists rather than serious reformers. Read Peter Marin's article in the *Saturday Review* ("Has Imagination Outstripped Reality?" July 22, 1972) about a representative group of radical deschoolers and free-schoolers who gathered at a New Orleans conference and you will see that many of them are prima donnas who can't agree among themselves and show little grasp of the pragmatic reality of schools. Some of them want schools to liberate the blacks or the poor (liberators are apt to have generous traveling grants); some want schools to foster the counterculture; others are social perfectionists who can't bear to face the fact that joy and ecstasy are not constant factors in the lives of teachers and school children; still others want the schools to help overthrow the present economic order.

 Most of the reformers described by Marin are on the far-out fringe of the alternative schools movement, but even among the more reasonable advocates there is a tendency to erect hypotheses and conjectures about learning and the nature of youth into a fairly rigid set of neoprogressive doctrines. The foremost doctrine, especially on the elementary school level, insists on the necessity for "informality." Its lack, according to Charles E. Silberman, has made American classrooms dour places, "killers of the dream," and its presence in some British primary schools has turned them into places of great joy and spontaneity and creative activity. Silberman is unable to point to any data suggesting that informal schools increase achievement, but then he agrees with an English research report which suggests that "the consequences of different modes of schooling should be sought less in academic attainment than in their impact on how children feel about themselves, about school, and about learning."[1]

This last remark suggests another item in the doctrinal litany of many alternative-schoolers: the importance of "feeling." One would suppose that children who achieve well academically would have a good feeling toward themselves, toward schools, and toward learning, but those who are keen on "affective" learning—I use the currently popular jargon—rarely see that it is enhanced by accomplishments in the "cognitive" realm. Some of the alternative school prophets seem to think that there is a fundamental conflict between emotion, or feeling, and intellect, failing to perceive what would seem to be an obvious truth: Feeling and intellect complement each other, the mind providing a guide for the feelings.

After "informality" and "feeling" come a string of doctrines: Children should be allowed to do their thing as the spirit moves them; they are naturally good until corrupted by the outside world; they must never be told things but should discover them on their own; the teacher who asserts authority, either over conduct or in teaching subject matter, is no better than an authoritarian dictator; the right relation between teacher and pupils is that of equality and palship; and—one of the hoariest of the progressive bromides—the school must bring "real life" and "the real world" into the classroom.

With such a set of governing doctrines many alternative schools tend to be antibook learning and indifferent to the basic skills and to any kind of "structure." Many go in for no grades and no failures, no bells between classes, handlooms and gerbil cages, and guitar playing in the halls. The "educational" program runs heavily to courses in macrame, tie-dying, karate, yoga, urban renewal, and wilderness survival. And over all there waves that banner with the strange device: Relevance!

Not all alternative schools, of course, are such caricatures of real education. Strangely enough, Jonathan Kozol, who considers our school system, to say nothing of our society in general, to be rotten and corrupt, runs his free school in Roxbury, Massachusetts, along rather structured

---

1. Charles E. Silberman, *Crisis in the Classroom* (New York: Random House, 1970), pp. 228, 262.

lines, teaching the basic subjects in a purposeful and sequential manner and soft-pedaling the paeans to Joy. He knows that the parents of the poor black children who go to his school want them to learn skills and he is impatient with young affluent white teachers who think such children will be better off making clay vases, weaving Indian headbands, playing with Polaroid cameras, and climbing over geodesic domes.

Several public schools that claim to present alternatives have also managed to be innovative and to meet the interests of students without abandoning the school's fundamental purpose of education. And of course many of the original alternative schools—the private schools—have for a long time been combining learning with practices that would be considered unorthodox in the public school system. With honorable exceptions, however, the alternative school movement seems to have fallen into the hands of either the more *avant garde* of the free-schoolers or the neoprogressives who are busy rediscovering William Heard Kilpatrick.

The alternatives movement in my view falls far short of providing the realistic reforms that many educators and laymen have long been demanding. Consider a little history. In the 1950s it became apparent that American public education was badly in need of change. There was widespread evidence of lowered academic achievement, eroded standards, poor teacher preparation, the proliferation of trivial courses, and the domination of the schools by an unimaginative and stand-pat establishment consisting of the schools of education, national teacher association, state departments of education, and the U. S. Office of Education. An amorphous something known as "life adjustment education" was in the air which seemed to be reducible to the notion that the majority of American youth were uneducable and that therefore the schools must provide a substitute for education for this majority. The founding of the Council for Basic Education in 1956 was the first organizational effort on a national scale to call attention to these conditions and to suggest plans for reform. After the alert of the first Sputnik, even before, many academicians who had formerly been aloof from the schools started work on curricular changes, especially in math, in the sciences, and in languages. Some of the reforms of the fifties and early sixties had an impact and some never got off the ground, but there is no doubt that the agitations of the period did much to stem the anti-intellectualism which stressed the social adjustment function of the schools over the primary educative function.

In the middle sixties (roughly) we discovered the "disadvantaged" and the reform clock was turned backwards. For every educator like Kenneth

Clark, who considered our first duty was to teach black children to read and write so they might enlarge their horizons, there were a dozen, usually white, who assured us that what we needed to stress in ghetto schools was informality, nongrouping, unstructured programs, the dialect of the streets, and the supposedly superior energy and spontaneity of the culture of poverty. This attitude was infectious and many educators began to apply these criteria for ghetto schools to all schools. In other words, they joined Silberman in suggesting that universally the consequences of schooling should be sought not in academic attainment but in how students feel. This seems to be the attitude of perhaps the majority of the philosophers of the alternative school movement.

The turn that much school reform has taken in the last five years or so cannot but make unhappy those of us who still believe that the schools must fulfill their obligation "to provide the essential skills of language, numbers, and orderly thought." We agree with the alternative schools advocates that many schools (surely not all) are dreary places that fail to reach the students, that many schools are bad schools run by administrators and teachers who are indifferent to, or contemptuous of, the students, and that public education often presents a bureaucratic side that is repellent. We cannot agree that the solution is to insist on a false teacher-student equality or to let the kids run the school or to foster feeling over thought or to value lightly the role in education of books, language, standards, and disciplined knowledge.

Those of us who cling to the historic idea of what schools should be are having a rough time of it these days, battered on the one side by the joy-and-ecstacy boys and on the other by theorists like Christopher Jencks who tell us that what the schools do doesn't make any difference to the future lives of those who attend them. The Council for Basic Education will continue to hold to the faith that true education is essential for all youth and it will continue to point out that if schools are to foster such education they cannot be indifferent to change and innovation but must at the same time operate within some rational organizational framework. I know that such a word as *efficient* will cause some of the advocates of loosely organized schools to bristle, but if we are to have efficient schools —i.e., functional schools—we must find some operating principles on which the majority of reformers can agree.

Sentimental utopians and perfectionists (and they abound in the alternative movement) will be in pained disagreement, but I suspect that pragmatic reformers can agree on certain propositions about schools: 1) While independent schools should be encouraged, a public system of compulsory education is a social necessity and convenience and will continue for a long time to come to be the dominant system. 2) Schooling has to be formalized, with required attendance and sequential courses and schedules, but the formalities should be governed by common sense, flexibility, and sympathetic understanding of the child. 3) Inescapably, the teacher is an authority and not an equal partner of the student. 4) The economics of the situation determine that some large-group instruction is inevitable. 5) Ability grouping in one form or another is fair and beneficial to all students. 6) Examinations and other forms of measurement are essential for judging the effectiveness of instruction. 7) Schools must provide a background of common knowledge if they are to play their proper role in helping to form a community or society of shared interests and ideals.

These are some of the necessities we must face in devising any program of realizable reform for the schools. There is no indication that any considerable number of the advocates of alternate schools would find these propositions congenial. Until they do, and until they are willing to acknowledge that the school's main function is the training of the mind, their movement will remain well-intentioned but essentially quixotic.

It is hard to judge whether or not the movement is a permanent one. Innovations in education have a habit of flourishing for a period and then gradually withering away, and founders of glamorous alternatives to conventional schools tend to weary after a while and move on to new schemes of regeneration. I wish the idealism and energies of the advocates of reform could be enlisted in behalf of changes for which there is an imperative need and for which there can be reasonable expectation of success. We need desperately to improve reading instruction, to devise workable programs based on higher aspirations for children of the ghetto, to establish clearer and better measures of academic achievement, and to give more attention to critical evaluation of current innovations before we move on to new ones. Above all, we need to give serious thought to the greatest of our problems, how to find good natural teachers and then change our present unsatisfactory way of training them.

In education we need always to reexamine our practices and to be willing to change them when necessary. Not to do so would be foolhardy, even suicidal. But change must be based on something more substantial than the slogans, ideological zealotry, and utopian sentimentality that all too often mark the movement for alternative schools. I think it would be unfortunate if this sort of change gained wide favor, for there is a Gresham's law in education, too, where bad reform drives out good.

6

Alternatives in the Public School
by Mario D. Fantini

Alternative forms of education are springing up in public schools all over the country. I call my plan for alternatives Public Schools of Choice.

This plan calls for cooperation of teachers, parents, and students in the development of a variety of legitimate educational options within our public schools. Choice is a key term in this plan. Each of the participating groups —teachers, parents, and students (the agents closest to the action)—have a choice of the option that best supports their style.

Public Schools of Choice is also based on the assumption that each teacher has a style of teaching and each student, a style of learning. Providing opportunities for a more compatible matching of teaching-learning styles can help further the long-held educational ideals of individualization and personalization. Teachers will perform a key role, not only in deciding which of the alternatives best supports their teaching style, but also in designing options. Since parents, students, and teachers are brought together by mutual consent and not by chance, the mismatches of the past which led to frustration for both teacher and student can be avoided.

Public Schools of Choice establishes standard education as a legitimate option. We have overloaded the standard pattern of education, expecting this approach to reach all teachers, students, and parents. No one pattern of education can reach everyone, and in a diverse society such as ours, a responsive system of public education provides a range of options and choices, including the standard.

To get any new system to operate, participants must agree on ground rules. To make Public Schools of Choice work, the following ground rules are essential.

*From *Today's Education*, September-October, 1974. Reprinted by permission.

No alternative within a public system of choice practices exclusivity.
No school or alternative can exclude a child because of race, religion, financial status, or—within reason—the nature of previous educational background. The schools must be truly open, able to survive on the basis of their educational merits and their ability to meet the needs of the students and the parents they serve.

Each school works toward a comprehensive set of educational objectives. These objectives or educational goals must be common to all schools within the system of choice. They should include mastery of the basic skills, nurturing of physical and emotional development, vocational and avocational preparation. The student must be equipped with a broad range of skills so that he will have as many alternatives and opportunities as possible for social and educational mobility.

Within a system of Public Schools of Choice, the real issue is not what goals to set, but how best to achieve the goals set. The system itself seeks out new means of increasing the chances for the student to mature as a maker of choices rather than to be a mere victim of circumstances.

A ground rule intrinsic to the idea of a free and open society and, therefore, to the notion of Public Schools of Choice is that no person or group imposes an educational plan or design. Within a system of choice, the consumer shops around as in a supermarket or cafeteria, choosing, testing, and finally settling on a school or learning environment that appeals to him.

If 90 percent of the consumers settle on approach A and only 10 percent want approach B, then 90 percent of the system's schools provide approach A and 10 percent, approach B.

Each community has to determine how many consumers are necessary to warrant setting up a new alternative. The point here, however, is that once the minimum percentage is established, the individual consumer can choose his own option, rather than having to accept one program because there are no alternatives.

Similarly, teachers are free to choose the alternatives that best support their styles of teaching. No one alternative is imposed on a teacher.

Obviously, new approaches will necessitate the retraining of teachers, but this can become an integral part of the staff development program of the school district.

Each new alternative can eventually operate on a financial level equivalent to the percapita cost of the school district as a whole. Although each new option may be permitted some additional costs for initial planning and development, it must conform to the standard perstudent cost of the total system within a reasonable period of time. This ground rule insures that a public school system of choice results in a wiser, more productive use of existing monies.

Some may ask whether a Nazi school or an antiwhite one for Blacks could exist within the framework of a public system of choice. Obviously, it could not. The concept speaks to openness. It values diversity, is democratic, and is unswerving in its recognition of individual worth.

Within these bounds, however, there is a full spectrum of alternative possibilities with new educational and learning forms. Schools could, for example, emphasize science or languages or the arts; they could be graded or ungraded, open or traditional, technical or non-technical; they could seek a multicultural approach or work to strengthen particular ethnic and group identities. Each, however, must meet the standard principles which are fundamental to a public school system of choice.

Respecting the rights and responsibilities of others, for example, cannot work if the option being promulgated is based on a system which advocated the imposition of one's own values on others.

Each alternative provides another approach to education alongside the existing pattern, which continues to be legitimate. Every legitimatized educational option is equally valid. The standard approach to education, therefore, is an important alternative and should not be eliminated or forced to take the brunt of criticism.

Each alternative includes a plan for evaluation. Since each alternative needs to achieve the same ends, assessment is essential for at least two reasons: to gather evaluation information as a basis for continuing to improve the option and to help determine the relative effectiveness of each option.

What constitutes a legitimate educational option under these rules is a critical question.

Public schools have a responsibility to equip each learner with the skills needed for economic, political, and social survival. At the same time, they must provide him with the tools needed for improving, transforming, and reconstructing elements of the environment generally recognized as inimical to the noblest aspirations of the nation or as detrimental to the growth and development of the individual.

Speaking practically, public schools must provide opportunities for each learner to discover his talents. Our public schools are necessarily talent development centers, linking talent to economic careers. As such, public schools encompass economic "livelihood" objectives as an important set of educational ends. If an educational option discounted this set of objectives, it would be suspect as a legitimate alternative within the framework of public education.

Public Schools of Choice can work only when students, parents, teachers, and administrators all have equal access to educational options at both the conceptual and operational levels. But, unless the parent or consumer is aware of the existence of new alternatives, he is left with only the ones with which he is familiar and is forced to play by the ground rules established by the existing system. Then the question which must be posed is: What mechanism must be developed to bring relevant educational information to the public?

The administration of a school system might assume the leadership role by arranging informational meetings with the groups involved. Such meetings could lead parent associations to hold more meetings to explore educational options. Student groups at the elementary, junior high, and high school levels and teacher organizations could do the same thing. After careful planning, the school system could launch trial programs, either in one school or in a cluster of them. Under certain conditions, a whole district could mount a special program.

While Public Schools of Choice works best when an entire school goes into the plan and provides many options for all students and teachers, it may be desirable to start by trying options not too dissimilar to the school's present operational style.

Developing choices at the individual school level can, however, pose a number of problems. For example, as the different segments of the public explore new options, a group might find itself involved in scanning an almost endless list of reading materials. This would not necessarily be bad, but it could leave the participants with a narrow view of the learning process.

If, on the other hand, a community undertook a conceptual examination of educational alternatives, participants might indeed achieve a better background for decision making. It is one thing to become knowledgeable about a concept or idea and quite another to become familiar with the intricate details that go into making the idea work. While it is obvious that some knowledge of detail is necessary, students, parents, and citizens in general need not be as well-informed about the subtleties of pedagogy as are professionals.

Professional educators have the responsibility for the substance and techniques of education, but the consumers must be responsible for determining the kind of education they want. They must, therefore, have the opportunity to perform this crucial policy role. Thus, a new standard of professional and lay participation could lead to more sensible educational conceptions, supported by both groups.

One way to consider alternatives is to place them on a continuum on the basis of how much freedom a student has to choose the elements of learning, i.e., how much freedom he has to choose the teacher, the content, the learning methodology, the time, the place.

At one extreme, the learner selects what he will learn, with whom, when, where, and how. At this end of the continuum, he has the greatest freedom. At the other extreme, he has no choice of teacher, content, methodology, time, and place. Institutional procedures and requirements predetermine the conditions of learning for him.

Between these extremes, there is a range of possibilities. The learner can be free to choose certain content areas, but not others, which are required for everyone (reading, writing, arithmetic, physical education, health). He may have some freedom in how he wishes to approach these content areas (by reading a book, by viewing videotapes, by doing research, by listening to a lecture, by discussing with others). He may have some freedom to choose the time and place to learn. For example, he may enter into a contract with the teacher to accomplish a project by a certain time.

There are obviously different types of free school alternatives—ranging from an Illich/Reimer model, which de-emphasizes schooling, to a Summerhill model, which uses the school as a type of self-governing unit. Free school alternatives are the most difficult to legitimize under a public school framework at this time and will probably remain outside as private alternative schools, since they run counter to the emerging ground rules for alternative public schools.

The open phase of the continuum overlaps with the free, but limits the range of choice the learner has. Thus, while a student can choose when and how he will learn science or math, they are, nevertheless, still required subjects, and the teacher helps guide the student in various content areas.

Such an educational continuum can be charted briefly as indicated below.

The British infant school, Montessori, and schools without walls could be examples under the open category. Ungraded continuous progress, modular scheduling, and behavior modification are possible alternatives under the modified. Formally organized, age-graded schools and uniformly regimented academies tend to fall into standard options.

There are various ways of providing educational options based on choice: Options can be based on (1) existing teacher styles; (2) classroom patterns, e.g., standard, Montessori, behavior modification, British infant; (3) teams of teachers forming schools within schools, e.g., Quincy (Illinois) Senior High II has seven subschools—standard, flexible, independent, fine arts, career, special, and vocational; (4) "new" school options which are housed in a setting apart from established schools. For example, in Los Angeles, there are four "off site" alternative schools located in different areas of the school system.

Once optional education and the ground rules of the choice system are understood, an entire district may want to develop a framework of alternatives for its schools. The following is a typical list from which parents, students, teachers, and administrators can choose.

Alternative 1 is a traditional approach. It is graded and emphasizes the learning of basic skills by cognition. The basic learning environment is the classroom, which functions with one or two teachers instructing and directing students at their various learning tasks. Students are encouraged to adjust to the school and its operational style, rather than vice versa. The sudents with recognized learning problems are referred to a variety of remedial and school-support programs. A central board of education determines the entire educational and fiscal policy for this school.

Alternative 2 is nontraditional and nongraded. In many ways it is like a British primary school with lots of constructional and manipulative materials in each area where students work and learn.

The teacher acts as a facilitator—one who assists and guides, rather than directs or instructs. Most student activity is in the form of specialized learning projects carried on individually and in small groups. Many of the learning experiences and activities take place outside the school.

Alternative 3 emphasizes talent development and focuses on creative experiences, human services, and concentration in a particular field, e.g., art, media, space, science, dramatics, music. The school defines its role as diagnostic and prescriptive: It identifies the learner's talents and orchestrates whatever experiences seem necessary to develop and enhance them. It encourages many styles of learning and teaching. Students may achieve by demonstration and by manipulation of real objects as well as by verbal, written, or abstractive performances.

Alternative 4 is more oriented to techniques than the others in the district. It utilizes computers to help diagnose individual needs and abilities and provides computer-assisted instruction based on the diagnosis for individuals and groups.

The library stocks tape-recording banks and has carrels in which students, on their own, can "talk" to and listen to tapes or work with manipulative objects. In addition, wide use is made of educational media which enable students and teachers to individualize many of the learning tasks. The school also has facilities for closed-circuit TV.

Alternative 5 is a total community school. Operating on a 12-to-14-hour basis at least six days a week throughout the year, it provides educational and other services for children of varying ages from the neighborhood and evening classes and activities for adults.

Services in such areas as health, legal aid, and employment are available within the school facility. Paraprofessionals or community teachers contribute to every phase of the regular school program. A community board governs the school.

Alternative 6 has a Montessori environment. Students move at their own pace and are largely self-directed. The learning areas are rich in materials and specialized learning instruments from which the student can select as they wish. Although teachers operate within a specific, defined methodology, they remain in the background, guiding students rather than directing them. Special emphasis is placed on the development of the five senses.

Alternative 7, patterned after the Multi-Culture Institute in San Francisco, may have four or five ethnic groups equally represented in the student body. Students spend part of each day in racially heterogeneous learning groups. During another part of the day, students and teachers of the same ethnic background meet together. In these classes, all learn the culture, language, customs, history, and heritage of their ethnic groups.

A policy board made up of equal numbers of parents and teachers runs the school and is only tangentially responsible to a central board of education.

Alternative 8 is subcontracted. For example, a group of teachers, parents, and students could be delegated authority to operate a particular alternative. Or certain private schools alternatives can petition to become part of the public schools.

Alternatives help give new direction to pre- and in-service education of teachers. If some options are in greater demand than others, then certain teachers (perhaps those who express the desire) can be helped to staff them. After all, even if there were no options, teachers would still require inservice education.

Public Schools of Choice can encourage closer ties between community and schools, professionals and laymen. Without professional leadership which promotes cooperation of all parties concerned, alternatives can be imposed and often opposed.

The Public Schools of Choice system would be a renewal system, that is, the options under a broad public framework would be judged by results. As the results associated with quality education were realized more in one model than in another, the attractiveness of the successful model would grow. The options that were more successful would most likely be in more demand, thus triggering a self-renewing process.

Alternatives on a Freedom-To-Prescription Continuum*

Free	Free Open	Open	Open Modified	Modified-Standard	Standard
Learner-directed and controlled. Learner has complete freedom to orchestrate his own education. Teacher is one resource.	Opening of school to the community and its resources. Noncompetitive environment. No student failures. Curriculum is viewed as social system rather than as course of studies. Learner centered.	Learner has considerable freedom to choose from a wide range of content areas considered relevant by teacher, parent, and student. Resource centers in major skill areas made available to learner. Teacher is supportive guide.	Teacher-student planning. Teacher centered.	Prescribed content is made more flexible through individualization of instruction; school is ungraded; students learn same thing but at different rates. Using team teaching, teachers plan a differentiated approach to the same content. Teacher and programmed course of study are the major sources of student learning.	Learner adheres to institution requirements uniformly prescribed: what is to be taught—how, when, where, and with whom. Teacher is instructor-evaluator. Student passes or fails according to normative standards.

*Mario D. Fantini, "Alternatives Within Public Schools," **Phi Delta Kappan**, Special Issue on Alternative Schools, March 1973, pp. 447-448.

Part II
REALITIES

Only so much can be learned about an educational reform movement from its underlying ideologies. Perhaps a more important question is just how these ideologies are translated into practice. The implementation process often undermines even the most coherent educational ideology.

It is a statement on the newness of the alternative school movement that in our search of the literature, we found few good, detailed case studies of alternative schools. Consequently, most of the nine case studies presented here were especially prepared for this book.

We have included examples of alternative schools which are different in many respects. The schools represent different ideologies, structures, and student populations. The schools are located in diverse community settings. Some are independent institutions; others are part of existing high schools. Some are public; others are private. While most succeeded, some failed. We have also attempted to include material which describes these schools from different perspectives. These case studies have been written by alternative school administrators (most of whom also taught in their schools), a student, a teacher, a parent, and an outside observer.

The first three case studies are of alternative schools in different types of communities: suburban, urban, and small town. "The Murray Road School," by Ronald Barndt, is the history and philosophy of one of the first public alternative high schools in the United States. Still operating in a suburb of Boston, the Murray Road School has served as a model for many other public alternative schools. Murray Road is also significant in that it was founded as an alternative to Newton High School, long considered one of America's outstanding public high schools.

MaryFrances Crabtree in "Chicago's Metro High: Freedom, Choice, Responsibility," presents a more personal account of another pioneering alternative school. Metro, one of the first urban "schools-without-walls," has proved that the alternative school concept is as viable in the inner city as in the suburbs.

Terrence E. Deal, in "Muddling Through: A School Above a Bakery," describes the beginning struggles of a public alternative school in a small town. By tracing the trial-and-error development of the Community School, Deal aims to "stimulate ideas about what to do and what to avoid in the inaugural year of an alternative school."

The next two selections focus on "schools-within-schools"—public alternative schools which are founded and operate within the physical context of a regular public school. Robert Nolan in "Student Power: A Case Study" presents the story of the Roslyn School-Within-a-School as an example of a student-run public alternative school. Based on this experience, Nolan ventures some conclusions about students assuming responsibility for their own education. David Murphy, in "Trauma and Renaissance: A Case History of an Alternative School's Evolution," concentrates on the complex structures and processes which allowed the Alternative School in Cubberley eventually to succeed.

Most alternative schools give students more freedom and options than traditional schools. In contrast, "The Hoover Structured School" is a public elementary school which provides a highly structured, teacher-directed education with a strong emphasis on "the basic skills." Founded on the belief that professional educators know best, Hoover discourages direct parent involvement in the operation of the school. The Hoover model is becoming an increasingly popular alternative for parents who believe that most public schools have become too permissive and rigorless. It is noteworthy that the Hoover Elementary School is located in the same school district as the Alternative School in Cubberley.

Contrary to Fantini's plan for public schools of choice, many individuals are unwilling or unable to establish their alternative schools within public school systems. In "A Student's View of the Successes and Failures of an Alternative School," Kathy Gross tells why she felt compelled to leave her public school and help set up a private alternative school. Like a number of alternative school students, Gross became disillusioned by her experience but more knowledgeable about her own educational needs and abilities. Daniel Linden Duke, in "Great (And Dissimilar) Expectations: The Growth of the Albany Area Open School," gives the history of a private alternative elementary school. From the perspectives of a parent and educational researcher, Duke notes many of the problems parents face in founding their own school outside the public system.

The factors that account for alternative schools' successes are complex. Similarly, such schools can fail for a variety of reasons: parental discontent, loss of key staff members, ideological conflicts, funding problems, and staff "burnout" are among the most common. In "Casa de la Raza— An Alternative School for Chicano Students," Francisco Hernandez tells the story of a public alternative school serving an ethnic minority. Casa de la Raza was closed because the federal government ruled that it was racially segregated. Casa de la Raza began as part of the Berkeley Experimental Schools Program which sought to provide a districtwide system of educational options. As the Casa experience suggests, the concept of providing schools tailored to the needs of minorities remains a promising yet controversial part of the alternative school movement.

7

The Murray Road School
by Ronald Barndt

A Brief History of the Program

Beginnings. In September 1967, the Murray Road Annex of Newton High School in Newton, Massachusetts, opened its doors to students for the first time. One hundred and seven high school juniors, five full-time faculty members, and a secretary comprised the population of the Annex. No administrators or guidance counsellors were assigned.

The building, located about two miles from the high school, had been built in the early 1950s as a 150-pupil elementary school. The building had been offered to the high school in the spring of 1967 to relieve over-crowding until the opening of the new high school planned for the early 1970s. The high school administration had then held a series of meetings with interested members of the high school faculty to discuss possible uses for the building. Finally it was decided to use the building to house a program whose purpose would be to explore educational innovations which might later influence the program of the new high school.

The principal of Newton High School, Richard W. Mechem, outlined the plan in a memorandum distributed to the high school faculty on May 31, 1967:

> students will take a minimum program of four and one-half major subjects, including English, Social Studies, French, Mathematics, and Physical Education. These major subjects will be scheduled rigidly into three mornings of the week, thereby giving the students and teachers the opportunity to do additional work in these areas or to

---

*From a booklet prepared for the Murray Road Annex of the Newton North High School, 35 Murray Road, West Newton, Massachusetts (February 1975). The material in this booklet was originally part of a doctoral thesis prepared in 1972 by Ronald Barndt. Revisions were made to bring the material up to date. Reprinted by permission of the author.

pursue other projects during the remaining periods of the week. In these subjects students will do homework, take examinations, receive grades, and be given Newton High School credits.

During the rest of the time, and this is meant to include afternoon and evenings and weekends as well as weekdays, the students and faculty will be free to plan and work together and to execute ideas as they develop. . . .

This proposal is highly tentative, and part of the project will be the self-determination by student and staff. During the year 1967–1968, this self-determination will be within the framework mentioned above. . . .

The staff at Murray Road will elect their own director. . . .

Thus the administration declared its intention of delegating the primary responsibility for the planning and implementing of the program to the faculty members involved, within a rather broad framework. From among the high school teachers interested in such a program, a staff was selected and assigned to the school. There were two teachers from the department of English, and one each from the departments of Social Studies, Foreign Language, and Mathematics.

The 107 students who enrolled in the program were recruited from the sophomore class of Newton High School in the late spring of 1967. The high school principal and the newly chosen faculty met with groups of interested students and their parents to outline and discuss the tentative plans for the program, and those students who volunteered and obtained parental permission were admitted to the program.

There were two principal reasons for the decision to limit the program to eleventh grade students: (1) Selection had to be made from among students already at Newton High School. Recruiting began so late in the spring that it was not practical to contact students in the various junior high schools of the city; this effectively eliminated the forthcoming sophomore class from consideration. (2) It was felt that students who were about to enter their senior year were too firmly committed to their present programs; furthermore, many of these students were making plans for post-high school education which were predicated upon their completion of their current programs of study.

Although the faculty of the Murray Road program had hoped to obtain a student body representative of the entire junior class of Newton High School, this did not in fact occur. The plan had been to select 150 students from among those who volunteered. But only forty-seven boys and sixty girls volunteered, so all of them were accepted for the program. As it turned out, the Murray Road student body contained a higher proportion of academically oriented students than the junior class of Newton High School: 59 percent of the Newton High School class of 1969 had taken sophomore English in a college-preparatory section (either curriculum I or advanced placement), but of those who enrolled at Murray Road fully 84 percent had taken sophomore English in a college-preparatory section.

The members of the faculty did their preliminary planning for the program during a three-week workshop in August 1967. During this workshop two of their principal aims were to explore and clarify their purposes and to find ways of structuring a school to carry out their purposes.

Developments during the first year. When the program began, the administration of Newton High School assumed that (1) the Murray Road faculty would elect a program director, (2) students would receive grades in all major courses, and (3) the students would spend their junior year at Murray Road and return to Newton High for their senior year. Before the first year was half over, all three of these assumptions had been reexamined and changed.

Rather than choosing one member of the faculty to serve as the director of the program, the faculty tried to learn to function without a formal leader. It proved to be a difficult task, but at the same time it had certain advantages. It assured each member of the faculty that his ideas and concerns would be taken into account in decision making. It enabled each member of the faculty to understand more fully why and how a decision was made, and this in turn made it easier for him to commit himself to the decision.

This style of faculty operation has continued, although there were several times during the first two years when the idea of choosing a director was again discussed. But in each case, the problems which gave rise to the discussion were dealt with in other ways. Currently, the faculty has divided the more routine administrative responsibilities among its members, and policy decisions are reserved to the faculty group as a whole. On most occasions decisions are reached by consensus, but on those occasions when consensus cannot be reached, decisions are made by majority vote.

During the first few months of the school's operation, the faculty discussed the matter of grading students. The faculty was concerned to focus student attention on the processes they considered essential to self-education: self-assessment of one's personal needs, interests, and goals, consideration of alternative courses of action, choice of a course of action, and self-evaluation of one's progress. It appeared clear that giving grades to students would be inconsistent with this emphasis. The faculty felt that awarding grades to the students would encourage them to direct their efforts toward pleasing the teacher rather than toward setting and meeting their own learning goals. The faculty feared that the progress of students toward self-directed learning would be severely inhibited if they felt that the only thing that really counted for the record was the teacher's appraisal of their work. Consequently the faculty proposed that no grades be awarded at Murray Road School, but that instead the student's record consist of (*a*) an evaluation of the student's progress written by the teacher, together with (*b*) an evaluation of his progress written by the student himself. The high school principal accepted the proposal, and rescinded his original directive that grades be given in all major courses.

In giving initial authorization to the Murray Road program, the high school administration had assumed that the group of juniors chosen would spend one year in the program and then return to Newton High for their senior year. But during the late fall, the faculty proposed that the students at Murray Road be offered the option of returning for a second year. In their position paper, *Where Do Present Murray Road Students Spend Their Senior Year,* presented to the high school principal early in January, the faculty gave its reasons for recommending that the Murray Road students be allowed to return:

> First, is the question of adaptation. Murray Road is a new educational environment, and newness itself often causes a drop in achievement as measured against achievement in a normal high school environment. The students in the new environment are occupied with the learnings which come from exploring and adapting to the new environment. But as they learn to live in the new environment and take advantage of the opportunities it offers, their achievement level rises, often dramatically. . . .
>
> Second, is the question of the length of time necessary for the student placed in a new environment to begin to use it to meet his educational needs. We feel our students need a second year of exposure to this new environment if they are going to be given the opportunity to work through the adaptive phase of the program into that phase where they will take increasing advantage of the environment in need-meeting ways. Third, and finally, is the question of how our students' present thinking about next year influences their ability to adapt positively to the Murray Road environment this year. Faced with having to return to the main high school next year, much of their attention would go towards preparing for next year at the high school, instead of adapting positively to the Murray Road environment and learning to use it to meet their needs.

Following several weeks of discussion of the issues involved, the faculty's recommendation was accepted.

In late January the students were informed that the decision whether to return to Murray Road or to Newton High for their senior year was theirs, and that their decision had to be made by the first week of April. When April came, 90 percent of the students elected to return for a second year.

The faculty now proposed to the high school administration that twenty-five new students be admitted to the school for the following year and that two new teachers be added to the faculty. When this plan was approved, it was decided to solicit applicants from the sophomore class at Newton High School and to select the new students from among them. This produced a student body for the second year of about ninety seniors and twenty-five juniors, thereby giving the faculty an opportunity to explore ways of working with students without regard to grade level.

In deciding how to allocate the two new faculty positions, the staff at Murray Road decided that the priorities were (1) a teacher whose background was in psychology, guidance, and group dynamics, and (2) a science teacher. The current faculty was given the responsibility of interviewing and recommending candidates for these positions. At the same time, the secretarial position was dropped and replaced by an aide position. The responsibilities of this position included managing the school office, working with students to prepare formal transcripts from their evaluations, answering inquiries about the school and handling other public relations matters, and supervising students who were tutoring in elementary schools.

Toward the end of the first year, the Murray Road faculty requested and obtained funds for a workshop to be held in August, before the second year began. Since then, there has been such a workshop each summer. The purposes of these workshops, as set forth in a memorandum to the Newton superintendent of schools, reflect the ways in which the faculty members attempt to revise the program in the light of their experience:

> We believe that a summer workshop is essential for the continued development of the program at Murray Road. It is essential because the problem is not to produce a "product" such as a set of instructional materials or a curriculum which can be reused from year to year, but to deal with current and continuing matters like the following:
> 1. Evaluating the current state of the program.
>   a. Sharing our perceptions of the experience of the school to date.
>   b. Identifying and examining questions raised by our experiences.

2. Reassessing our goals and determining our priorities.
   a. Reexamining and clarifying our assumptions.
   b. Using the lessons learned from the preceding year to determine relevant and realistic goals for the coming year.
3. Promoting faculty growth and faculty unity.
   a. Continuing to work toward a sense of shared purpose as a faculty.
   b. Continuing our efforts to recognize the strengths and interests of individual faculty members and to assign responsibilities so that we capitalize on them.
   c. Improving our skills at working as a team.
   d. Integrating the new faculty members into the faculty.

In order to remain responsive to the needs, wants, and feelings of our students and at the same time to exercise responsible leadership, we must devote a great deal of thought and discussion to matters like these throughout the year. But in order for us to give them the serious and careful attention they require, we need time free of the obligations and duties which arise in the day-to-day operation of the school. Thus, the workshop is essential.[1]

Subsequent developments. During the first year, all students were required to take courses in English, social studies, mathematics, and foreign language. These courses met on Monday, Wednesday, and Friday mornings. Nothing was prescribed for afternoons or for Tuesday and Thursday, and it was here that the students and faculty were expected to develop new ideas and approaches. This time was used in various ways: teachers, students, and parents offered various courses to those who were interested, some students tutored in elementary schools, and some students brought in resource people from the community to work with them on their special interests.

The courses on Monday, Wednesday, and Friday mornings, though required, were by no means traditional. There was a good deal of emphasis on student planning and participation—even more than in some of the elective courses. But there was a tendency for some of the students to regard the required courses as the "real school," which they had to endure in order to get the electives they really wanted, and this attitude sometimes interfered with their making effective use of the courses. Some students found it easy to avoid thinking about the meaning of the required courses —they had to take them, and that was that.

---

1. Memorandum to Superintendent Aaron Fink from the Murray Road faculty, dated May 12, 1970.

For these reasons, the faculty decided that, beginning with the second year, the distinction between required and elective courses would be eliminated wherever that was possible. The only requirements retained were those established by state law—U. S. history and physical education—together with a Newton High School requirement that each student enroll in an English course each term. Even these requirements were eased by providing alternatives: students could fulfill the requirements by choosing from a variety of appropriate elective courses or by independent study.

At the same time, the students were invited to participate actively in planning the whole program of the school for the second year. Each term since that time has begun with a series of all-school meetings whose purpose is to organize the school for the forthcoming term. In group discussions and in individual conferences with faculty advisors efforts are made to help individuals decide what they want and need from the school. Faculty members and students propose courses which they wish to offer or participate in. The number of courses proposed has sometimes approached one hundred. Groups meet to describe and discuss each of the proposed courses, and students select those they want. Then a student scheduling committee does its best to arrange all of the thirty or more courses which have survived the process so far into a schedule which allows most people to have the program they desire. This whole process, which may take two weeks, is regarded by the faculty as an integral part of the program of the school, for it encourages students to think seriously about their goals and different ways of reaching them, and it encourages them to assume responsibility for the program which results.

The school now exists as a three-year school with a 100-member student body comprised of sophomores, juniors, and seniors (in proportions which vary somewhat from year to year). Each spring as the senior class prepares to graduate, the school sets about recruiting new students. During the first five years, about twice as many students applied for the program as could be accepted. Applicants are classified according to sex and high school curriculum.[2] Equal numbers of boys and girls are accepted, and an attempt is made to have each Newton High curriculum proportionately represented. The actual selection of students within each category is made randomly.

---

2. Curriculum classifications used are: Ia—Honors; I—regular college preparatory; II—all other. (In actuality the high school has more than three curricula; this scheme is used only for Murray Road admissions purposes.)

The faculty has not abandoned its intention of obtaining a student body reasonably representative of Newton High as a whole, but so far this intention has been only partially realized. Despite concerted efforts to interest and recruit others, the school continues to have a slightly disproportionately high number of students from the college-preparatory curricula. Since 1970, teams of Murray Road students and teachers have made recruiting visits to potential applicants through their classes at the high school, making special attempts to interest those who are not academically oriented. Nevertheless, the percentage of these who apply has remained below the proportionate response of about 40 percent. Murray Road has tried to compensate by accepting all of these who apply.

Some possible causes for this lack of response from those who are not in the college-preparatory curricula are: (1) Students tend to apply who have had friends at Murray Road. Thus the present population tends to perpetuate itself. (2) The school has acquired a reputation of a "freak" school. Although "freaks" are probably no more common at Murray Road than at Newton High, this reputation repels many of the students the faculty would like to reach. (3) The process of planning, acting, and evaluating which is basic to the school has usually taken a very verbal form, and this sometimes intimidates less verbal students who are otherwise attracted to the school. (5) Parents with limited education tend to distrust innovative schools. The program is voluntary and the students who apply must obtain parental permission; consequently, some who would like to enroll are prevented from doing so.

Indications so far are that those noncollege-preparatory students who do come respond well to the program; for this reason the faculty continues to make an effort to recruit them.

For the 1969–1970 school year two groups of students were admitted. One group was recruited as usual from the sophomore class at Newton High, but the other group came directly from junior high school. This made it possible for the faculty to explore the desirability of mixing students in groups without regard to age difference, allowing students to select themselves into classes on the basis of their own needs, wants, and readiness. Also, the faculty suspected that younger students who came to Murray Road directly from junior high school would respond more quickly to the environment than students who had spent their sophomore year at Newton High School. But at the end of that year, the decision was made by the students and faculty to return to a two-year program by admitting only juniors for the following year. The chief considerations which led to this decision were: (1) The presence of three different age and experience levels in the school greatly expanded the diversity of student demands on the small faculty and forced some faculty members to make a great many uncomfortable choices about which needs to neglect. This problem was notably severe in mathematics, foreign language, and social studies, despite the addition of teacher aides in these fields. The faculty felt it could better serve the students if the diversity of demands was reduced by eliminating the sophomore class. (2) There was concern that continuing to accept students directly from junior high school would weaken the ties between Murray Road and Newton High, and this was considered undesirable because there was (and is) a desire to maintain communication with Newton High in order that the two schools may influence each other. Because of the decision-making process at Murray Road, which involves students and faculty working together to reach consensus, this decision has been reviewed each year. Currently the school is functioning as a three-year program.

Some Unusual Features of the Program

One of the most natural ways of introducing the program of the Murray Road School is to present some of the features which distinguish it from most other secondary schools. The following paragraphs describe some of the more unusual features of the program as it exists now.

1. A high degree of student freedom. The school is operated on the "open campus" model: a student is not required to be present at the school except for his scheduled classes. There are no school regulations restricting student dress. Required courses are few. Students take English every term, one year of United States History, and must fulfill the physical education requirement. Otherwise, they may plan their program as they choose.

2. Student involvement in the school decision making and school operation. All-school meetings are held to discuss issues facing the whole school, and students are encouraged to take the initiative in trying to find ways of dealing with these issues. Most of the limitations imposed on student decision-making power are consequences of laws, ordinances, and regulations to which the school system as a whole is subject. Examples of such limitations are attendance laws, fire regulations, and high school graduation requirements. Students are involved in determining how these requirements might be met.

Following is a selection from the long list of responsibilities in which students have been involved:

—proposing and organizing new courses. This includes actively seeking resource people for those things which cannot be offered by the regular faculty.

—planning and scheduling the program of the school. Within the framework of the school calendar (opening, vacations, closing) students and faculty work together to determine how blocks of time should be used for learning. A student group works out the scheduling of classes, etc., which will allow the maximum number of students to have the classes which they want.

—proposing and implementing different ways of organizing the program of the school as a whole. For example, in one term, time was set aside so that one subject could be studied in concentrated fashion for up to three hours a day, five days a week. Later, classes were suspended for a longer period to allow groups to devote all their time to a single topic of interest to them through various classroom and nonclassroom activities. This form of concentrated study has existed for periods of one, three, and six weeks.

—participation with the faculty in presentations of the program of the school to outside groups such as faculties of other schools, seminars and courses at nearby schools of education, student-faculty-parent planning groups in other school systems contemplating changes in their schools, and various educational conferences.

—scheduling, greeting, and hosting visitors to the school.

—participating with the faculty in presenting the program to prospective students and their parents.

—working with the faculty to determine criteria for the selection of new faculty members, and participating in the interviewing of candidates for faculty positions. (Final decisions about faculty appointments are made by the continuing faculty, from among candidates proposed by a faculty-student committee.)

—preparing transcripts of their own work at Murray Road by choosing representative comments from the more lengthy evaluations prepared by them and by the faculty. (This is done under the supervision of a faculty member to ensure that selections made from the teacher's evaluations are representative of the whole in tone and content.)

—sounding out colleges on their receptivity to graduates of a program such as ours, and organizing a committee to compile this information.

—devising a means of fulfilling the state physical education requirement. (The school lacks a gymnasium and a staff person in this area, so this was a real problem.)

3. Student involvement in classroom decision making and evaluation. In many classes, students are involved in the planning of the content and organization of the course. Topics for study are chosen, goals are set, and a means of proceeding is hammered out. An important part of the evaluation procedure in each course is the student's written self-evaluation of his work in the course, which, together with the teacher's written evaluation of the student's work, becomes part of the student's record. The final step in the evaluation process is a meeting between the student and his adviser to discuss his own and his teachers' evaluations.

4. Deemphasis on ability grouping and curriculum designations. After the first year, nearly all such distinctions were eliminated, even in mathematics and foreign language.

5. Student involvement in the community outside the school. Some forms this has taken include tutoring in elementary schools (which at its peak had nearly 75 percent of the student body participating), working for community service organizations, and working with action groups concerned with such problems as the Vietnam war, the ecological crisis, etc.

6. No designated program director. The faculty functions cooperatively as an administrative team to make policy decisions for the school, and day-to-day administrative responsibilities are divided among the faculty members. Technically, the Newton North High School principal has veto power over any faculty decisions, but he never exercised it. Decisions which are made by the faculty include selecting new faculty members, and deciding who will receive tenure.

7. A high degree of mutual commitment of the faculty members to their continuing growth and development as teachers. There are three meetings of the entire faculty each week, each meeting at least an hour and a half in length. One meeting deals primarily with administrative issues. A second meeting is held to discuss individual students, their response to the program, and any special problems

they may be having. The purpose is not only to share information which will help the faculty to deal constructively with the student, but also to gain more insight into the strengths and weaknesses of the program at the school as it is experienced by the individual student. The third meeting is intended to explore basic issues in teaching and learning which seem important in the operation of a school of this kind. An important function of this meeting is to allow faculty members to explore and clarify their assumptions and attitudes in order to help one another increase in effectiveness as teachers.

The Aims and the Program

Educational Aims and Educational Programs. The Murray Road School shares its primary aim with many other schools: to help its students acquire a general education:

> General education deals mainly with preparation for life in the broad sense of completeness as a human being, rather than in the narrower sense of competence in a particular lot [Harvard Committee 1945, p. 4].

> General education is that education which presumably every man *as man* should have, as distinguished from specialized education which some men need by virtue of some function that they but not all individuals have to perform [Broudy 1961, p. 292].

This does not mean that the school does not encourage, or provide resources and facilities for, specialized learning. In fact, it is ordinarily the case that students are encouraged to discover and explore areas of specialization which are of interest to them. What it does mean is that the school is primarily engaged in providing the individual with experiences which help him to identify and develop his own potentialities.

It might be supposed that differences in the programs of schools have their roots in fundamentally different interpretations of what a general education is. If this is so, however, the differences do not often manifest themselves clearly in the written statements of philosophy which schools produce. For example, the stated philosophy of Newton North High School is one to which the Murray Road faculty can readily subscribe, for there is nothing in it antithetical to their purposes and beliefs. To understand the real differences in the philosophies of schools it seems necessary to pursue the answers to two questions: (1) What is the relative emphasis among the basic concerns which are expressed? and (2) What means of implementation have been chosen as appropriate?

The first question reflects the fact that no one sees all of his aims as equally important, and consequently some aims assume centrality. This effect can be illustrated by a comparison of these two interpretations of general education:

> The basic concern of general education is to help each student realize and accept the challenge of his individual potential and lay the foundation for successful pursuit of his full status as a responsible citizen. The purposes of general education are thus fourfold: (1) to contribute to the preparation for life needs, not only those which the student realizes but also those which he must be taught to realize; (2) to establish basic relevance between knowledge and everyday experience; (3) to provide a nonspecialized type of training characterized by wide application, universal value, and great intellectual appeal; and (4) to lay the foundation of basic information essential to later intelligent pursuit of individual interests and special aptitudes [Butler and Wren 1965, p. 44].

> ... the goal ... is to assist students to become individuals
> who are able to take self-initiated action and to be responsible for those actions;
> who are capable of intelligent choice and self-direction;
> who are critical learners, able to evaluate the contributions made by others;
> who have acquired knowledge relevant to the solution of problems;
> who, even more importantly, are able to adapt flexibly and intelligently to new problem situations;
> who have internalized an adaptive mode of approach to problems, utilizing all pertinent experience freely and creatively;
> who are able to cooperate effectively with others in these various activities;
> who work, not for the approval of others, but in terms of their own socialized purposes [Rogers 1951, p. 387].

A reading of these two statements does not compel the conclusion that the writers are advocates of different programs, or that they are in disagreement about the aims of general education. But there are differences of emphasis between them, and these differences are likely to lead to differences in programs which grow out of them. For example, Rogers specifically sets forth as objectives the ability to cooperate with others and the habit of working for one's own purposes rather than for the approval of others. Although these same goals may be implied in the Butler and

Wren statement (perhaps item 1 of that statement), the fact that Rogers chooses to emphasize them probably means that we would be more likely to find conscious efforts to achieve these goals in a program of his. It seems reasonable to suppose that differences of emphasis in objectives will lead to significant differences in programs.

The second question—concerning the means of implementation chosen —has two aspects, which I shall call *external* and *internal*. In its *external* aspect, this question involves such external constraints as the resources available to the program, the amount of freedom the planners are allowed to exercise in implementing their ideas, and the previous experiences of the students who enter the program. This aspect reflects the effect of the external environment within which the planners must build their program.

In its *internal* aspect, this question primarily reflects the assumptions the planners have about students, about teachers, and about the nature of learning. What is the role of the student? How much responsibility is it reasonable to give him? How capable is he of participating actively in the planning of his own educational experience? How large is his intellectual capacity? What is the role of the teacher in the classroom and in the school as a whole? How should teachers relate to students? How much creative behavior is it reasonable to expect of a teacher? How does learning occur? What constitutes evidence of learning.

The importance of this aspect can be seen by considering what may happen in a program one of whose objectives is to foster greater student responsibility if a teacher in the program has limited faith in student ability to assume responsibility. His means of implementation will no doubt be quite different from that of another teacher who has greater confidence in the potential responsibility of his students.

The second of these two questions—the means of implementation chosen—is dealt with in the earlier part of this paper by describing some details of the program at Murray Road. The first question—aims which have been emphasized—is the subject of the remainder of this section.

Educational aims which have been emphasized at Murray Road.   John W. Gardner has said, "The ultimate goal of the educational system is to shift to the individual the burden of pursuing his own education." [Gardner (1965, p. 12)] Presumably the individual is to assume this burden as part of his responsibilities as an adult; therefore it is essential that secondary schools, which deal with students who are making the transition from childhood to adulthood, recognize the importance of this goal. Since adolescence is a period in a person's life when he is striving for greater independence and responsibility, it is an opportune time in his educational experience to provide constructive channels through which to develop these traits.

Adolescents are trying to define an adult role for themselves, and they often respond positively when they are accorded the rights and privileges of adults. Perhaps this is one reason why the Murray Road planners find themselves exploring some of the same ground as workers in the field of adult education.[3]

Knowles has written of the implications for adult education of the adult learner's need to be treated with the respect due a person capable of self-direction. He sets forth five implications:

> 1. Great importance is placed on the establishment of a *social climate* that is characterized by informality, concern for human comfort, respect for individuality, ease of interaction among students and teachers, and a sense of mutuality.
> 2. The students are involved in a process of *self-diagnosis of needs for learning,* with the teacher taking responsibility for providing models of desirable content, an example of objective self-analysis, and resource information.
> 3. The students and teacher engage in a process of *mutual planning* in translating the diagnosed needs into objectives and learning experiences.
> 5. Evaluation is a process of *self-evaluation,* or more specifically, a process of reself-diagnosis, in which the same tools and procedures that were used for diagnosis of needs for learning are now repeated to measure gains in learning [Knowles 1968, pp. 2–3].

At the Murray Road School there has been a serious attempt to implement a classroom climate and procedure similar to that described by Knowles. This attempt grew out of the faculty's belief that students would respond positively if they were granted more responsibility, and also from their concern that students gain experience in the exercise of responsibility. At times the faculty's faith in this approach has been sorely tried, for students seem frequently to prefer a passive role in the classroom. When

---

3. It is interesting to note that certain workers in the field of adult education have found that commonly accepted principles of pedagogy did not seem appropriate to their task. As appropriate principles began to emerge, the term *andragogy*—the guiding of adults—was coined, to distinguish this set of principles from those of *pedagogy*—the guiding of children. But as Knowles has noted, "the enthusiasm of both students and teachers for the new technology [*andragogy*] has caused the question to be raised, Wouldn't it work equally well with younger students? [Knowles 1968, p. 6]."

teachers have told students that they were to participate in the planning and evaluation of courses, the result was often that described by Rogers:

> However, this is not to say that things will run smoothly. In students who have, for anything from one to twenty years, experienced a class as a passive experience, such an opening of a course is at first puzzling, then downright frustrating. Negative feelings, often very strong ones, are aroused. At first they are not expressed because one does not "talk back to" or correct the teacher; but as the tension mounts, some bold soul bursts out, "I think we're wasting our time! I think we ought to have an outline and follow it, and that you ought to teach us. We came here to learn from you, not to discuss among ourselves!" [Rogers 1951, pp. 393–94].

Murray Road faculty members have responded in various ways to these expressions of student frustration. Sometimes they have ridden out the storm and have been rewarded eventually by exciting student-led classes. Sometimes they have attempted to ride out the storm but have found that the storm never abated and the course never really got moving. Sometimes they have yielded to the pressure from the students and have offered more conventional courses. Most of the teachers have sought to be patient with a class while its members learn the skills and attitudes necessary to proceed effectively in a spirit of mutual inquiry. They recognize that it takes some time for students to learn a new style of classroom interaction, and they believe that the expenditure of time is justified in the light of the kind of learning which then becomes possible.

The teachers have not insisted that students assume responsibility for all aspects of their learning at once. If, at a given time, students seem unable to manage a certain responsibility, the teachers sometimes allow them to relinquish it in order that the students can be free to learn to deal with other responsibilities. For example, a number of students who had had a frustrating first term because their English class seemed unable to plan together effectively approached two English teachers and asked them to plan a course based on books which the teachers liked. The students made it clear that they would read and discuss whatever the teachers thought worthwhile. The teachers responded to the students' self-diagnosis of their needs by consenting to offer such a course,[4] and it turned out to be rather successful. It is important to note that, although the teachers had consented to select the materials for the course and to do some of the plan-

---

4. The students promptly named the course "Like It or Lump It."

ning, they did not abandon their concern that the students engage in mutual inquiry as they discussed their reading, nor did they abandon their concern that the students evaluate their own experience in the course.

The importance of the role of self-diagnosis and self-evaluation in the program must be emphasized. If continuing self-education is to become a possibility for students, they must learn ways of finding out where they are now in relation to their goals. Students often know neither what they do not know, nor what they need to learn to reach their goal. Worse than this, in fact, in most school situations teachers attempt to teach without first trying to find out where their students are at the start. Thelen, in his article, "The Triumph of 'Achievement' Over Inquiry in Education," points out that the emphasis in educational practice often seems to be on the final state of a student's knowledge, without regard to how much he actually *learned*:

> If learning were the goal, achievement would be measured as the difference between pre-tests and post-tests on the material of the course. Since pre-tests are seldom used, the teacher has no way of knowing how much the pupil learned [Thelen 1960b, p. 191].

Therefore, if evaluation of *learning* is to be undertaken either by the teacher or by the student himself, diagnosis is a necessary step.

But this is not the only reason that self-diagnosis is stressed as a basic step in the educational process. As Knowles says, if a class is to work together in a spirit of mutual inquiry, then it is essential that the group find out what its collective resources are. Those members of the group who find that they have relevant resources to contribute to the other members are reinforced in their commitment to the learning group. Knowles (1968, p. 3) points out that an adult has a reservoir of experience and knowledge which is important to his self-identity, and which is a rich resource for further learning. If his experience is ignored, the individual is likely to feel rejected as a person of worth.

One of the chief reasons for stressing student self-evaluation rather than evaluation by the teacher is that it tends to foster habits of learning which are genuinely educational. Thelen has enumerated some of the antieducational consequences of evaluation solely by teacher-given tests:

> In class discussions and class projects, the teacher seems to want class members to share ideas. But on tests, pupils see their classmates as rivals who are required to get the better of one another . . .
> The purpose of learning is to gain status, symbolized in a mark, rather than to master the discipline of the subject. . . .

Often the main object of inquiry in the classroom is the sort of question the teacher is likely to ask, the bases he uses for marking, his biases and enthusiasms.... In good teaching the demands the pupil faces come from the problem situation, not from the teacher. . . .

Once knowledge is tested, it can safely be forgotten. . . .

Pupils learn that specific information is an end in itself rather than the means to broad understanding of universal principles.

. . . Our procedures for measuring achievement do not help the pupil find out who he is or discover his strengths and weaknesses as a person. Our tests only tell us how well the pupil is conforming to a specified 1960 super technical model [Thelen 1960b, pp. 191–92].[5]

When the student must evaluate himself, he is forced to consider the relevance of what he is doing to the rest of his experience and to his own personal goals. The self-evaluations the students write at the end of each semester present convincing evidence that many students are learning to think in these terms.

Many of the current educational innovations which stress student responsibility place their chief emphasis on the development of programs of independent study. At Murray Road, however, there has been a great deal of emphasis on *mutual* inquiry: inquiry undertaken by a group. Part of the reason for this emphasis is the concern that students learn the skills and attitudes of group interaction which are valuable in a wide variety of settings. But perhaps the chief reason for this emphasis is one which has been well stated recently by Bruner:

A community is a powerful force for effective learning. Students, when encouraged, are tremendously helpful to each other. They are like a cell, a revolutionary cell. It is the cell in which mutual learning and instruction can occur, a unit within a classroom with its own sense of compassion and responsibility for its members [Bruner 1971, p. 21].

The central concern of the classroom learning group, then, is *mutual inquiry*. The process of inquiry has been described as taking place when the individual initiates ". . . the processes of giving attention to something; of interacting with and being stimulated by other people, whether in person or through their writings; and of reflection and reorganization of concepts and attitudes, as shown in arriving at conclusions, identifying new

---

5. Thelen adds wryly: "But we do have a conscience. Having conditioned the pupil, through awards and other forms of social approval, into submissiveness, we then propose to put him in a liberal arts college to develop his human spirit."

investigations to be undertaken, taking action, and turning out a better product [Thelen 1960a, p. 85]." Inquiry is much the same process that Dewey has called reflective thinking, and that others have variously termed critical thinking or problem solving.

The cultivation of the spirit of inquiry is a central task of education. But all too often schools construe their task as no more than the communication of the results of inquiries of the past. Unfortunately, what Schwab has said of the traditional science course is true of teaching practice in other fields as well:

> ... It has tended to treat only the outcomes, the conclusions of inquiry, divorced from the data which support them and from the conceptual frames which define—and limit—their validity.
> The result has been to convey a false image of science as knowledge that is literally true, permanent, even complete. This misleading image is reinforced by the neatness with which our courses are usually organized and expounded. We tend to provide a structure which admits of no loose ends. We minimize doubts and qualification. We strive for exposition characterized by an almost artistic beginning, middle, and end [Schwab 1962, p. 3].

It is bad enough that the absence of the spirit of inquiry in education can cause a distorted view of the nature of the various disciplines of learning, but there is a worse danger: that the learner's natural curiosity and willingness to explore may be crippled. No doubt the exaggerated emphasis on the learning of "content" is responsible for many such casualties. Einstein is said to have remarked that after studying intensively in order to pass his university examinations, he was completely unable to engage in inquiry for a full year. He continued, "It is in fact nothing short of a miracle that the modern methods of instruction have not entirely strangled the holy curiosity of inquiry; for this delicate little plant, aside from stimulation, stands mainly in need of freedom. Without this, it goes to rack and ruin without fail."[6]

What is a classroom like which provides the necessary freedom for inquiry? Of course there is no single pattern of behaviors which characterizes mutual inquiry; the pattern depends on the subject, the teacher, the members of the class. In an English class studying poetry the members may agree to discuss among themselves the meaning of a particular poem,

---

6. Albert Einstein, quoted by Carl R. Rogers in a lecture given at Harvard University, April 12, 1966.

and try to explore the relationship of the meaning to the form, style, imagery, and technique employed by the poet. The procedural emphasis is to explore together, to discuss. References may be consulted, and information may be sought from the teacher. But the teacher is no longer at the center of everything: students typically address remarks, opinions, and questions to each other rather than to the teacher. The tendency of students to direct most of their effort toward obtaining the "right" answer that the teacher had in his mind at the outset is reduced or perhaps, we may hope, even eliminated.

In a mathematics class the focus of discussion may be upon a problem brought to the attention of the class by a student who was unsuccessful in solving it on his own. As the class tries to solve it, or to help the student understand a solution, inquiry may focus on one of two problems, or perhaps on both at the same time: how can we solve this problem, or how can we help the member of the class who posed the problem understand how to solve it? At times when a problem has been solved, it leads to a new inquiry. For example, a student may look at the solution and, observing a certain pattern, raise the question, "Does it always happen that . . .?" A generalization is born, and an inquiry can be launched to determine if it is true.

Besides the mutual inquiry which takes place as students attempt to help each other make knowledge their own, there are two other kinds of inquiry which Murray Road seeks to foster. Thelen (1960a) has called these *personal inquiry* and *reflective action*. *Personal inquiry* involves the attempts of the individual to achieve some sort of self-understanding and integration between himself and his knowledge. This is a delicate area because it involves very personal concerns of the student, and perhaps for this reason schools have tended not to concern themselves with it directly. Murray Road attempts to foster this kind of inquiry by (1) attempting to provide an atmosphere in which the student feels free to explore his own thoughts and feelings about himself and what he is learning, and also (2) by requiring every student to write a self-evaluation from time to time. In writing his self-evaluation the student is asked to consider what he has learned, to compare that with what he ought to have learned (by his own standards), and to describe areas in which he is conscious of personal growth. This is a lot to ask of students; most of us never had it asked of us in the course of our own schooling. "Know thyself." Self-knowledge has been recognized as a goal of education for millenia, but typically our educational institutions have assumed that it would emerge of itself.

Reflective action is the sort of inquiry which the individual interacts with his environment in order to change it and to learn the skills necessary to change it. The concern to foster this kind of inquiry has led at Murray Road to the practice of involving the students in the planning and operation of the school as a whole and in the planning and operation of courses within the school.

Some of the elements of the process of reflective action appear to be these:[7]

1. Forming thoughts and feelings into a statement of a question or problem.
2. Considering alternative ways of solving the problem.
   a. Collecting evidence bearing on the potential effectiveness of alternative solutions.
   b. Hypothesizing about the potential effects of an alternative solution when factual evidence is not available.
   c. Identifying the limitations within which the problem must be solved.
   d. Weighing possible consequences and deciding if they are willing to live with them.
3. Choosing an alternative and acting.
4. Evaluating the action taken, perhaps with a resulting statement of a new problem which begins the process again.

These elements are important not only in reflective action, but in the other types of inquiry as well.

But there is an element in the inquiry process which has not been made explicit in the foregoing list: the creative element. Possibly the most important element in the process, it is also the hardest to foster. Much has been written about creativity in recent years; some of the available evidence suggests that schooling in general has been more destructive of creativity than encouraging of it:

---

7. Adapted from *Where Do Present Murray Road Students Spend Their Senior Year*, a position paper by the Murray Road faculty written in January 1968.

The intent of this list will be misconstrued if it is assumed that this is a *method* students are expected to follow. Like the so-called "scientific method," or the *heuristic* of Polya (1945), it is not a method which is explicitly followed; it is a list whose purpose is to focus attention on the salient features of a process which is actually carried out informally and somewhat intuitively.

Years ago some psychologists at a university were discussing creativity and age. They agreed that by age forty-five, one is over the hill, and creativity is pretty much gone. They decided it would be useful to establish this fact experimentally. They selected test instruments and tested a universe of forty-five year olds. To no one's surprise, only 2 percent were highly creative. Discussing the results one psychologist suggested that it would be interesting to find the age when creativity seemed to "ear out." The others agreed and they tested a universe of forty-four-year-olds, forty-three-year-olds, and so on. This proved to be a monotonous task because the 2 percent highly creative remained the same until the weary psychologists reached the universe of seven year olds. Highly creative jumped to 10 percent. At five years old the figure was 90 percent highly creative [Papanek 1964, p. 170].

Perhaps because creativity is so little understood, or perhaps because it cannot be taught by lecture or explanation, or perhaps because most teachers are themselves not creative individuals, education has given little attention to the encouragement of creativity:

Dr. Weisskopf observes[8] that while the social science literature contains considerable information about creative thought and the conditions of its growth, educators have strangely not taken it much to heart. Dr. Weisskopf for example grants that industry, regular study habits, and a critical and controlled attitude are necessary attributes of successful intellectual work, and that those creative individuals who eventually learned the values of relaxation, irregular habit, and periodic abandonment of criticism and control have usually spent years exercising the virtues advocated by traditional educators. "Yet," she observes, "the question remains unanswered why, among the four stages of the creative process, namely, preparation, incubation, illumination, and verification, we prepare children for the first and last stage only, and completely ignore the other two stages" [Jones 1962, p. 214].

Perhaps the answer is that students do not need to be *prepared* for these two stages, incubation and illumination; they merely have to be *freed* to engage themselves in them. Students frequently have little idea what creative inquiry is like. Because their schooling has usually been concerned solely with the *outcomes* of inquiry, they have had the opportunity to engage only in the preparation and verification stages. They often regard the other stages as necessary only to the uninformed and uneducated and

---

8. In Weisskopf (1951, p. 188)

hence inappropriate for use in school. One of the tasks of the school is to show that these stages are legitimate and necessary parts of the process of creative inquiry.

Holt (1964, pp. 88–91) has observed that the sheer volume of work we give students tends to inhibit creative thinking by making the students *answer-centered* rather than *problem-centered*. When the student feels he has too many problems to do, his attention is shifted away from an attempt to understand the problem, away from an attempt to get himself into it, toward an attempt to get an answer as quickly as possible. This produces the demand, "Tell us how to do these." And then the student does not exercise his own creative resources to seek an answer; he follows a set procedure which produces the answer. The set procedure becomes the objective of the student's learning, rather than the ability to attack and investigate problems effectively.

Another reason that students become answer-centered is found in their need for the security of knowing what to do, of having a set procedure to cope with all situations they might encounter. Rogers (1951, pp. 384–428) has noted that this need often arises if the student feels that his acceptance by others, and perhaps by himself, depends upon his success in producing the response he believes is required. Engaging in inquiry entails a risk: the risk that the result desired may not be achieved. A student who feels that he will be rejected if he fails will tend to avoid the risk.

Rogers also lays stress on the fact that significant learning is by its nature a threatening experience, for it involves the student's reorganization of his present perceptions and understandings; in short, it involves reorganization of self. He believes that the evidence available to him shows that learning is facilitated when an atmosphere is created in which the individual's anxiety about the threat implicit in learning is minimized.

To achieve this classroom climate, the teacher's specific teaching techniques seem to be secondary to the teacher's attitude:

> If teachers accept students as they are, allow them to express their feelings and attitudes freely without condemnation or judgment, plan learning activities *with* them rather than *for* them, create a classroom atmosphere relatively free from emotional strains and tensions, consequences follow which are different from when these conditions do not exist. The consequences, on present evidence, seem to be in the direction of democratic objectives. It is apparent that the above conditions can be achieved in more than one way—that the climate for self-directed learning by students is not the result of only one kind of practice [Paul E. Eiserer (1949), quoted in Rogers 1951, p. 392].

Apparently teachers have a wide latitude in developing a style or set of techniques which is their own while attempting to implement these ideas. But there are certain aspects to the teacher's role which Rogers considers essential. The teacher must take pains to establish the acceptant climate which is necessary. He must set an example of respect for the ideas and feelings of group participants. He helps the participants state and clarify their aims. He endeavors to make available resources which students may use for learning. He regards himself as a flexible resource to be used by the group in any way which seems meaningful to them insofar as he can operate comfortably in these ways. He acts as a facilitator of the learning process and as a participant, but not as a goal-setter, teller, and evaluator.

When the teacher assumes this new role, the relationships between the students in the classroom are altered. The focus of attention is no longer on the teacher and his thoughts and actions. Students relate to each other in various new ways: teaching one another, learning from one another, and exploring ideas and their implications together.

Students seem to be able to work together in these ways even when they are of disparate achievement levels and ability levels. The amount that each brings and the amount that each takes away are different, but there is not a sense of the slower student holding back the faster. For the faster student the learning which takes place is different from that for the slower, to be sure; for example, the learning of the faster student may involve the things he discovered in trying to clarify an idea for someone else.

This was one of the considerations which led to the deemphasis of ability grouping at Murray Road. But the faculty was also concerned about a practical problem: the deceptive nature of the curriculum "ability groups" at Newton High School. Casual observation at the high school seemed to support the belief that the curriculum levels reflected ethnic, social, and economic factors at least as much as ability factors. This could have come about because of the tendency on the part of many students to find their way into the "ability" group to which most of their friends belonged. It seemed reasonable to hope that many students would respond very favorably to the stimulation of being in classes where no distinctions based on ethnic, social, economic, or ability considerations were observed.[9]

The faculty's responsibility to the students. From the beginning of the

---

9. Bettelheim (1958) observes that ability grouping has not been empirically shown to be good practice, and in addition presents some theoretical objections to it.

program, one of the chief concerns of the Murray Road faculty was to foster responsible action on the part of the students. In order to give the students the opportunity to learn to exercise responsibility, the staff gave them extensive freedom to make decisions for themselves and to participate in the operation of the school, along the lines already described. People who are new to the school, both students and visitors, often assume incorrectly that this freedom was established as an end in itself; but to the teachers it is primarily a means to an end. They make the assumption that their responsibility to the students begins, not ends, with the freedom they offer the students. They feel a responsibility to help the students to learn to use their freedom in productive ways. They do not regard all the directions in which students can choose to move as equally valid, even though on many occasions they have agreed in advance to live with any choice the students make. The teachers do not simply stand back and wait to see what the students will choose; instead they participate with them, offering their ideas, their cautions, their perspectives, and their support through the sometimes complex and frustrating process of making the school work.

Some books on education published in the last few years are suffused with a romanticism which seems to hold that if teachers only leave students alone to develop themselves in accordance with their innate motivation to learn, they will flower into happy, mature, and responsible human beings. The Murray Road staff doubts the validity of this. They believe that education must be purposive, and that they as educators must have purposes for their students. This means that the encouragement which the faculty offers to the student is not bland, noncommittal support for any choice he makes; instead, they try to support him by offering understanding and counsel, while not denying their own values. In short, the faculty has acknowledged a moral responsibility to the students.

Consequently, there are certain responsibilities which the teachers assume on behalf of the students whether or not the students ask them to do so. Some of these are:

   1. Attempting to make the students accept responsibility for their actions, choices, and assumptions. This often means confronting students with the consequences of the things they think and do. Thus, a teacher may initiate a discussion with a student about the effect of his behavior on others in the school or the consequences of an opinion he has expressed.

2. Supporting students as they learn to live with the consequences of the choices they make. For most students, making significant choices for themselves is a new and unsettling experience, and it helps them to know that there are sympathetic and concerned adults who will not abandon them if things do not work out as they hope.

3. Bringing to the students' attention ideas and possibilities which would not otherwise occur to them as possible choices. It is not enough to ask students what they want to do. Often they have no idea of the richness of the possibilities. Thus the faculty often takes the initiative in presenting them with possible conceptual frameworks or possible models for action.

As the teachers try to meet these responsibilities, they face certain problems inherent in the process. For example, if the faculty allows students to make choices which affect a class or the whole school and simultaneously assumes the responsibility of confronting the students with the consequences of their choices, this raises the possibility of subtle manipulation of the students by the faculty. It would be unfortunate indeed if the teachers were, in reality, maneuvering the students toward predetermined outcomes, thereby offering the student only the *illusion* of responsibility. The teachers guard against this possibility to the best of their ability by remaining aware of the danger and by consciously examining their own motivations and actions.

Another problem is created by the responsibility to make students aware of new possibilities and new ideas. On one hand, the faculty feels that students learn best the things they discover for themselves and that they pursue goals they have developed for themselves more ardently than they pursue those suggested by others. On the other hand, they want to make the student's experience as rich and productive as they can. Sometimes they seem to be forced to choose between these two values. For example, a teacher may see that a class is on the verge of a major insight which has as yet occurred to no one there. From experience the teacher knows that if the class gains the insight on its own, there will be a great deal of excitement and the insight will be internalized by many students. But it may take an indefinite period of time for the class to arrive at the insight on its own, if indeed it arrives at all. The problem confronting the teacher is whether to intervene and, if so, when it is appropriate and how it can be done most effectively.

A word is in order about the basis of the authority the teachers exercise as they seek to carry out their responsibilities to the students. Fundamentally, the authority is based on the respect the students have for their teachers—respect for their competence as teachers, respect for their fairness and openness, and respect for their other human qualities. In most situations the faculty suggests or urges, but does not demand, for they attempt to base their authority on respect rather than power.

References

Bettelheim, Bruno (1958): Segregation, New Style, *School Review,* v. 66, 3, Autumn, 1958, pp. 251–272.

Broudy, Harry S. (1961): *Building a Philosophy of Education.* Englewood Cliffs, N.J.: Prentice-Hall.

Bruner, Jerome S. (1971): *The Process of Education Revisited, Phi Delta Kappan,* v. 53, 3, pp. 18–21.

Butler, Charles H., and Wren, F. Lynwood (1965): *The Teaching of Secondary Mathematics.* New York: McGraw-Hill.

Eiserer, Paul E. (1949): The Implications of Non-Directive Counseling for Classroom Teaching, *Growing Pains in Educational Research.* 1949 Official Report, Washington, D.C.: American Educational Research Association.

Gardner, John W. (1965): *Self-Renewal: The Individual and the Innovative Society.* New York: Harper and Row.

Harvard Committee, Report of (1945): *General Education in a Free Society.* Cambridge, Mass.: Harvard University Press.

Holt, John (1964): *How Children Fail.* New York: Pitman.

Jones, Richard M. (1962): The Role of Self-Knowledge in the Educative Process, *Contemporary Educational Psychology: Selected Essays* (Richard M. Jones, ed.). New York: Harper and Row, 1966.

Knowles, Malcolm S. (1968): *The Application of Andragogy to the University Classroom.* Prepublication manuscript.

Papanek, V. J. (1964): Solving Problems Creatively, *Management Views,* v. 9 (Part 3). Selected Speeches, Academic Year 1963–64, U.S. Army Management School, Fort Belvoir, Va., pp. 169–196.

Polya, G. (1945): *How to Solve It.* Princeton, N.J.: Princeton University Press.

Rogers, Carl R. (1951): *Client-Centered Therapy.* Boston: Houghton-Mifflin.

Schwab, J. J. (1962): Science as Inquiry—An Answer to the Dilemma of Today's Teacher, *Teacher Topics.* New York: Harcourt, Brace, and World. Science Materials Center, Spring, 1962.

Thelen, Herbert A. (1960a): *Education and the Human Quest.* New York: Harper and Row.

Thelen, Herbert A. (1960b): The Triumph of "Achievement" over Inquiry in Education, *Elementary School Journal,* v. 60, pp. 190–197.

Weisskopf, Edith A. (1951): Some Comments Concerning the Role of Education in the "Creation of Creation," *Journal of Educational Psychology,* v. 42, pp. 185–189.

8

Chicago's Metro High: Freedom, Choice, Responsibility
by MaryFrances Crabtree

The buildings that line the 500 block of Chicago's South Dearborn Street have a desolate sameness about them: scarred, smoke-grayed brick facades, storefront windows opaque with grime, dingy portals with chipped gold-leaf numbering. Metro High's address is 537, up a flight of dilapidated stairs. The once-painted, now graffiti-decorated walls bear smudged hand prints and battle scars from past encounters with immovable objects and very movable young people, some of whom line the stairs in various poses, laughing and talking.

The school office is one large room built around pillars wrapped in announcements, ads, and posters, and partitioned by file cabinets top-heavy with papers. At one end of the room, the principal, Nathaniel Blackman, is seated at his desk surrounded by an animated group of blue-jeaned students. This unusual principal's office, minus the usual reception room and closed doors, houses the entire administrative staff in one room. The city is ever-present—there is continuous movement and constant noise from within and from without. The windows overlook a typical Chicago landscape: a patch of gray sky, worn buildings, sooty panes, the ubiquitous maze of fire escapes—all orchestrated to the sound of an air compressor at a nearby construction site.

Lee Alo, assistant to the principal, allowed me to visit Metro not on the basis of educational background or teaching experience, the usual criteria, but because, as he put it, "you sound nice." This informality, friendliness, and unqualified acceptance of the individual are basic to Metro's style.

The Chicago Public High School for Metropolitan Studies, popularly

*From *Phi Delta Kappan* LVI, 9 (May 1975): 613–15. Reprinted by permission.

called Metro High, is an experimental four-year "high school without walls." As a result of a kind of natural progression, it is now considered an alternative to traditional secondary education in Chicago.

Metro resulted from negotiations between the Chicago Board of Education and a firm of management consultants, the Urban Research Corporation, hired (for $10,000 a month) to design a program resembling Philadelphia's Parkway Program. The involvement of outside consultants from initial planning stages to final program evaluations is a significant aspect of the school. The Urban Research Corporation approached the Board of Education with the idea for an urban school, "a community of learners" in which education could occur in real-life situations, where a student with the help of a skilled teacher could learn from people with varied talents and interests—from businessmen, lawyers, electricians, artists, newspaper reporters. The Board of Education paid the Urban Research Corporation a total of $150,000 to plan and implement all phases of the Metro program, including contacts with participating organizations, curriculum planning, staff development, teaching classes, student counseling, development of administrative procedures, and evaluation.

Originally located at 220 South State, Metro High opened its doors in February 1970, with 150 students and seven teachers. In June it moved to its present location in a neglected office building whose sole renovation seems to have consisted of meeting fire code standards. It is here that some of the basic "learning units" are taught.

However, only a small percentage of Metro classes meet at the South Dearborn address. Most classes meet in space donated by institutions— the cafeteria of the Prudential Building or Adler Planetarium, for example. This is the "school without walls" concept, and it results in an unusual schedule.

There are five class periods on Monday, Wednesday, and Friday, and four on Tuesday and Thursday—but as much as thirty minutes' travel time is allowed between classes. The Metro student learns to be proficient in intracity travel and its hazards, which have little to do with "changing" neighborhoods or traffic delays: Police often stop a Metro student en route from one class to another on suspicion of truancy. Public transit personnel often refuse to honor half-fare cards or tokens from Metro students coming from the zoo, not understanding that the student can be coming from "school."

The learning units taught at Metro include the traditional subjects, but the majority are in areas not usually covered in a high school curriculum:

ethnic cooking, puppet making, and reading music lyrics as literature. Exemplifying the school without walls concept, there are regularly scheduled ancillary courses taught by businessmen, librarians, curators, and individual volunteers: studying marine life at Shedd Aquarium, writing for a large magazine under the guidance of a staff writer, broadcasting at one of Chicago's major radio stations, or acting with a professional theatrical group at Second City.

Every Metro student is also required to enroll in the Concentrated Experience program, which allows him to do intensive work in an area of interest. Each staff member is responsible for teaching one concentrated experience. Some projects presently being developed are a recycling center, flying instructions, newspaper production, videotaping, and working in politics.

Each one of these learning units fulfills requirements for graduation in a major subject or in an elective. Metro satisfies all state requirements; its full-time staff has Board of Education certification; it is accredited by the North Central Association.

As in any high school, the students choose their courses on a variety of bases: interest or ability in the subject, or simply to fulfill state requirements. Choice and decision making are not limited to selecting a program, however. Students often suggest courses to faculty members, resulting in some unusual offerings—"Plain Old American History" and "Making It," for example. The latter offering is clarified by the question: "Are you preparing to get a good job, or will you be forced to work just to feed your face?"

There are other components of the diverse Metro program: independent study; individual placement in various occupations—all nonpaying activities for credit outside school, from working in a secretarial pool to assisting at the Lincoln Park Zoo; and cooperative work training to explore possible vocations and to develop a marketable skill.

Finally, there are counseling groups consisting of fifteen to twenty students who meet one hour each week for personal encouragement, support, and individual counseling. The counselor helps plan a student's schedule and provides registration materials and weekly travel tokens for public transportation to and from classes. He also keeps the student's records and makes announcements about school business. An added educational resource derives from the counseling group: Students from diverse backgrounds share ideas and interact in discussions of school policy and curriculum in a kind of group forum.

The school year at Metro is divided into four ten-week learning cycles. At the end of each cycle, the student meets with each of his teachers, who make a detailed evaluation of his work. Teacher and student decide if "credit" or "no credit" should be given for the preceding 10 weeks. Though there are no grades and no class ranking at Metro, the student must have "credit" in order to receive points toward graduation. Thus one of Metro's prime lessons: Freedom entails responsibility.

This environment of freedom/responsibility, with a minimum of "checking up" on student actions, fosters openness and friendliness in the students. Moreover, Metro is the only school in the city that lets the students take an active role in administration. The school functions in part through four standing committees: curriculum, staff selection, student selection, and evaluation-registration. Students are invited and expected to participate actively in committee meetings and procedures. Thus teachers and students cooperate in defining their goals, and the student is responsible for his part of the bargain. All of this is important in encouraging an outgoing student attitude. But it is also a result of the type of students enrolled and the way they are chosen.

There are presently 350 students at Metro—49 percent black, 41 percent white, and 10 percent from other minorities. The staff of twenty-five teachers, including two counselors and three aides, results in a pupil/teacher ratio of approximately 15:1. Per-pupil cost is $980, and the budget allocation for the 1974–75 school year is $573,703, according to Board of Education figures. The students come from every neighborhood in the city, reflecting the ethnic, racial, and academic diversity of Chicago's high school population. Although students may be admitted because of extraordinary circumstances, through recommendation by local authorities or by a social agency, or because of an unusual level of commitment to this type of self-propelling education, most of Metro's student body is chosen randomly in a yearly lottery from thousands of applicants who want to be a part of Chicago's school without walls.

Alo invited me to observe a learning unit in session at Metro headquarters, a class in trigonometry. However, it was not the intricate formulae that impressed me. Nor was it the unconventional classroom: desks of various models and in different stages of disrepair scattered haphazardly around the room, students sitting on the floor. It was the fact that the teacher was a student.

Marshall had the rapt attention of the class, except for one girl, who oblivious to the beauties of the number of permutations of four integers, was engrossed in a book. About midway in the class, she gathered her belongings and left. A young man entered and went to the row of lockers along one wall, opened one locker, and rattled around a bit. There was a glance of annoyance from Marshall, who doggedly continued his explanations. When the young man left, Marshall went to the door and firmly closed it.

"O. K., guys, I have a ditto to pass out—I'll wait until you've finished looking it over. Does anyone want to see any more examples?"

"Not really. . . ."

"All right, then. The first few minutes on Friday, we'll have a quiz."

"Oh no. . . ."

"Can we use the book?"

"Do we have to memorize the models in the book, Marshall?"

"Well, you should sort of memorize. . . ."

"Why?"

"Because Cramer (the textbook) is God—that's why!"

(Laughter)

The "real" teacher, who had been sitting among the students, indistinguishable from them, explained to me that at the beginning of the cycle each student had picked a topic he wanted to teach for one week. However, students at Metro are also allowed to teach a course for an entire ten-week cycle. The interested student requests permission from the department concerned. If it is determined that the course should be taught, a sponsor from that department is appointed to assist the student in preparing the course form. This sponsor is present during all class time, and the teaching student receives full credit for the course, plus one bonus point toward graduation.

The students in Marshall's trig course, all college-bound, were of different competencies and at different age levels. "But they've all had some trig," explained the teacher. "We just fill in the gaps according to individual needs. I list the basic requirements for the course in the catalogue, and the kids sign up. But I know each of them, and where they are."

An unorthodox classroom in a seemingly impossible learning atmosphere, yet in spite of the formlessness, the casualness, not only was there no anarchy, but there was quite a bit of subtle organization. The students seem to have a pact of mutual respect and mutual learning with each other and with the teacher. And whoever said that education was all dry formulae in an orderly classroom presided over by a teacher who wouldn't be caught dead in Marshall's tie-dyed shirt?

Alo admits that Metro High is not free from criticism. "The learning units dealing with remedial work in the basic skills of language and mathematics are weak," he says. "They are not providing enough intensive, sustained work to affect achievement marks or to raise the scores on standardized tests."

"The teachers should not have to be amateur psychologists. Often a teacher's involvement with a student becomes too 'heavy,' leading to an unhealthy relationship for student and teacher."

Moreover, the basic concept of the school without walls, using the entire community for learning, seems to be in serious difficulty at Metro. Participation by the outside community has diminished from 35 perecent to 20 percent. Alo puts some of the blame on the public relations people: "They aren't contacting enough outside staff." But he realizes that the difficulty lies more with diminishing community interest than with public relations. "Not enough business and professional people want to be involved anymore. Everyone has a stake in education. Without the help of the community which provides us with meeting space, resources, instructors, even with whole programs, Metro cannot exist."

However, one can neither criticize nor praise without first asking some questions regarding Metro's concept of education. What kind of person is it we are educating, and for what kind of society? Because· ultimately education is a social process. How can education help us to find "the good life?"

"Man is basically good," says Alo. "Therefore, education can never be reform, but rather direction or guidance. We can only alter behavior insofar as motivational attitudes are concerned. Education then becomes a problem of finding a starting point, of introducing the student to a community of learning, and letting him direct himself to a rich and satisfying life."

Metro's starting point for learning is "to teach the student that freedom, which allows choice, also entails responsibility." Alo points to the "credit" or "no-credit" evaluation as an example of this teaching.

"Education should enable man to work within his intellectual and social limits. But 'survival skills' are more important than intellectual ability for coping with our society with its complexities. Man has found 'the good life' when he has the knowledge and ability to perform efficiently, to make a constructive contribution to society, and to gain personal satisfaction from his efforts."

Chicago's Metro High: Its curriculum is the city; its learning laboratory is the community; and its lesson is freedom, choice, responsibility.

9
Muddling Through: A School Above a Bakery
by Terrence E. Deal

In the late 1960s and early seventies, a new breed of secondary schools surfaced in diverse locations throughout the country. Some of the new schools were private; others were public. Some were located on existing high school campuses; others were housed in warehouses, storefronts, and private residences. Some schools encouraged personal growth and development; others emphasized vocational and career training. The new breed thus contained a variety of species. But all were lumped into one genus— "alternative schools."

This is the story of one alternative school's first year. A publicly funded alternative to the traditional high school, the Community School was headquartered above a bakery in a small California community. Its story has five main parts: (1) developing and "selling" the original idea, (2) planning for September, (3) implementing the plan, (4) revising the plan, (5) assessing the results and "reselling" the school The main purpose of this case history is to stimulate ideas about what to do and what to avoid in the inaugural year of an alternative school. Consequently, in a final part some implications are suggested for other newly-established alternative schools.

In addition, many of these ideas may be applied to current efforts aimed at the revitalization of established secondary schools. Signs suggest that the reform of secondary schools may be entering a second stage, during which ideas underlying alternative schools will expand. Current sponsorship will differ, however, in that many state governments will help to encourage—if not to mandate—major changes in the organization and instruction of high schools.

As alternative ideas move from small experimental settings to large high school campuses, it seems wise to heed the lessons of the "pioneers"— both the successes and failures. This is a story of one such pioneering effort, which despite torturous progress, ended in success. Its telling will reveal strategies and pitfalls through which a smoother implementation of change might be recommended for other schools seeking to implement: (1) a closer relationship with the community, (2) an individualized and competency-based approach to instruction, (3) new roles for teachers, students, administrators, parents, and community members, (4) new relationships among these various roles, and (5) new patterns of governance and management.

Developing and 'Selling' the Original Idea

The original idea for the community school came from two sources: (1) a conference convened by a progressive superintendent of schools putting state funds to the purpose of generating ideas for the redesign of secondary education and (2) a Ph.D. student (a former teacher of the district) whose research and studies had crystallized some concerns about the nature of high schools and some possible directions of reform.

A discussion between the two principal actors led to the appointment of the doctoral student as administrative assistant to the superintendent. Together, the two developed a preliminary plan for a new district high school which would be funded by state "necessary, small high school" monies. Essentially, the school's primary purpose was to be "closely engaged with the community" and to provide a "human, authentic and stimulating environment." Its characteristics were to include:

(1) Independence from short-term funding, (2) small size, (3) a heterogeneous student population, (4) flexible, warm, highly organized teachers, capable of relating to adults as well as to students, (5) a sound image, (6) well-designed goals, and (7) an individualized curriculum and systematic evaluation.

This preliminary plan was submitted to the district's governing board. The immediate response was "why do we need another high school, when we already have one?" However, the board—persuaded that there might be a student population whom the high school was not serving—agreed to authorize a study. The study, consequently conducted by the superintendent's administrative assistant, involved research and a dialogue between students and community members.

The research phase of the study included two steps. First, dropout rates for several years were compared to see if there had been an increase. There had not. Second, yearly rates of "early" graduates were compared and proved that from 1965–68 there had been a 300 percent increase in students who graduated either a semester or year early. Personal interviews revealed that nearly all of the 1966 early grads had left high school, feeling that it had no more to offer them. In nearly every case the emphasis was on getting away—not moving on to something else. Many, after graduating, were doing nothing.

Discussion groups provided an arena for dialogue between "bored" students and community opinion leaders. A sociogram was conducted to locate students in the high school who were bright, but alienated or "turned off." A research study had previously suggested that 23 percent of the 1,200 student population was highly alienated from the authority structure of the high school (Henderson 1971). The poll produced 100 names of students, after which another such poll located influential adult members of the district's community. Largely conservative with a high proportion of retired people, the community has also a sizeable "artsy-craftsy, avant-garde" contingent. Influentials were selected from all the important subgroups.

The community influentials and "turned off" kids were invited to several small discussion meetings, where main questions were posed: "Is the high school serving all students' needs?" and "Is there a need for an additional high school?" Discussions were lively and heated. After the meetings, most community influentials left convinced that the regular high school was not responding to the needs of all students. Many called individual board members to suggest that a new approach to secondary education in the community be explored.

The original proposal was resubmitted to the school board, and many community influentials attended a board meeting in support of an alternative school. With a vote of 4-1, the board passed a resolution establishing the new school for a year's trial period, despite board president's feeling that "it won't work, but we'll give it a try." The administrative assistant was then named principal, or "head teacher," of the school.

Planning for September

The proposal approved by the board was intentionally vague. The strategy was to leave the students and teachers considerable latitude in designing a school compatible with their own goals, interests, needs, and talents.

The first act of the new principal, in consultation with the superintendent, was to establish a community advisory group. The purpose of this group was to provide broad guidelines for the selection of students and teachers, and for the further elaboration of concepts to characterize the school. The advisory group represented all factions of the community and included many of the influentials who had attended discussion meetings. Also included in the group were a student and teacher from the traditional high school.

At its first meeting the advisory group discussed the individual functions of its members and subdivided into special committees where members would actively participate in the formation of the school. For the most part, however, group members were to provide, collectively and individually, general advice, assistance, and support when needed. The advisory group identified the selection of students as the top priority task.

The student selection process began by "spreading the word." Announcements of the new school were sent to all students in the regular high school. The new principal met with all social studies classes to describe the projected school and answer any questions. Out of a student population of 1,200, 60 students applied.

Each student applicant was interviewed by a subcommittee of the advisory group. Students were selected on the basis of three criteria: (1) alienation from the traditional high school, (2) enthusiasm for the new school, and (3) inaccessibility to another existing alternative program in the district. Additionally, the selection committee aimed for a "mixed bag" of students, selecting those with a wide range of attitudes, orientations, and styles. The only common element among students was dissatisfaction with the regular high school. It was for a variety of reasons, however, that the thirty selected students were dissatisfied.

Since the main purpose of the school was to provide an alternative program for students unable to learn in a traditional environment, the tentative list of students was submitted to the regular high school's assistant principal to see if it included those it could benefit most. Skimming the list, he smiled, and simply replied "good luck."

Next was the task of selecting teachers. The advisory group agreed that the students and principal should be primarily responsible for this. The two openings announced received 120 applications, mainly from outside the district. Selection criteria established by students and principal were: a demonstrated ability to work closely with students, successful teaching experience in math or English, and breadth of interest and preparation. On the basis of their confidential files, twenty-five applicants were selected for interview. The superintendent trained the principal and students in interviewing, and both interviewed each of the prospective teachers in what one applicant characterized as "the most grueling hour I've ever spent—those students cleave right through the educational bullshit."

In one eight-hour session the decision was reached through consensus. Chief influence in this decision was the applicant's perceived ability to work as a team (with the principal), a balance of teaching strengths, and salary. Two male teachers were selected despite arguments for a "token" female. Of the two, one was an older (ergo more expensive) social studies and English teacher from the regular high school; the other was a young (and consequently, cheaper) math and science teacher, just graduated from a teacher training program.

An immediate problem was that neither of the new teachers could begin until September. The form of the new school thus remained diffuse and amorphous since its design was to evolve from an interaction between students and staff. Logistics reduced the planning activity to a summer school class in "educational philosophy." Twice a week the principal and most students met to formulate plans for the new school.

There were two main foci of the skeleton planning process: (1) specific "nitty-gritty" projects, and (2) the philosophy of the school. The projects involved student identification of community resources, the location of a suitable site for the school, and location of curriculum materials. The projects were seen as a mundane "burden" which students were, nevertheless, willing to undertake for the "cause." All projects proceeded in a slow, erratic fashion. Finding a suitable headquarters was an especially difficult task, not resolved until September.

The philosophic side of the summer's planning included discussion of the latest educational critiques and the evils bred by traditional high schools. Discussions highlighted what the school would *not* be. The discussions took place twice a week, and set the tone for subsequent schedules—which occurred early in the morning, in the evening, and at various odd times of the day. At the end of the planning process there was only high agreement on what the school was *not* to be and that was: "anything resembling the traditional high school." Despite an explicit negative profile, however, only vague, diffuse images arose to usurp the throne.

Toward the end of the summer, the advisory group encouraged the principal to begin informing the community about the school. The first attempt at this was a presentation to the local Rotary Club. Four students, who were briefed beforehand, accompanied the principal to discuss the rationale and emphasis of the school. The long hair of two and the failure to salute the flag of three, however, inspired only audience contempt. Instead of obtaining much-needed community support their appearance spawned rumors about the "communist" principal and the "subversive" school. Several advisory members attempted, but were impotent, to patch up the torn quilt of confusion and flying feather.

In sum, the summer's planning process ended with an unimpressive record: half-completed projects, a negatively derived philosophy, no place to house the school—and a tainted image to boot. It was August 25; school was to begin August 31.

Implementing the Plan

The three staff members met together for the first time on August 26. The principal had developed an impresive list of issues for discussion. Among these were: What is the purpose of the Community School? What are we trying to do? What kind of students do we eventually want to produce? In what ways can we organize ourselves to accomplish our objectives? What guidelines and procedures should be developed? What rules and procedures should not be developed? How will decisions be made? How will students and teachers be evaluated? Apparent to principal and staff alike, was how useless discussion (or even resolution) of these issues was in solving their most immediate crisis, however. With no headquarters and few ideas about "what to do on Monday," basic issues took top priority.

Before school opened officially, the staff met with the students in a "get acquainted" session and announced the temporary headquarters of the school as the local Episcopal Church. Students were unanimous in voicing their dissatisfaction. A church is not exactly the place to begin a revolution against a traditional institution.

School began officially August 31. Following a strong appeal by the principal to accept "challenges and opportunities," everyone agreed to accept immediate responsibility in two areas: (1) for themselves and (2) for a particular aspect of the school's operation. Several committees were established, whose functions were: evaluating the school, identifying community resources, and locating a headquarters site. In addition some preliminary rules were established: students were responsible for keeping the staff informed of their whereabouts and students were to devote their time to "scholarly pursuits" during "traditional" school hours. Later that day, the headquarters committee located a site for the school: one purple and two orange rooms above a downtown bakery.

The school was thus launched. In essence, it began as the "flip side" of the traditional high school using, as a basis for the comparison, six dimensions for learning. The character of the community school in its initial days is nicely captured in the table.

In the next two months the school passed quickly through three stages: Euphoria, Psychic Upheaval, and Dissatisfaction.

Table 1

Differences between the Community School

and Traditional Secondary Schools

on Six Important Dimensions of Learning*

Learning Dimensions	Conventional Secondary Schools	The Community School
Who is involved in the learning process (roles)	Certified teachers, counselors, administrators, students. All have relatively well-defined role expectations.	Teachers, administrators, parents, community members, students—anyone who has something to teach. Certification requirements relaxed; role distinctions blurred.
What is learned (curriculum)	State- or district-prescribed curriculum. Knowledge divided into subject areas. Special programs for non-college-bound or other ''special'' students. Emphasis on cognitive learning.	Wide variation in educational substance, dictated largely by interest of students; may encompass areas usually taught in school but also extends into many other areas. Emphasis on affective learning.
Why it is learned (authority)	Extrinsic motivation; learning to fulfill requirements, to pass tests. Authority vested in teacher: ''do what you are told.'' Teachers directive.	Intrinsic motivation; learning because of interest or need to know, to learn a skill or to acquire knowledge. Authority vested in students. Student choice. ''Do what you want.''
How it is learned (methods)	Emphasis on reading, writing, listening; group presentation; lecture by teacher common; some audio-visual aids; some discussion.	Methods vary as widely as curriculum; reading, writing, listening not excluded, but emphasis on doing and experiencing; all senses involved.
Where learning takes place (location)	Learning takes place on campus, in classroom. Some field trips, but these are exceptional.	Wide variation in location of learning: private homes, beach, forest, libraries, businesses. Instruction in formal classroom is the exception rather than the rule.
When learning takes place	Instruction typically between hours of 8 and 4; day segmented into periods or modules.	Learning takes place anytime, depending on nature of learning task; infrequent scheduling, no time segmentation.

*From Terrance E. Deal, ''An Organization Explanation of the Failure of Alternative Schools,'' Stanford Center for Research and Development in Teaching, Stanford University, 1975, p. 5.

Euphoria. The first few weeks of the community school were joyful, triumphant, and rewarding. The experiment seemed to be a complete success.

Students were busily engaged in planting organic gardens, building geodesic domes, sharing innermost feelings, walking on the beach, learning history from retired citizens, extolling the virtues of alternative education to their friends at the traditional high school, and otherwise living out the fantasies they had created in days of "incarceration" in more formal classrooms. Community meetings proved a lively vehicle for discussing and resolving school wide problems.

The staff was pleased, enthusiastic, and somewhat pompous. Their fantasies of creating a human institution where both teachers and students could reciprocate learning were fulfilled. The principal began to outline a treatise on secondary school reform.

Parents, too, were overjoyed. Their kids were happy and doing well in school. Years of coaxing and cajoling, frantic calls from the attendance office, teacher-parent conferences, visits to the vice president's office, and just plain worry vanished into a new set of positive experiences. One parent donated $50 to the school board, wanting to contribute something to the institution that had redeemed her "lost" son.

The superintendent was pleased, board members felt the glow of having made a good decision, and community members were energetically involved or passively accepting of the "weird" school above the bakery.

The traditional high school staff seemed chagrined that such a school could actually work.

Psychic Upheaval. The euphoric stage, however, quickly gave way to depression, gloom, tears, and emotional crises.

Nearly all the students were affected adversely during this period. At the headquarters, many cried, confessed insomnia and depression; others were simply listless and asocial. Some students regressed into childlike behavior. More alarmingly, one student attempted suicide.

The staff quickly shifted roles from fellow learners to counselor-confessors. They discussed adjustment with individual students and convened small group sessions, but no general course of action was established. Community meetings were held infrequently. When they did occur, discussions were stilted and not very productive. In meetings, it was not unusual for one student to break into tears and to have the rest of the group fumble to provide comfort and support.

Though assistance was quickly provided the staff members felt occassionally depressed themselves. Their depression was offset, however, by the rewards of helping someone else "work through things."

While most parents were concerned about the rapid shift in student behavior, they retained their confidence in the staff. The students were attending school and receiving support and counseling under the supervision of well-trained professionals. Some parents also began to show symptoms of depression and pyschic stress, and it was not unusual for staff members to counsel parents during the evening. The sessions with both parents and students produced insights into some major conflict areas. The staff, as confidants, even became privy to some festering family difficulties.

The superintendent and board were relatively unconcerned during this period. After all, the school was established "for kids who were unable to adjust to the traditional environment." Erratic behavior was to be expected as such a school developed.

Some community members were alarmed to see students skipping arm-in-arm, hugging one another, and openly crying or otherwise publicly showing emotion.

The traditional high school staff smiled a collective "We told you so."

Dissatisfaction. The psychic upheaval stage melted quickly into rampant dissatisfaction. The students were openly hostile in expressing their dissatisfaction with the school. Absenteeism rose. Several students returned to the traditional campus just to "see their friends and sit in on some classes." One student observed that if the students had the right to hire teachers, they also had the power to fire them.

Community decision making was undermined as well. During one community meeting, the staff tossed fifty $1 bills (the mother's contribution) on the floor and gave the students the task of redecorating headquarters with it. The staff left; the students deadlocked and split into factions. The end product was a couch cover, and some curtains. The walls remained purple and orange. Some of the students bought wine with the change and got drunk.

Parents also began to actively express their concerns. The issues were never specific, but generally seemed to boil down to "the kids are not learning anything."

The superintendent, hearing reports from the principal, became sensitive to the new shift in the community school. He decided that the board needed to be informed—not collectively, but as individual members. He and the principal, during one week, held five successive "cocktail hours" in which the principal candidly informed the board members of the difficulties. The board members were not alarmed, but echoed their former response: "What can be expected from kids who have difficulty adjusting to a traditional setting? If you are getting to 10 percent, you're doing okay." The board member who voted against the school was more concerned than the others, due to his having been confronted by the conservative of one student's parents. He asked the principal to take some action to reduce the parents' anxiety. This resulted in a conference between the principal and the student's grandfather, a local merchant and pillar of the community. During the conference, the grandfather said to the principal, "If I ran my business like you run your school, it would fail." The principal replied, "If I ran this school like you run your business, they would fire me." The grandson transferred to a private school.

During the dissatisfaction period, those in the community who were supportive of the school remained so. Some conservative members of the advisory council expressed some concern, but still defended the school to its critics. The passive objective of the conservatives became more active, however, one citizen complaining to the fire department that the school violated fire codes. The fire inspector (a member of the advisory council) inspected the school and made some simple suggestions of how to remedy the problem.

This heightened activity of the conservatives and the continued support of others polarized the community and made the school a subject of controversy. During a Rotary meeting one Rotarian publicly said to another, "What kind of books do the kids who attend that school where they smoke pot and teach the forty-six positions buy from you—things like *I Was a Teen-Age Werewolf?*" The other Rotarian (the owner of a bookstore with which the school did a sizeable business) replied: "Most of the books they buy from me, you probably wouldn't be able to read."

The traditional high school staff were not only reassured in their approach to instruction but as pompous as had been the alternative staff during the school's euphoria.

During the dissatisfaction period, the alternative school staff began to meet more frequently and to discuss the problems more openly. Previously, schoolwide issues had been discussed in weekly community meetings where decisions were made by consensus. As the dissatisfaction mounted, the principal convened the staff separately from students, arguing that community meetings could not handle such enormous problems. The staff had to take a more active role in decision making. The younger teacher was initially opposed, but agreed to go along.

Revising the Plan

The staff unanimously agreed that a return to traditional patterns, even though it would be eagerly received by a majority of the students and parents, would not work. The staff felt committed to "failing for the right reasons." They wanted to maintain the alternative character of the school. But despite their willingness to "go down with the ship," they wanted also to create an alternative school that worked. The dilemma was to develop a balance between the "unwanted either" and the "unworkable or," yet no one knew quite what the balance point was.

The staff developed five strategies for stabilizing the situation temporarily. First, they decided to survey the parents and students to identify problems more clearly. Second, they agreed to meet as a staff with individual students to discuss high school credits. Third, each staff member agreed to establish at least one formal class. Fourth, each staff member agreed to take specific responsibility for a group of students. The students were divided on the basis of interest and compatability with a given staff member. Fifth, the staff admitted self-satisfaction in playing the father confessor role, and confessed they were rewarding students for negative behavior. The staff decided not to respond to student problems and to focus instead on rewarding initiative and positive action.

The temporary plan, with its associated behaviors and overtones, was greeted with mixed reaction. Some students saw it as a sell-out; others plunged eagerly into very traditional tasks, counted Carnagie units, and enrolled in classes.

The students unanimously agreed to the survey. A subcommittee composed of three students and the principal developed the questions and summarized the responses. The principal developed a parent questionnaire. All parents responded and their opinions were also tabulated.

The students and the parent surveys obtained perceptions of both the positive and negative aspects of the school. The parents felt students were happier, interested in school and learning, and more self-confident than they had been a year before. They expressed concern about the large amount of unstructured time, how well the school was preparing students for college, how much students were learning, and the lack of a definite curriculum or coure of study. A number of parents felt uninformed about the progress of the school.

The students expressed more concern than parents about the state of the school. Nearly all agreed that the school was experiencing difficulties. Student responses were consolidated on three problem areas by a smaller subgroup.

Problem Area #1

How do we get people in the Community-Centered High School to know one another?

Many of us who listed the problems of the Community-Centered High School expressed the feeling that there is a lack of trust, sharing, and tolerance among us; that some of us do not feel like part of our school. Is this one of the reasons some do not attend on a regular basis? Should we do more together? What?

Problem Area #2

What is the purpose of our school?

Some of us indicated that we have either forgotten why the school was established—or never really knew. Many people stated that: "Nothing is happening," "We've come to a standstill," "We're not exposed to enough academic subjects," "We're not using the community enough." Is this why people are not personally committed to the school? Is there anything to be committed to? Or, has lack of commitment prevented us from establishing a purpose?

Problem Area #3

How should our school be organized?

Some people complained that the school is disorganized; that there is no communication about classes (interests), no direction provided, nor any real structure. What kind of organization is needed? Who should provide direction? Is structure necessary?

Many of the comments about the general meeting; for example, "No one talks in general meetings" or "No decisions are ever made in the larger group" may show that very few are aware of what general meetings are all about. Why do we have them?

It is also not clear that many people in our school don't know what their roles or responsibilities are. Some asked, "What the hell is the teacher for?" Others asked, "What is the responsibility of a student?" Well?

The results of both surveys were discussed in community meetings. These produced a better understanding of the school's problems. Some problems were solved by stop-gap solutions. For example, most parents reported being worried about how much students were learning. The students decided that their parents equated learning with homework and agreed to take home books and to spend at least one-half hour alone in their rooms each night. One problem was thus solved.

But, although many problems were better defined, most solutions were still elusive. The central dilemma of how to synthesize traditional and alternative patterns into a unique school were all that remained.

The catalyst that produced the synthesis was a visit from a university professor. Retained as a consultant by the principal, the professor was a renowned educational philosopher steeped in the traditional of John Dewey. The professor spent two days at the school visiting with students and staff. A dinner meeting provided an opportunity for an informal exchange between the professor, the superintendent, and school board members.

In a wrap-up meeting the professor summarized his visit and outlined two concerns. First, he noted a gap in the assignment of responsibility for learning. The staff, in his view, had delegated the responsibility for learning to students. But the students were experiencing difficulty in knowing how to assume or share the burden of developing (1) the goals and objectives of learning, (2) learning tasks, and (3) criteria for evaluating progress. Second, he detected a feeling among students that the school was either granting them freedom or permitting them to take it as their natural right. Contrasted to this view, the professor emphasized a definition of freedom as the power to choose from known alternatives with responsibility for the consequences. From this perspective, he argued, freedom must be vigorously claimed or worked for.

The summary session initially confused and disappointed everyone. The students felt that the school was not given proper credit; the superintendent had expected more concrete suggestions for improving the school; and the staff—especially the principal—was frustrated because the void between the rigid traditional and the unworkable laissez-faire approaches remained unfilled.

In subsequent staff meetings, however, the light suddenly flashed. The community school had been established on a premise of freedom which, in fact, constricted students and staff alike. If freedom is the power to choose among known alternatives with full responsibility for the consequences, the school had granted the power but had deemphasized the act of generating alternatives and had shielded students from the consequences of making choices.

The philosophical shift permitted the staff to fill the middle niche, particularly in terms of what is learned, why it is learned, and the role of the staff and students in defining learning goals and objectives, establishing tasks, and evaluating the results. Table 2 contrasts the compromise position with the two extremes.

Table 2
Contrasting Experimental with Conventional
and Laissez-Faire Schooling

	Conventional schooling	Experimental alternative schooling	Laissez-faire alternative schooling
What is learned	Determined by state- or district- prescribed curriculum.	Determined by an interaction between the students' short- and long-term interests and the goals of the school.	Determined by student interest.
Why it is learned	Do what you are told.	Do what has been jointly established.	Do what you want.
Role of the student	Passive; learns pre-scribed curriculum; no choice.	Active; learns what is needed to accomplish short- and long-term objectives.	Active; learns anything that is intrinsically interesting. Full choice.
Role of the staff	Active; teacher directs learning by deciding what is to be learned, developing learning tasks, and evaluating the results.	Active; teacher and student interaction directs learning. Student decides what to learn, but teacher takes an active role in formulating goals and objectives generating alternative learning tasks and using predetermined criteria to evaluate the results.	Passive; student directs learning by individually deciding what is to be learned, developing learning tasks, and evaluating results.

The new philosophy became the guiding principle for revising the community school. The first step in the process of reorganization was to establish goals for the school. The original goal statement was written by the principal and a small group of students. It was subsequently revised in a series of small meetings which included all the students and staff. Next, the goals were formally discussed and adopted in a community meeting. Finally, the goals were approved by the parents and board of education. The goals provided the new direction for the school.

Goals for the Community School

1. To develop problem-solving competence through experiences in seeking solutions to personal, community, and academic problems.

2. To develop, with conscious knowledge of the full range of alternatives, a cohesive set of values which, although subject to continuous reappraisal, provide a philosophical base for making present and future choices.

3. To use, whenever desirable and possible, the human, environmental, and institutional resources of the community as an aid to learning.

4. To assume the main responsibility for learning including: the development of goals and objectives considering personal interests, aspirations, and parental expectations; the identification of desirable processes and resources; and the selection of standards, in keeping with the goals and objectives, by which progress can be evaluated.

5. To develop positive feelings of self-esteem and self-worth to a sufficient degree that internal emotions, feelings of efficacy, and the ability to relate to any situation allow for present and future goals and aspirations to be realized.

6. To develop the skills and abilities in communication that are necessary to effective and satisfying relationships with individuals and ideas.

7. To develop the attitudes, skills, competencies, as well as the "inquisitive spirit" necessary to assume a satisfying role in a society.

8. To grow in self-direction while sharing responsibility as a member of a heterogeneous group.

9. To develop at least one cultivated enjoyment.

The second step in the school's reorganization was to use the goals as a framework for developing a learning plan or objectives for each student. The learning plan was developed jointly by a student and staff advisor. The process involved intense discussion of long- and short-term plans, alternatives routes for accomplishing objectives, and the criteria which would be used to evaluate learning activities.

The tentative plans were then reviewed by other staff members and the students' parents. The process was different for all students. Many students were hazy and undecided about their long-term aims. These students were encouraged to undertake experiences that would yield some options. Other students realized that college was a necessary step. Some students became excited and anxious to develop vocational possibilities.

Several examples illustrate the importance of the planning process and resultant plan.

During the initial days of the Community School, Joseph was a member of the "Fun Cult," a group of hedonistic students who spent a large proportion of their time embalmed in alcohol. After the school goals were developed, two members of the group developed plans which provided a new direction for their heretofore inebriated energies. Virginia decided to go to college and plunged energetically into mastering the necessary academic "survival" skills; Mary decided to test her interest in nursing by volunteering in a local convalescent home and enrolling in the nursing class at a nearby community college.

Seeing his support group dwindle spurred Joseph into action. He had read Thoreau and developed an idealized longing for a simple life as a farmer in a pristine setting. He decided to test this direction by going to a farm in Maine. He and his advisor worked out a plan whereby Joseph could accomplish the Community School's goals by living on the farm for three months. In a lengthy session, his parents approved the plan. Joseph then left to become a farmer in Maine. His "contract" included specific objectives for each of the school's goals.

Four weeks in the nippy early spring of Maine burst Joseph's bubble about the rewards of life on "Walden Pond." He called the principal to renegotiate his contract, and specified the elements of an alternative plan. The plan was approved by the principal and Joseph's parents had a revised "contract" mailed to Joseph. He returned to the school disappointed, still somewhat confused about his life, but certain that one alternative could be discarded.

Tom was a student whose parents had pressured him toward college since early childhood. In the first months of the Community School, Tom was apprenticed to a local Porsche mechanic. He had a strong aptitude in mechanics and in short time was able to take an active role in the shop. As months passed, however, Tom began to question whether the work and lifestyle of a mechanic would satisfy him. As he and his advisor worked to develop his plan, Tom decided that he wanted to attend a state university. His plan outlined a series of activities which included developing a minimum competency in algebra, geometry, and English, and writing a term paper which would meet first year standards at a state university. Although he had completed classes in those subjects with a satisfactory grade in the conventional high school, Tom's skills were initially very low. Within one semester, however, he was able to demonstrate acceptable levels in algebra, geometry, and English. He submitted a well-organized and well-written term paper comparing the 1965 and 1966 Porsches. He passed the college entrance exams and was accepted to the state university.

As Sally worked with her advisor to develop a learning plan, she was unable to decide whether or not college was in her future. But she was certain that she did not want to rule out the possibility. Her plan therefore included work experience and some traditional course work in Spanish. To satisfy this latter requirement, Sally was assigned to a local college student with a strong background in foreign languages. A performance contract was developed between the two which specified the desired level of competency and a time frame. A teacher in the conventional high school was hired as an independent evaluator to determine whether Sally had actually achieved the desired level at the end of the contract. The college student was to receive a minimal amount if Sally had not achieved the level at the end of the time period. But if Sally achieved or surpassed the level, the student would receive a proportionately higher honorarium.

These are only three examples. Other students developed plans which included: taking art lessons from a local artist, tossing pots with a famous sculptor, recreating the life of a Castanoan Indian, and hewing a chair from a redwood log. For all students, however, these activities were linked to objectives developed from a dialogue between students and their advisors using the school's goals as a basis.

At the end of the year, each student was evaluated by the three staff members as a group. The evaluations took place in a three-hour conference between the students and the three teachers. In this session, the advisor was the student's advocate, the other two teachers challenged goals, objectives, and activities. Using the predetermined criteria, they pressed hard for evidence that learning objectives had been met. The session ended in one of two ways: (1) the student graduated; (2) the staff suggested specific goals and activities for the next year. Of the original thirty students, seventeen graduated. Of these, ten were seniors; seven were juniors. One senior was "retained."

The third step in the school's reorganization was to change the community meetings. Staff decision making was heightened and most decisions were made consensually by the staff. The principal was given authority to make decisions in schoolwide areas such as community-school relations and the relationship between the school and the district office. Just a few general policy issues were reserved for the all-school meetings with the decision rule: consensus is desirable, but when impossible decisions will be made by majority vote.

In sum, the net impact of these three changes was a school character faithful to the spirit of the original plan but more formalized and "bureaucratic" than originally intended. Goals were established which endowed the school with a purpose. The goals were not that different from the traditional high school. But they were different enough to make the school unique. And everyone—students, staff, and parents— had some influence in developing the goals. Instructional activities, linked to the goals, were tailored to each individual student. No two students were alike. Consequently each instructional plan was different. But each plan had a definite structure and progress was assessed regularly using specific criteria.

Roles and relationships were clarified and formalized. The authority of the staff was greater than anticipated—both over individual student learning and the overall operation of the school. The general meeting was convened infrequently and the community as a whole made only general policy decisions—such as the adoption of schoolwide goals. The staff made key decisions about evaluating learning, hiring community personnel, and referring students to community resources. But in the area of instruction, the students were still the prime decision makers even though the staff played an active role in generating options and evaluating progress.

As the school changed and stabilized, the environment became less polarized and more favorable. A member of one conservative group, a vocal opponent of the school, unknowingly complimented two Community School students in the town newspaper. The students established and operated a Saturday matinee for children which the conservative thought "was bringing our children closer to God in a time when violence and sex pervade television and movie screens." The principal sent the citizen a letter in which he thanked him for recognizing the achievements of two Community School students in a time "when many adults focus undue attention on the negative exploits of adolescents." The citizen responded with complimentary meals for the students at one of his restaurants and gave them helpful advice on running their matinee business (which, incidentally, eventually ended in bankruptcy.

The local Kiwanis Club invited the principal to make a luncheon presentation. This time three students accompanied him; only one had long hair and all three saluted the flag. At the end of the presentation, one Kiwanian suggested that the school seemed to be training the "businessmen of tomorrow." It was as close as many would get to understanding the school, and Kiwanis Club members were almost unanimously supportive.

Most of the traditional high school staff still publicly ridiculed the school, but many began asking questions and silently incorporating some of the Community School ideas into their own classrooms.

Assessing the Results and 'Reselling' the School

As the school year drew to a close, the Community School staff and students began to pull together an assessment of the initial year. The evaluation consisted of several parts.

1. Tests measuring student attitudes and alienation.
2. Letters from parents.
3. Letters from students.
4. Letters from experts.
5. Uses of community resources.

Tests. Although academic achievement test results were unavailable, two formal tests were used to measure change in student affective growth during the year. The first measured alienation. The results were quite favorable. Initially 56 percent of the Community School students scored high on their overall alienation from the authority system of the traditional high school (compared to 23 percent of the total high school population). At the end of the year 12 percent of the Community School students were highly alienated—a significant reduction. Similarly favorable change occurred for most of the individual alienation scales.

Community School students also took personality tests at the beginning and at the end of the school year. The adjective check list has six scales including: favorable and unfavorable self-image, aggression, self-control, personal adjustment, and self-confidence. During the year students shifted in a favorable direction on five of the scales. Student self-confidence, as measured by this instrument, did not change. See Table 3.

Parent letters. At the end of the year the superintendent sent a letter to parents asking them whether the program should be continued and the reasons for reaching their conclusions. Of thirty-four sets of parents, twenty-nine responded favorably; five did not return the questionnaire. The parents were unanimous in stating that if the decision were theirs, they would continue the Community School. The parents' rationales were categorized into five main areas. Chief among their reasons were responses which indicated an improved attitude toward learning. One parent said:

> We have noticed a tremendous change in her personality and attitude toward school after being involved with the Community-Centered High School. She has matured and has a desire for learning and going on to school. A whole new world seems to have opened up for her.

Quality of the professional staff and program, improved student attitudes toward themselves, other students and parents, were listed as second and third most important reasons for continuing the program.

> She will never again be lost enough for drug abuse or for generally hostile behavior; but she was. And that school was important in her overcoming those things—by helping her learn who she is and what she wants.

> Although our daughter has always been a good student, we really didn't realize how suppressed her personality had been. She became (this year) outgoing which she was not before; she talked more which she did not before.

> . . . during the past school year, we have observed noticeable changes. We can communicate with much more ease. She has voluntarily assumed many of the home chores.

> My son spends a great deal of extra time dealing with some kind of the administrative problems of the school. The kind of work he has produced in the stimulating atmosphere of the school has been remarkable in quality. The maturity of some of his writings approaches the quality of an upper-level college student term paper.

Acceptance of responsibility, an improved attitude toward the community, and interest in further education and vocation were the fourth and fifth areas listed by parents as reasons for continuing the program.

> The evident close-knit relationship of this small student body has made our son more aware of the problems and needs of other individuals, and we feel this has broadened his perspective toward life in the community and towards his place in life itself.

> It takes a little time for a student to find himself and to adjust to a learning program wherein he virtually dictates his own rate of progress. After the novelty and possible abuse of the system passes, the student can progress at a fairly rapid rate perhaps even with greater understanding than in a conventional high school. This appears to be true in our daughter's case. Scholastic achievement still must have a final evaluation, but her studies have been approached with enthusiasm and a sincere desire to learn with continuation on to the college level. This is almost a complete reversal of attitude.

Student letters. The superintendent also asked students to submit a letter stating whether the program should be continued and giving reasons for their conclusion. Twenty-eight of the thirty students responded. All wanted to see the program continue. Their reasons were categorized into areas which included the high quality of the program, an improved attitude toward learning, acceptance of responsibility, interest in further education in a vocation, and the high quality of the staff. One student articulately captured the sentiment of the others in a summary statement.

> My life is mine.
> I need to feel its source comes basically from my own energy, that my education is my responsibility and that I have a hand in the "real world" of making myself live. The reason I say "real world" is because at my age I am not *only* a child. Usually in the regular high school I was forced to play a child's role. Being told that I had to do this and be here at a certain time, wear certain clothes, talk politely, sitting in an impersonal room doing homework or studying something I thought irrelevant . . . when outside there are war, pollution, family struggles, a lot of learning to do and there I'd sit bored and unhappy. I'd have deep relations with a person outside school or go hiking way out in the woods with a lot of serious taking care of myself. Then think about going back to school and being talked down to just because of age difference. I don't want to wait. I want to live now. This is a great age to go out and try things. And that is what I did this year.
> My (our) school gives the chance, almost demands straight communication. This means dropping fears of being close and open with people, dropping competition, comparison, and judgments of right and wrong. It means adding goals of meaningfulness, and values of people in the true meaning of brotherhood, nature, and joy in living.
> In my school is the concept of caring. I am special, needed and not only care for others but also for myself. So many things I can do when I like myself.
> The school automatically seems to breed independence and motivation. With all that I have talked about you don't need rules or authority. No need for authority means that it doesn't come from one point but all points with understanding. We all have the child, adult and parent in us. Some might know a lot about some things while others are able in another field regardless of age.
> This culture is very complicated. One system cannot satisfy many many people. There has to be several concepts in the system or several systems to meet the needs of people. This high school, the regular high school and other programs are all important and needed.
> All that I have said takes a lot of struggling and hard work. We have all gone a long way. Of course anything that goes on in the school can only be so from what the people make it. And so, from a year's

experience I conclude that the Community School leaves all doors open. From it comes stability, creativity, independence, honesty, communication, love and growth. These do not make jails, asylums, as many hospitals, murders, pollution, nervousness, "rape" or unhappiness.
Some necessary improvements
1. I would like more space around and inside the building.
2. The age 16 law banished.
3. A place or more ways to get out pent up emotions—dancing, running, painting, time for talk sessions specifically for just talking about what I'm doing or feeling. Anything so long as it interacts with other people.
   I hope you feel the sincerity and great feelings from this letter.

Love,

Expert testimony. Two psychiatrists, a probation officer, a university professor, and a consultant for the National Commission on Resources for Youth wrote testimonial letters commenting on the favorable and positive climate which the Community School provided for young people.

Uses of Community Resources. The evaluation included a list of community resources which students used during the year. The list included several institutions and long lists of individuals, including: teachers, retired people, housewives, artists, laboratory technicians, lawyers, and archeologists.

The evaluation was presented to the school board by the principal and several students. Prior to the meeting, the board was provided a written report, in which results of the evaluation were highlighted. At the end of the presentation, board members asked several questions, proceeding publicly to extol the virtues of the Community School. The conservative board member who had voted against the original resolution stated emotionally: "I voted against the school and I want to say that I was wrong. Maybe what schools need is a little more humaneness and love."

By a vote of 5 to 0 the board resolved to continue the Community School. It still exists today.

Implications for Newly Established Alternative Schools

The problems experienced by the Community School in its formative months were probably similar to those experienced by many other alternative schools.

Organizationally, alternative schools were new institutions with vague, diffuse goals and an underlying ideology which emphasized individual freedom, unique experience, and humanistic values. The schools often existed in hostile, "establishment" environments and because of frequent criticism closed themselves off except to those in the environment who believed as they did. The educational program of these schools, following the goals and ideology, was highly individualistic and discontinuous, and both the techniques of teaching or learning and ways to judge progress and success were underdeveloped or nonexistent. The authority granted to students in selecting learning activities, the "do your own thing" character of the schools, not only increased the diversity of curriculum and instruction but made it difficult for teachers to play much of a role in student learning. The instructional tasks of any one student often involved input from several teachers and, as a result, the efforts of teachers, as well as students, were highly interdependent.

Any successful combination of these organizational features required a highly developed structure to coordinate, support, and evaluate a highly complex instructional program in an often hostile environment. Yet structurally, alternative schools were primitive, undeveloped, fragmented, and highly informal. The counterculture ideology abhors organization, routinization, and bureaucracy, and as a result decision making in the alternative schools was participatory, consensual, cumbersome, burdensome, and ineffective. Problem solving was laborious, although enough problems existed to keep even a well-oiled system working at full capacity.

Using the organizational character of alternative schools as a framework, one may explain the developmental stages of the Community School and others like it somewhat as follows.

In the "euphoric" stage there was no need for organization. Students and teachers were busily engaged in living out their personal and educational fantasies. Students were able to do what they had formerly dreamed of in classes where instructional activities had been meaningless to them. Teachers were able to provide instruction without the constraints of the conventional system. But as time passed, there were no formally recognized standards to judge such activities, nor was there any feedback for highly individualistic accomplishments.

The psychic upheaval stage was a normless, listless, confused reaction to the lack of formal feedback for the learning activities of the first stage. The goals of alternative education were vague and diffuse. In living out their personal fantasies, students and teachers soon began to look for formal validation indicating that their direction was "appropriate." But as they looked for such recognition within the school, they found no goals or consensus, and as they turned their attention outside, they found little if any environmental support for their activities. This situation threw students (and teachers) back on their own resources, and they looked inside themselves for the validation they had expected from without. Such introspection produced a predictable trauma; as its intensity increased and extended to many of the students in the school, the organization began to reward disturbed students by giving them feedback about their personal difficulties through the teachers—ostensibly the formal and legitimate evaluators. This, in the absence of other feedback, quickly led to a negatively based system of evaluation and rewards—having a personal problem was formally recognized and rewarded.

At the same time, teachers were overloaded. They were required to provide counseling, to provide educational leadership for a school whose leadership was supposed to flow from the collective, and to develop and coordinate numerous and highly diverse instructional activities, many of which were neither routine nor within the purview of their professional preparation. Moreover, they were faced with the reality that collective decision making was not working and were frustrated by the power of an ideology which suggested that this was the only way in which problems could legitimately be resolved. Few activities were routinized; this inevitably overloaded the only accepted decision-making apparatus, making it difficult for any problems to be solved. Teachers became overworked, but unable to make needed changes since their proposals were modified or aborted by the consensual decision-making process.

Students, receiving little feedback from teachers, turned to their peers who, like them, were too wrapped up in personal problems to offer support or assistance. The peer group was highly inconsistent in its values but tended to stress the norms of the counterculture. Students began to dress alike, talk alike, and act alike. In frustration, students (and teachers) reached outside to parents and others for some assurance that they were achieving educational goals. But in a relatively hostile and unsupportive environment, they found only criticism and an exhortation to return to conventional patterns. This pattern led quickly to stage three.

The dissatisfaction stage forced upon alternative schools and realization that their organizational shift to the status of counseling or crisis center was unsatisfactory. For some students, the schools had provided a temporary "way station." Now these same students were requesting, even demanding, some highly conventional instruction. But how could this become both a crisis center and a conventional high school? Or even if this were organizationally feasible, how could consensus be reached in a highly individualistic setting with the determination of policy in the hands of the entire population of the school?

Clearly, continuing the status quo would result in severe internal splits or in destruction. But, on the other hand, if the faculty or someone else in the school took over, would not that act in itself destroy the integrity of the school? In the absence of clear goals, in an environment which rejected the main learning activities, without a history, without clear means for accomplishing learning or measuring success, without the internal support of individual or informal group norms, without adequate time for the professional leadership to develop direction, how were alternative schools to maintain their organizational integrity?

For many schools the answer was clear: they either went down without striking their colors or returned to the safety of a familiar and friendly port. These were the alternative schools that dissolved or reverted to a highly centralized and conventional system.

Those schools, like the Community School, that "made it" did so because they were able to find a philosophical middle ground. This philosophical compromise was then reflected in an organization that maintained a highly individualized or pluralistic structure but one that was also well integrated and formalized. A division of labor was made. Roles were clarified. Students were given considerable autonomy in choosing learning activities, but teachers were formally given the responsibility for expanding the base of alternatives. Goals were specified, evaluation processes were regularized, and decision rules were established to centralize some decisions while keeping others decentralized and consensual. Boundary-maintenance activities were developed to control and process the flow of negative information from the environment, while specific attempts were made to persuade the parents and the community that the alternative program was highly desirable educationally—by any standards. In short, the successful alternative schools developed a well-knit, sophisticated organization capable of supporting the highly complex instructional program they had chosen to operate. They had compromised somewhat their original participatory, democratic, "hang loose" approach to organization but were able to maintain the integrity of the other elements in their alternative approach to instruction.

As new alternative schools begin and as existing high schools "coopt" many alternative school characteristics some lessons can be learned from past experiments. First and foremost, changes should be carefully planned in advance. The community school and other alternative schools were often launched with only vague ideas about what the school would not be. Developing a clear idea about the school's basic form and anticipating the consequences of making changes will help prevent some problems.

Second, despite the importance of planning, it is probably more realistic that alternative schools or reforms in existing high schools will begin without specific, well-formulated plans. Schools will undoubtedly follow

Table 3

Percentage of Students High on Alienation Scales for Total High School Last Year, Community-Centered High School First Year, and Community-Centered High School Second Year

SCALES	Percentage of community school students highly alienated	Percentage of traditional school highly alienated	Percentage of community school highly alienated after one year in the program
Authority granted to teachers	40	34	76
Expertise granted to teachers	60	42	64
Authority granted to school officials	96	77	80
Favorability of attitude to teachers	44	20	4
Justice of teachers	24	17	0
Participation in school activities	84	17	0
Liking for school	60	44	0
Achievement orietation	68	41	30
Concern with grades	68	33	52
Conformity to school rules	20	17	8
TOTAL ALIENATION INDEX	56	22	12

the planning scheme of "muddling through." As they "muddle," schools will be able to use previous experiences to stabilize a school as changes are implemented. Such schools should develop organizational properties that will enable them to avoid either falling apart or returning to a highly centralized system.

Third, the prior knowledge that the formative months of alternative schools may encounter certain stages, may prevent the teachers and the staff from rising and falling with the natural development of the school. They can bring some degree of rationality to the situation as well as being able to manipulate aspects of the structure to minimize the effects of the various predictable stages.

There is probably not much that can be done in planning or implementation to avoid the problems of changing schools. There is much that can be done to develop structures and procedures for resolving problems in schools, once problems arise. Reinventing the wheel is not necessarily a bad strategy—if you have a hub and some spokes.

References

Bennis, Warren G., and H. A. Shepard. "A Theory of Group Development," in *The Planning of Change.* Ed. W. G. Bennis, K. D. Benne, and R. Chin. New York: Holt, 1961.

Bredo, Eric R., and Anneke E. Riemersma. "A Study of Authority in Three High Schools." unpublished paper, Stanford University, 1971.

Deal, Terrence E. "An Organizational Explanation of the Failure of Alternative Schools," Stanford Center for Research and Development in Teaching. Stanford University, 1975.

Henderson, Judith. "Adolescent Alienation from Authority and Educational Aspirations Before and After Changes in the High School Authority Structure." Unpublished Dissertation, Stanford University, 1971.

McCauley, Brian L., Sanford M. Dornbusch, and W. Richard Scott. "Evaluation and Authority in Alternative Schools and Public Schools. (Stanford Center for Research and Development in Teaching, Technical Report No. 23) Stanford University, June 1972.

Mills, Theodore M. *Group Transformation: An Analysis of a Learning Group.* Englewood Cliffs, New Jersey: Prentice-Hall, 1964.

Smith, Louis M., and Pat M. Keith. *The Anatomy of Educational Innovation: An Organizational Analysis of the Elementary School.* New York: Wiley, 1971.

10

Student Power: A Case Study
by Robert R. Nolan

"End The War!" "Education, Not Racism!" "No Military On Campus!" "Power To The Students!" Such was the campus rhetoric of the 1960s and early 1970s. First college, and later high school students became more critical and vocal about social and political issues, especially the institution of which they were an integral part—their school. While a case can be made that students were instrumental in bringing about Lyndon Johnson's decision not to run for reelection, the end to the Vietnam War, and even consumer reforms (Nader's Raiders), there is less evidence that students significantly altered their own schools and colleges. Most schools and colleges today have more minority teachers, more liberal student-conduct rules, and less restrictive graduation requirements, but the essential organization of most schools and colleges looks much the same. Day-to-day decision-making authority remains in the hands of administrators with ultimate authority in school boards or trustees. Key budget, personnel, and curricula decisions are normally immune to direct student input.

However, in a few rare cases, students were able to win significant power over decision making in their school. This is a study of one of those cases. This paper traces the struggle to establish the Roslyn School-Within-a-School (Roslyn, New York) and follows the struggle through the first year of the school's operation. Based on this experience, some conclusions about student control of a public alternative high school are presented.

The Initial Struggle

The idea for an alternative school in Roslyn originated with sophomores and freshmen from the only high school in the district. The regular high school was generally liberal in its philosophy with no dress code, many electives, and an emphasis on preparing students for college (over 90 percent of the graduates went on to some form of higher education). But, one small group of students was openly discontented. They felt that the curriculum, varied as it was, was teacher determined and directed. Students could pick only from electives which were offered by regular teachers. This offered little opportunity for students to design their own educational options. Only limited use was being made of the rich resources of the community and nearby New York City. These students felt a need for a far greater range of learning opportunities. Stimulated by such books as A. S. Neill's *Summerhill* and the establishment of alternative schools in two neighboring school districts, they set out to work for an alternative high school for Roslyn.

Their first efforts were sporadic. A series of after-school meetings, also attended by a few interested teachers, revealed widespread interest in such an idea but harnessing that interest proved difficult. While some students had read a number of books on educational reform and visited alternative schools in the area, other students understood little about the concepts underlying alternative schools. In addition to an uneven level of awareness, the organizers were hampered by ignorance of the procedures of running large meetings. The first meetings resulted in great frustration and charges that the small, but ill-defined, group of organizers were ignoring the input of other students and were making all the decisions themselves. The students could not get together on anything but the need for a new school where the students could determine and manage the curriculum. A number of meetings with school and district administrators further accentuated the students' lack of organization and clearly defined goals. While these administrators maintained an open-door policy to students, they were more concerned with other demands for student power which focused around racial issues (more black teachers, more black theme courses) and the antiwar movement (the right to attend demonstrations, the right to distribute radical literature). Philosophically opposed to students "running their own education," the administrators saw no need for another high school. Little was done that first year.

The following year a number of teachers were asked to join the small organizing group. Believing that this should be an all-student project, these teachers maintained low profiles with only an occasional question or suggestion. Feeling somewhat pressed by accusations that they were being unresponsive, the district administrators arranged for one of the high school's vice principals to work with the interested students and teachers to explore their ideas. This particular vice principal was new to the high school and was therefore reluctant to champion any controversial causes. The choice of this vice principal was a setback for the students. He insisted that most discussions be held with interested teachers without the presence of students. His attitude was "convince me." He argued every point and spoke vaguely of some "workable compromise." Seeing that valuable time and effort were being wasted, the group of students began to limit their work sessions to a small group of committed students and interested teachers. A written proposal, based on the writings of several education critics and the proposals of other alternative schools, was drafted and submitted directly to the board. It was debated in open session with a number of parents, teachers, and students speaking in its favor. No school or district administrator was in favor of the alternative school. From the start of the debate, the board members were obviously opposed to the idea of an alternative school.

One influential board member urged that the proposal be defeated on the grounds that it was budgetarily extravagant. When a plan to finance it by shifting funds on a per pupil basis from the regular high school was submitted, another board member argued that it should be defeated because it was improperly drawn up (an eventuality that the vice principal was supposed to prevent) and philosophically unsound. The proposal was defeated 7-0.

The following year the issue of an alternative school seemed to be dead. Two years of effort had resulted in a unanimous defeat by the school board. Most of the original student organizers were now seniors, occupied by applying to colleges, and with no hope of ever attending a Roslyn alternative school. Most were convinced that "working within the system" had failed again. Nevertheless, a core of five seniors wanted to try again. They wanted to rework the proposal and resubmit it to the board. They first went to the high school principal and made their intentions known. He required that they have an advisor. The students asked me to serve in this capacity. I refused. I had been one of the teachers who had worked on the original proposal and was now as discouraged as most of the students. Faced with the open opposition of the board, I didn't believe that it had a chance and told these seniors so. They persisted. Their determination and altruism were convincing. I agreed to serve as their advisor only under certain conditions: we would set deadlines and keep them; in a time of explosive rhetoric and confrontation, we would work quietly and behind the scenes to gain support; my role would be supportive and not directive.

Their first step was to begin rewriting sections of the original proposal. They carefully outlined staffing assignments and budgetary requirements so that the teacher/student ratio would be equivalent to that of the regular high school. Since staff would come from the regular high school faculty and funds from the regular high school budget, the alternative school could be no "richer" than the regular school. They decided that students for the alternative school would be picked by lottery from volunteers. The method of selection had been a divisive issue among those previously planning for the alternative school. Those who worked hardest for the cause wanted a guaranteed place in the school while those not part of the planning group considered this unfair. Since the alternative school could only be implemented the following year and the planning group was now entirely seniors, they were able to settle on the equitable system of a lottery. They also reduced the planned initial size of the school to sixty students because experience had shown that the smaller the group, the easier it is to organize. Other alternative schools had become fragmented when they became too large. The Roslyn alternative school initially would be limited to juniors and seniors because both would have finished most of their required courses and the juniors would provide continuity for the following year. The statement of philosophy was shortened and clarified to say:

> Our proposed program will be an experimental alternative in education. In general, its purposes will be to help students assume responsibility for their own learning and to allow students and teachers to create a school community of their own design. Toward this end, both students and faculty will play a role in forming policies, procedures, and curriculum which will satisfy the mandates of New York State law.
>
> It is our belief that the traditional approaches to education do not meet the needs of all students. In order to provide for an alternative educational experience, our school will explore other approaches to learning. We will attempt to establish an environment which will enhance learning by placing an emphasis on the individual's interests and needs. Students, for example, may partake in tutorial or independent study, small group seminars or workshops. Most importantly, they will be encouraged to take advantage of the resources outside the school building, perhaps nearby museums or universities. Some may even wish to undertake paid or volunteer work. This living-learning situation will, it is hoped, prepare students to deal effectively with the many changes taking place in the world today.
>
> Because of their structure, traditional schools, while providing

for learning of cognitive material, often do not involve one's feelings and personal interpretations. According to Carl R. Rogers in his book *FREEDOM TO LEARN*, "When we put together in one scheme such elements as a prescribed curriculum, similar assignments for all students, lecturing as almost the only mode of instruction, standard tests by which all students are externally evaluated, and instructor chosen grades as the measure of learning, then we can almost guarantee that meaningful learning will be at the absolute minimum." For those people who do not function under those circumstances but might otherwise, we are proposing a feasible alternative. Therefore, the purpose of the school will be to free the student to experience learning as a whole individual whose feelings and cognitive aspects are involved.

Freedom to make decisions and assume responsibility for the consequences will be a means of developing responsible adults. In removing some external restrictions, experience under the guidance of involved teachers in a supportive atmosphere, will lead to the kind of self-restraint that makes the imposition of restrictions by others unnecessary.

Our philosophy, therefore, is based on the belief that all people, of all ages, are naturally curious and do want to learn. It must be understood that no one school or system of education is best for all. We firmly believe that given the opportunity, students will realize their own interests which will encourage learning for the most valid reason there can be—because the student wants to learn.[1]

During the time we were rewriting the proposal, we planned our strategy to get the school board to accept it. We knew that it was critical to gain the Parents' Association's support. The previous year they had shown some interest in the idea of an alternative school. We contacted them early in the year and, on their suggestion, we helped them plan a conference on alternative education. Parents, teachers, and students from nearby alternative schools spoke to a large audience of interested community members. This conference showed the community that responsible people were running successful alternative programs. Thus, our efforts for a Roslyn alternative school gained legitimacy and support.

Since most other alternative schools were sponsored by a key administrator, we chose the principal of the regular high school to be the first to win to our side. We emphasized that there were successful alternative schools operating in neighboring districts. The "let's keep up with the Joneses" argument was effective with our district administrators who were

---

1. "Alternative School Proposal," Roslyn School District, Roslyn, New York, February 14, 1973, pp. 1–2.

very proud of the district's educational offerings and didn't want to become a second-rate "educational power." In meeting with the high school principal and other administrators, we followed a few guidelines. We made no demands. Our meetings were discussions of our requests. We kept the meetings small. No administrator had to face more than two or three students at once. We did not try to convince the principal in just one meeting. We tried to deal with just a few issues at a time.

Concurrently, we had to contend with another district power, the head of the teachers' union. The students would have to pick the teachers for the alternative school among volunteers from the regular high school staff. (The students knew that they would not be able to hire new teachers due to a very low district staff turnover and stable student enrollment.) This was contrary to the teachers' master contract which stipulated that all staff assignments must be made by the district administration. Due to the sensitive nature of this topic, this was one of the few meetings in which I spoke for the students. An unofficial agreement was reached: as long as no jobs were eliminated or threatened; no official complaints made by any teacher; all tenure and seniority rights were protected; and all assignments were officially made by the district administration, the union would make no moves to block the alternative school. Shortly after this agreement was reached, our tactics with the high school principal brought results. He agreed to support the proposal for the alternative school with the implicit understanding that we would continue to work through "proper channels."

With the help of the high school principal, the students then met with the district superintendent. Since the high school principal had taken the first step, the district superintendent was not long in agreeing to support the proposal. Here again, the fact that other districts had functional alternative schools and that ours would require no new money was critical. The alternative school proposal was placed on the agenda for the next school board meeting. A copy was sent to every board member with a supporting cover letter from the high school principal. The students had some of their parents meet individually with board members to discuss the proposal. The Parents' Association, before which we had made presentations on the proposal for the alternative school, voted to officially support the proposal.

Everything was set. We had worked quietly, excited no tempers, had the open or implicit support of key administrators, the Parents' Association, and a number of influential parents, and had tried to anticipate every possible objection. The night of the board's vote the students quietly filled the back of the meeting room. When the alternative school proposal was brought up, it was passed 7-0 with virtually no debate. We had won.

Implementing the Proposal

We had won the right to set up our alternative school, but only a month remained before summer vacation to choose the students and staff for the start of school the following September. The planning committee of seniors continued their work. After-school meetings were held to inform students of the new school, letters were mailed to the parents of potential students, a mandatory evening orientation meeting was held for interested parents and students, permission slips were distributed and collected. A lottery was unnecessary to fill the sixty student places. Only fifty-six students had chosen to brave the perils of setting up and being a part of a new experimental school.

The first real meeting of the new school was held just before the summer vacation to choose the faculty for the start of school in September. The planning committee of departing seniors chaired the meeting. The students were limited to the guidelines outlined in the proposal and they had to choose the staff from teachers who had volunteered from the regular high school staff. Almost a full day of heated discussion resulted in a formal recommendation on staffing. This recommendation was quickly approved by the high school principal and district superintendent.

Since the school was to be housed in the regular high school complex and, since most of the new school's faculty and students wanted to avoid antagonizing the regular school with a provocative name (for example, The Free School), the school was named the Roslyn School-Within-a-School (SWS). Negotiations were begun with the high school administration to secure quarters for the new school. As the regular high school was very large and the new school would effectively reduce the number of regularly scheduled classes, three classrooms were eventually allocated for the new school in a separate section of the regular high school building. Entirely separate quarters were impossible since the new school was to cost no more per pupil than the regular high school. Having quarters in the regular school complex had its advantages and disadvantages. Students and part-time faculty could move more easily to and from the two schools and special equipment (for example, motion picture projectors) and the library were more accessible. However, unannounced visitors were sometimes disruptive and extra effort had to be made so the special liberties granted the students of the alternative school did not subvert the rules and regulations of the regular school.

Governance and Structure

The main method of governance was the general meeting which was held weekly or more often when necessary. Decisions were made within the broad framework of state and district rules and the school proposal by a majority vote of those present. Decisions were binding on all school members, both faculty and students. The meetings were run by rotating chairpersons who were also responsible for organizing each meeting's agenda. Committees were formed to deal with transitory or on-going problems. Certain standing committees were established: a college committee polled colleges on what form of evaluations were acceptable since the School-Within-a-School would not award formal grades; a budget committee processed all requests for money from the school budget; a resource committee located people and organizations from the community who were willing to offer their services to the school. Committees made their recommendations to the general meeting where all final decisions were made. Committee membership was made up of whoever wished to work on a particular problem. During my association with the school, I never saw a complete student/faculty split on any committee or general-meeting decision.

The position of school director, the one for which I was chosen and held concurrently with that of the alternative school's social studies teacher, was meant to serve as liaison between the School-Within-a-School's government and the regular high school and district administrations.

Each student, in consultation with his/her faculty advisor and SWS guidance counselor, devised a program best suited to that student's talents and interests. The learning options open to students were virtually limitless—among the more popular being individual projects and tutorials, college courses, volunteer work, special lectures and trips, and regular high school courses. The alternative school students could take a maximum of two courses in the regular high school. This limitation existed so as not to overburden the regular high school staff. Furthermore, if the students wanted to take more than two courses in the regular high school, it was reasoned that they should remain in the regular high school because most of their time would be spent there. SWS courses for the first year included science fiction, the novels of Herman Hesse (student-taught), creative writing, selected plays of Shakespeare (taught by a student from the regular high school with minimal guidance from the high school drama teacher), educational reform, conversational French, philosophy, and math survey. Individual student projects included working at a local arboretum, teaching flute, working as a sculptor's apprentice, volunteer work at a geriatric center, making an electric guitar, designing a solar cell power system with the help of a local engineer, and studying Elementary Particles and Relativity at Columbia University.

The general meeting, acting upon the recommendations of an ad hoc rules committee, adopted a series of rules and obligations for every SWS student:

1. Sign in daily; call in when sick; bring an absent note in promptly.

2. Attend all General Meetings.

3. Meet with faculty advisor at times determined by the individual and the advisor. Inform the advisor of a schedule and any schedule changes.

4. Keep and revise a schedule sheet in the Master Schedule Book (SWS Activities Book).

5. Devote one period a week to office work.

6. Adhere to rules of the regular school.

7. Submit and have approved a physical education program by a date specified by the physical education committee.

8. Meet with the Review Board at a time specified by that board.

9. In addition to the above, contribute some substantial time and effort to the running of the SWS.[2]

Evaluation of students took place in a number of ways: student/teacher conferences; end-of-the-term evaluations of teachers, students, and courses; written evaluations of students (worked out by students and teachers) which could be used at the student's option for college admission purposes. A student-faculty review board was formed to periodically evaluate each student's program and determine if he/she was fulfilling the obligations of an SWS student. This review board worked in the following way:

---

2. "Rules Committee Report," passed by the General Meeting, Roslyn School-Within-a-School, October 22, 1973, p. 1.

Each SWS student will meet with the Review Board at a time determined by the board. (The student's faculty advisor will be present at this and any other meeting with the board.) The board will review the work and activities of the individual student and how that student meets the obligations and standards discussed above. If the board feels that the student is not meeting these requirements, the student will be called back to discuss the matter with the board. If at this point the board still feels the student is not fulfilling his or her responsibilities, the matter will be brought to a General Meeting, at which time both the board and the individual will present and discuss his or her case. The board and the General Meeting will decide if the next step should be taken.

If the situation still exists after the General Meeting, a member of the Review Board will contact the parents of the student to inform them of the situation. If there is still no improvement, the final step, which would be determined at a General Meeting, would be a recommendation to the parents and the administration that the student be transferred to the regular school. Any transfers will be made at the beginning of a semester.[3]

During the first year of the alternative school, it was necessary for this process to work to its conclusion in only one case—one student was returned to the regular school.

Conclusions

What can be learned from this example of student power?

● *Most importantly, students (at least high school students) can successfully take control of their own education.* Given the option, some, probably a minority of sixteen- to eighteen-year-olds, can manage and benefit from an essentially self-directed education. From cleaning classrooms to making the most minute (and necessary) budget decisions, such students can run their own school.

● *Students need time to learn the skills necessary to run a complex organization such as a school.* Few, if any, students normally possess the knowledge and skills to run large meetings, draw up and use an itemized budget, schedule classes, raise money, deal with administration complaints, etc. Initially, failures may outweigh successes. Parents, teachers, and administrators must be patient for growth to occur.

3. Ibid., p. 2.

● *Students have to learn to deal with adults as sources of expertise and assistance rather than authority figures.* Both adults and students are not always comfortable with this new arrangement where personal worth and abilities become more important than position.

● *Student-run schools should be kept small.* The larger the organization, the less personal it becomes and the more difficult to manage. The smaller the school, the larger the proportion of students who can make important contributions.

● *Students must learn that a student-run school (like other educational institutions) functions in a political environment where method and appearance are often more important that substance and reality.* One year the proposal for the alternative school was unanimously rejected by the school board, whereas the following year essentially the same proposal, but advocated by different methods, was passed unanimously. At times, one dramatic success or failure would mean more to those evaluating the school than a careful weighing of the school's merits and demerits.

● *Contrary to Lawrence Cremin's view,[4] reinventing the wheel can be a valuable learning experience.* In struggling to discover which methods of learning and governance were most suitable, SWS students tested, discarded, and modified a variety of methods. While they often adopted a procedure long used by others (for example, conducting most of the general meeting's work in committees), the process of discovery increased everyone's understanding of the various options and commitment to the one eventually adopted.

● *The rewards of a student-run school are probably the greatest for the initial group of students.* The whole process of struggling for and building their own school cannot be duplicated for later students. Some students even suggested destroying the whole school so that the new students would be forced to go through the whole building process themselves.

● *As it is true for students, not all teachers would function well in a student-run school.* Teachers must replace authority with persuasion and guidance. Moreover, as student learning options increase in number, preparation time, and the danger of teacher "burnout" increase.

● *Procedures must be available to advise and redirect students who*

4. Lawrence A. Cremin, "The Free School Movement: A Perspective," *Notes on Education,* No. 2, October 1973.

cannot function in a student-run school. Students who cannot assume the responsibility for their own education can hurt not only themselves but can threaten the very survival of the school. A few conspicuous "goof-offs" or troublemakers can do much to undermine the school's reputation.

● *Students and parents need to be educated as to the advantages and disadvantages of different educational methods and options.* Orientation sessions, special back-to-school night programs, mailings to parents, and newspaper articles serve to make the decisions of parents and students informed decisions. Nothing can be more disruptive to an educational program as unrealistic expectations or unwarranted fears. Since the SWS was under the critical eye of district administrators and community members, the extensive time spent on public relations was a necessity.

● *A student-run school can have a positive influence on the regular school.* The SWS served as a testing ground for new courses and forms of independent study, some of which were incorporated in the regular high school curriculum. In addition, the SWS acted as a "safety valve" for the regular high school in drawing off some of its most discontented students.

In sum, the greatest benefits of a student-run school are for the students. As one student wrote:

> The SWS has been one of the best learning experiences that I have ever encountered. The ability to create a school community and to assume responsibility for your own education is an unforgettable experience. The SWS has enabled me to pursue my interests that were somehow curtailed in the regular school structure. It has given me the chance to really see what kind of motivation and independence I can apply to my own learning.[5]

---

5. "Progress Report on the School-Within-a-School Program," Roslyn School District, Roslyn, New York, January 21, 1974, p. 6.

11

Trauma and Renaissance: A Case History of an Alternative School's Evolution
by David Murphy

Background

In 1970, Cubberley High School established a school-within-a-school. Like other "alternative" schools, the Alternative School in Cubberley (ASC) was a student-centered school, guided by the staff, but governed by students and staff. Unlike many other such educational experiments, however, ASC has grown and flourished. The reasons for its success are complex. But the most important factor has been the evolution of stabilizing structures and clear, systematic (yet fluid) processes for making decisions, resolving conflicts, and dealing with the ebbs and flow of life in a school.

ASC did not begin with these stabilizing structures or systematic processes. This article records their evolution, illuminating successes and identifying some near-fatal steps that could have tipped the delicate balance to a less successful outcome. The purpose of this article is to point out successful practices and to recommend some shortcuts that we can share with those who are about to embark on a similar venture. These practices and shortcuts are mainly a product of hindsight, as ASC is, and will continue to be, a fragile, constantly changing institution.

The article will follow the ASC through its several phases: preplanning, planning, the early beginnings, problems and stabilization, and finally institutionalization and legitimacy.

Preplanning

ASC's preplanning followed perfect theory. In the beginning, the new principal invited students and staff to brainstorm curricular changes for the entire high school. Several groups met monthly at first, then weekly. The frequency increased as people found it necessary to maintain momentum. These groups were supported by the active and encouraging presence of the principal. Anyone was welcome to participate, but as the groups worked harder and harder, the number of participants decreased. Finally a small core of students and staff remained. The staff group was led by the school psychologist, the student group by a few bright, but bored students. Independently, these two study groups evolved the same recommendations: change fundamentally the process by which curricular decisions are made and involve students in real decision making about their own education.

All members of the student and the faculty groups wanted something real to emerge from their efforts. The principal agreed with the spirit of the recommendations and promised support if the groups could develop a specific proposal.

The students and staff took the challenge and scheduled a weekend retreat to form the ideas into a concrete proposal. Student and staff credit that retreat as a turning point. In the atmosphere of rough cabins and bunkhouses set in the hilly trail-laden foothills, the students and teachers became comrades, cooking and cleaning together, playing and working together, sharing personal conversations and feelings on long walks.

The retreat produced more than teacher-student solidarity. By the end of the weekend an outline was developed for the proposal, and a small task force had agreed to write a preliminary draft. The proposal was to be specific enough to give substance, yet general enough to include divergent views at Cubberley. The key words for the proposal's tone were "inclusive" and "open." The tone was designed to attract a heterogeneous student population, ranging from mentally-gifted high-achievers to average intelligence low-achievers, from student body officers and career musicians to parking-lot hang-outs. It was also an expression of the belief that ASC was open to anyone committed to learning and working with others.

In retrospect several decisions contributed significantly to the success of the preplanning. The principal had decided that both the student committee and the teacher committee were important, and he attended most meetings, helping as needed. Essential to the success of the committees was the principal's decision to firmly support this process.

Second, the committees had decided to brainstorm the problems at Cubberley and to share the dreams of the committee members—all before any solutions or practical problems were discussed.

Third, the committees, although initially planning to meet monthly, decided to meet weekly in order to have the proposal ready before administrators had to determine the next year's budget, master schedule, and personnel placement.

The fourth significant decision was to go off campus for a weekend to a natural habitat to encourage sharing of all leads among all people of the school: students, teachers, and administrators.

Finally, permeating the entire process of preplanning was the most significant decision: The process and the proposal would be open-ended and include all interested students and teachers and, initially, all ideas.

Planning

The principal and the school psychologist strongly endorsed the proposal and took it to the faculty, temporarily allaying their many fears and reservations. Here the principal asked the faculty for support. It was weakly given. (Several faculty members felt they were given no choice.) Overall the faculty was skeptical, but tolerated the further development of the proposal. Twenty faculty members (25 percent) volunteered time and effort, but an equally strong minority opposed ASC's development.

The proposal was next taken to the second school constituency: the Cubberley students. Each Cubberley student was to be informed, and every student was to be given the opportunity to become involved in the development of the ASC. For several reasons, social studies classes were selected as the information forums: class sizes in social studies were small enough to allow for more informal discussions among the students; teachers in the social studies department were favorable to the proposal (two members of that department had been among the original faculty group preparing the proposal); and because social studies is a required subject, all Cubberley students could be reached.

Each ASC information team included one faculty member and a few students who had been involved in the development of the proposal. Role-playing prior to the presentations encouraged an inclusive and open approach form of presentation. The main purpose was to include many types of students.

During the presentations, answers to questions were open—"We want to give this proposal to you and have the people involved in ASC reach their own answers rather than our making them for you." The initial invitation to students thus paralleled the theme of the proposal: "People who are significantly affected by a decision should help decide it."

The parents were informed about ASC through the students. Every student was given a copy of the proposal and an admonition: "If you have any interest in what ASC might offer, come to the evening information meetings. You must come if you want to preserve your option to join later. One of your parents must come too." Most parents were reluctant but came to the meetings because students were excited and insistent.

At two major information meetings, the principal explained the legitimacy and need for ASC, its evolution from two curriculum groups, and its experimental nature. He emphasized that although ASC would have his full backing, ASC was a school in which students, parents, and teachers would work together in designing the learning program they thought best. The principal told those attending to receive the proposal as an idea—as a point of discussion. He urged them to explore its possibilities; the ASC information teams were prepared to help.

Half of the meeting was formal, didactic, as students and teachers explained the specific elements of the proposal. The second half was devoted to exhibits and discussions, each centered around a table labeled by its focus: curriculum, budget, transportation, community resources, staffing, et cetera. Parents were told to visit any table and there to help create ASC. Parents there volunteered to help organize the school and to collect resources. From this activity, ASC became theirs too, and this involvement and ownership by the parent constituency proved invaluable during two later crises.

About 125 families expressed interest. That was about ninety more than had been anticipated. About one hundred students showed substantial interest, but most still wanted to take some courses in the regular school—especially those courses either not offered by ASC, or not yet staffed by specific ASC teachers trained in those courses' curricula. ASC then changed from a self-contained school community of thirty-five to fifty students (which had been the conception of many planning team members) to a school community in which students could take a mix of ASC and regular school classes.

During the spring and summer before ASC's birth, a succession of crises nearly aborted ASC. The school psychologist who had been the prime staff leader for ASC (aside from the principal) developed glaucoma and dropped out for extended eye surgery, leaving ASC leaderless for two months—at a time when planning and direction were needed. Then a key English teacher withdrew, leaving ASC without an English program. Planning fell further behind.

But the student enrollment existed; enthusiasm remained in all three constituencies; a new English teacher was recruited; and a Cubberley social studies teacher wanted to assume staff leadership for ASC. These patches increased as more tears and holes developed in ASC's planning. Then a very conservative member of the Board of Education learned about ASC and demanded that the board take action about ASC's "secretive" development. (The CHS principal had kept the superintendent informed about ASC, but the superintendent had not felt ASC was a matter needing board approval.) ASC's current stage of planning was inadequate and "too general" to be approved, board members felt. They complained that ASC still didn't know what specifically happened at 8:35 A.M. on the first day of school. This board attitude angered both ASC parents and students who felt "their" community school attacked. Parents packed both board meetings; parent and student indignation and anger were obvious. The district administration further pressured the board, arguing that the planning would be completed later; that ASC included only seventy-five students—all volunteers, and all with parent permission; that no change or violation of board policy or state law would occur because of ASC; that ASC was a pilot, an experiment; and that essentially ASC was a minor matter of changing teaching methods to conform to research findings and was therefore an administrative decision, not a board one. Pressure on the board from the superintendent increased. At the second board meeting, one preceded by many discussions and struggles, the board agreed that ASC was an administrative, not a board, decision.

But the board strongly requested that the administration keep the board well informed about ASC's progress and evaluation, especially as that related to cognitive skill development. The administration promised to fulfill those requests.

Despite these onslaughts, the ASC plan still remained an idealistic, romantic novel of everyone doing what he knew to be right and humane. A year had been spent in planning; all three constituencies were involved; tacit board approval existed; central administrative office approval existed; the principal strongly backed ASC; part of the ASC staff and a few students had worked throughout the summer to build learning contracts; one ASC teacher had developed hundreds of objectives and methods for individualizing instruction; a variety of community resources had been identified for student use; and an evaluation of cognitive and affective domains had been prepared, complete with a control group in the regular school. As a model of planning, nothing seemed overlooked.

In retrospect, however, a few things were overlooked. First, we overlooked the impending master schedule construction and assumed that we could plug in our needs before the last master schedule was constructed. We were too late, and unwittingly overlooked the importance of arranging our students' schedules so that each student's ASC periods ran consecutively and so that all ASC students would have the same block of time free in ASC. As a direct consequence, we diluted the "community" concept, made chaotic the scheduling of students and learning groups, and severely reduced the flexibility for learning when and where we wished. Second, in our enthusiasm for ASC and in the dedication to ASC, we overlooked the administrative difficulties. We assumed that good intentions, hard work, and enthusiasm would cure all. Third, when the primary faculty leader behind ASC went to the hospital, we accepted the only other teacher willing to shoulder the responsibility for ASC and assumed that his enthusiasm, his dedication to ASC, and his student popularity would help him develop his skills to organize, to plan ahead, and to relate well to other adults in ASC and out of ASC. Finally, we overlooked the importance of teaching our ASC staff group process skills and personal communications skills. Instead, we again assumed that mature adults had these skills and that enthusiasm and good intentions would create good working relationships among staff members.

The year of planning and the proposal had not provided ASC with a practical structure or process, but that year did produce benefits: a sense of camaraderie—among ASCers, a sense of such loyalty to ASC that some staffers and students would work seventy to eighty hour weeks in an attempt to effect that romantic ideal proposal, and a belief that working together we could create a new way of learning which was more natural and fuller than the old. It was that faith and loyalty which welded that incongruous, distrusting, and unskilled group of people together during those first two years. Without that faith and loyalty, ASC would have collapsed from the weight of the patches alone, if not from the rips and tears themselves. Yet in a real sense, that year of planning was essential to build in all three constituencies of ASC the vision which fueled the ASCers' faith and loyalty.

Early Problems

Intrastaff Conflict

Staff incompatibility most severely affected ASC for the next three years, with negative influences which remain even now. Although the staff agreed with the proposal itself, the proposal was general enough to allow differing interpretations. The staff also had diverse styles and differing values about how to teach—all of which produced conflict. Concealed jealousies, and the failure by some to meet the expectations of others also contributed to the conflicts. The conflicts were rarely discussed, and the result was a brooding fear and tension in two of the major staff members. Trust and cooperation markedly declined, and intrastaff conflicts and power struggles diverted much energy from solving the many problems which "suddenly" appeared after the blush of three weeks. The two full-time ASC staffers could not work together, yet they had primary responsibility for guiding ASC.

This major staff conflict worsened with each month. One staff member felt that the other was neither a competent nor a responsible administrator of the program and was not giving credit where deserved. The other felt that the first staff member was usurping control of the program and covertly making decisions, rather than openly and cooperatively. Each of these two felt ambivalent about the other, but each wanted to get along and form a team. But the team concept was undermined by the opposing personal styles, and the associated conflicts. Each of the two distrusted the other, yet each felt committed to work things out in the best interest of ASC. These difficulties were compounded by a lack of openness about the differing beliefs and feelings.

Neither of the two staff members was well trained in communication skills or group process work. Their level of trust was abysmally low. Several temporary conciliations occurred. Most were private, some were tearful. But the conflicting styles and conflicting visions of what the school should be like were too strong. The conflict permeated the student body, with large minorities of students taking the side of each of these staff members. The split was obvious. It was the structured ("controlling") people vs. the freedom ("antisystem") people. The rest of the ASC staff, though aware of the conflict, preferred to stay out of it, hoping it would subside. It never did.

During the end of the first semester the conflict between these two staffers reached such a high level that everyone knew it had to be resolved.

This was done by order of the principal, who, although aware of the problem, had heretofore intentionally remained out of the internal affairs of ASC. He suggested the two staffers, being sincere and well-intentioned as they were, should divide areas of responsibility. They did. But most importantly, the school psychologist—whom everyone trusted—was asked to help. She met weekly with the staff during three-hour, Friday afternoon meetings to discuss the working relationships, difficulties, and problems to solve in ASC. That process was instrumental in helping the entire staff communicate more honestly, more immediately when troubled. From these sessions came a greater trust and flexibility among staff. The staff became trained to better listen, to accept differences of style, and to understand the other staffers' frames of reference and needs. Problem solving for ASC itself improved as the staff improved its own communication and group process skills, skills vital for a team to succeed.

Although one of those two staffers left ASC three years ago, the effects of the intrastaff conflict remain. ASC still has a federation of teachers, not a close-knit community, and ASC is more subject-oriented than interdisciplinary. But on the positive side, ASC has developed a highly structured but effective peer-evaluation process for a team.

Scheduling

Scheduling students, staff, and learning activities in ASC was a problem second only to the intrastaff conflict. Scheduling difficulties were not adequately recognized during the planning phase. ASC opened with a method for coordinating eighty individual schedules into common interest learning groups. On paper, the method seemed clear and easy. But variations in individual schedules, the diversity of interests, and the patience required exceeded human tolerances. During the first year, eight different scheduling methods were tried, and all eight failed. The failures included: a weekly detailed schedule distributed to all ASCers, a bulletin board and index cards, a plastic eraseable board, and a Thursday scheduling meeting of all learning group leaders. Two factors compounded the scheduling difficulty: widespread resistance to following any formal procedures, and an inability to gather all ASCers together to solve problems and make decisions. Confusion and frustration increased. Only the shared commitment to restore the ASC dream kept people trying. Finally, as hatred of all rules and procedures lessened, and as desires to learn prevailed, a ninth method succeeded, although even it required some patience. (For specifics, see the "institutionalization" section.)

Despite the moderate success of this method of scheduling, the original decision to allow students to take any number of ASC courses at times convenient to the regular school master schedule, still significantly affects ASC.

Not scheduling all those interested in a certain learning group is still a frustrating and disappointing activity because, for any group of ASCers interested in learning together, several have regular school class obligations which interfere with the learning group's activities. Regular school schedules also interfere with the length of the learning group meeting, and restrict off-campus activities.

Yet there are some benefits from maintaining a link with regular school classes. Students can choose their best learning situations from the entire selection offered by the high school, including regular school and ASC opportunities. Occasionally a small group of ASCers suggests a requirement that ASCers must take a half or more of their classes at ASC during specific times. But each such suggestion is quickly and vehemently opposed by the majority. They do not want to lose their freedom to choose from the best of both regular school and ASC.

Group Meetings

The lack of effective group process skills—among both staff and students—was the third major problem in the school's early days. This problem was inadequately addressed during the planning phase. Quakerstyle meetings ensured—at least on paper—that everyone would be involved in making decisions. In practice, however, such an approach exceeded people's patience and skills. The all-school meetings first attracted everyone, but dwindled to twenty-five people by the third week, and to four people by the third month. The meetings bogged down in numerous minor decisions, petty arguments, hard feelings, shyness, and a general sense that nothing significant ever happened.

Decision making was thus ineffective during the first year at a time when the need for resolving problems was enormous. The increasing distrust and tension between the two major staffers caused them to withdraw from taking the initiative in making decisions; and the other staff felt reluctant to intervene, partly because they were part-time staff, and partly because they felt they lacked required insight, as well as the necessary energy and time.

The decisions made by those few who continued to attend the "all school" meetings could not inspire sufficient recognition from the other ASCers to be implemented. In the absence of an effective decision-making body, a few ASCers became the actual decision makers but their power was even further restricted by the informal "rule" against formal rules and sanctions.

Various changes in decision making were attempted; but all failed. Finally after two years of inadequate solutions, of hard-bitten iconoclasts objecting strenuously to formalization, and of intense frustration, one successful method did emerge: a group of elected ASCers (twelve students and three staff) became responsible for managing the ASC decision-making process. A schoolwide referendum gave the group these powers: the governing group would make all minor decisions, distinguish between minor and major decisions, and conduct an information campaign leading to an all-school referendum (one person, one vote, staff and students alike) for each major decision. Decisions in the governing group meetings were made by consensus, but during the schoolwide referendums, a majority vote would prevail unless the governing group believed an issue's significance (like moving the school off-campus) merited a higher percentage for approval.

This process of decision making satisfied both the emotional and rational criteria: minor decisions would not waste everyone's time, students retained control over major decisions, students remained involved at all levels of decision making, the staff retained a guiding role over ASC's systems of decision making and thus over the school as a whole. ASC's system of decision making remained flexible enough to match the changing needs of future ASC's constituencies.

Because ASC's structure and process were fluid and capable of changing as ASCers' needs and ideas changed, immediate responses could be made to individual or schoolwide problems. No decision would or could be permanent. In fact, during that first eighteen months of turmoil and difficulty, decisions were made one week, reversed the next, and then reverses reversed until finally people began to trust one another more. During this process the antiprocedure sentiment mellowed somewhat, and people began to recognize the need for more consistent policies. Building expiration dates into decisions assured continuing review. But such stability began only after staff became more skilled in managing group processes and only after staff and students developed a heightened sense of trust.

Looking back, we realize that we made the mistaken assumption that because staff members and students cared about creating ASC and were "good" people, an effective process of problem solving and decision making would easily and joyously evolve. Only after this assumption was demolished, and only after we saw ASC's near demise, did we recognize and accept the idea that to make group decisions, students—and even mature adults—need formal training in group process skills and interpersonal skills. Fortunately, the former school psychologist, who had also been the first primary faculty leader supporting ASC, was available to help train us in these skills. But before such skills were firmly enmeshed in ASC processes only our commitment to the ASC dream enabled us to endure the frustration and trauma of those first two years!

Relationships with the Regular School

ASC's relationship with CHS faculty also took three to four years to stabilize. From the beginning, most faculty members tolerated ASC, although they were skeptical about its prospects. Twenty-five percent of the faculty volunteered to help in some way: teaching a small seminar or offering a one-time learning experience. But another faculty group strongly objected to ASC as a permissive, irresponsible influence on the school and on non-ASC students. This latter group created a good deal of political turmoil for the principal, and caused the ASC staff to become paranoid about their "enemies." Consequently, the school became increasingly insular. We were particularly afraid of the potential affects that the school grapevine might have on enrollment. What types and number of students would apply? Would grapevine "rumors" attract or discourage new staff members? Thus the school grapevine was a real concern to ASC. Because of these fears and our own preoccupations with internal conflicts, we built protective facades around the school.

But the faculty opposition could never find a cause célèbre or a violation of rules sufficient to damage ASC's credibility. Derogatory rumors— "it's a sandbox school," "it's for hippies only," "people there are into drugs"—did occur. Most of the faculty, though still skeptical about ASC's worth, ignored the rumors and adopted a "wait and see" attitude.

Whenever we acted or spoke of regular school disdainfully, or as a rigid, inferior institution filled with uncaring people (common rhetoric among alternative school people), our relationships with the regular staff suffered. Such attitudes did not accurately reflect reality, and insulted and demeaned other teachers.

The dominant "wait and see" attitude among the regular staff slowly became more accepting and positive. Individual ASC staffers developed positive, informal relationships with the regular school faculty. These relationships were made easily because a number of ASC teachers also taught in regular school departments: science, math, social studies, and PE. Other informal, trusting relationships developed from the interactions between the ASC staffers and regular faculty members in the lunchroom, or in the hallway. Overall, the more we mixed with the faculty, the more we were accepted and thus ASC was accepted.

The credibility of ASC as a responsible program at Cubberley also developed because ASC students were enrolled in regular school classes. During the first few years, regular school faculty members became increasingly aware that some of their brightest, most responsible students were also in ASC. Dialogues would ensue about ASC, and students would explain why they chose ASC and what they did in the program. The more the regular school faculty learned about ASC from these students, the more the faculty accepted it as a responsible program—for some students.

They were also other reasons for ASC's acceptance among the regular staff. Only about 10 percent CHS students were enrolled in ASC, and thus the fear lessened that all of CHS would become ASC, as did the threat that all of CHS would be troubled by ASC. Some faculty members believed that ASC made regular school classes easier to teach because students who disliked the regular school program could transfer into ASC. Some acceptance came because we gave a few formal presentations about ASC to the faculty. But the major reason for ASC's acceptance was the credibility of the program established by frequent, informal, positive interactions between ASCers and the regular school participants.

The counseling department also posed a unique problem initially. We were concerned that most students and parents could be influenced for or against ASC by the counselors. Because our "enemies" in the regular school sometimes sounded louder than our "friends," we were worried that the counselors would develop an unfavorable image of the school and thus use ASC as a "dumping ground" for problem students. To assure that ASC, as we knew it, would be presented accurately to potential students, we met with the counselors and agreed that interested students and parents would be directed to the ASC staff.

To help all counselors better understand what ASC was actually like and to more quickly gain their trust, we decided to allow each counselor to keep as counselees those ASCers who would normally be theirs. In addition the ASC staff met with the counselors to exchange information about ASC students, ASC's structures and processes, our respective evaluations of ASC, and ASC's relationship to the counseling department's procedures and responsibilities.

During the first year, counselors and ASC staff met to clarify the counselor's responsibility to student ASCers. We agreed that counselors would accept responsibility for the ASCers' graduation prerequisites, post high school plans, and regular school progress and problems. The ASC staff accepted responsibility for keeping parents informed about a student's progress and behavior in ASC classes.

Relationship with the Principal

The relationship with the principal was a top-priority concern in the development of ASC. From the preplanning stage through the stabilization stage, ASC's relationship with the principal was a model of trust, help, and pragmatism. Clearly ASC was a potential political problem for the principal, but he accepted the risk. He was confident that the initial planning (in which he was involved) and the process structure of ASC would be able to handle any emerging problems. In truth he probably had more confidence in ASC than we did. We needed his strong political and psychological support.

During the first two years the principal served as a buffer between antagonistic faculty members and ASC, declaring from the beginning that he personally was accepting responsibility for ASC and that the ASC coordinator would report directly to the principal and be evaluated by him. Without the principal's buffering, we could not have mustered the energy to constantly defend our program against outsiders and to solve our internal problems. Those first two years were like an incubation period for a baby born prematurely.

More than just a buffer, the principal met weekly with the ASC coordinator in order to discuss ASC's problems, solutions, processes, and plans. Although the principal would ask questions, give suggestions, and highlight problems he foresaw, he resolutely would not manage ASC's internal affairs, leaving that to the process which he knew would work over time.

Without the principal's strong support and confidence during those beginning years of political storms and frustrating circumstances, ASC could not have survived.

Relationships with Parents

During the initial year our relationships with the regular school became more active, but our relationships with ASC parents grew progressively more passive—in violation of our romantic proposal that ASC would be cooperatively run by students, teachers, and parents. However, whenever

ASC really needed parents, they rallied. During the planning-orientation meetings parents helped establish task forces and several completed their tasks. Second, the summer before ASC was to open, parents rallied to support ASC at Board of Education meetings which challenged ASC's right to exist. Third, a large-scale parent involvement occurred in response to an ASC staff letter which read: "If you think everything is working satisfactorily, then you don't really know what is happening. Come to the evaluation meeting." This announcement came nine weeks after ASC opened, in the midst of rising staff anxiety, because the "on-paper" dream was not working.

Parents came. But instead of attending the meeting to condemn the staff for its failure to produce the dream outlined in the proposal, the parents came to encourage. They told the staff that the students were in fact learning (even though not as much as the staff might have liked), working at home and at school, reading voraciously, and talking about school during the dinner table conversation. Parents spoke about changed students' attitudes and a greater sense of cooperation and well-being. Somehow parents felt that ASC was working. Although the staff had a hard time seeing the good shrouded by frustrated expectations, the parents told us that such a dream takes more than nine weeks to produce. Overall, the parents provided us with a needed vote of confidence.

In subsequent years some parents were sporadically active. In the third year, for example, a family initiated and organized a community potluck on the grounds of the youth hostel where the first ASC draft proposal began. In the fourth year another ASC couple, apprehensive about how much they didn't know about their "silent" daughter's ASC learning, talked with staffers and decided to help communicate about ASC to other parents. The results were a one-evening meeting and a newsletter, with promises of many more things to come. But the parent leader became overcommitted in his own work and the promises went unfulfilled. Toward the end of that year, the staff coordinator called several parents together to form a Citizens' Advisory Group to ASC. The parents responded, eventually creating and implementing a parent evaluation of ASC. The results, based on an 80 percent response vote, supported the success of ASC, but also uncovered a complaint: parents did not know enough about ASC and some believed that they were being kept ignorant purposely by the students. Although each student was given a progress report every quarter which was circulated among the staff, students, and parents, these reports were inadequate to bridge the gap. Students would not give the reports to parents, and the staff couldn't call each family. Today parents remain passively satisfied with ASC (of those ASC students returning to CHS for another year, 95 percent of their parents gave explicit permission to their students to again study in ASC), but the ASC staff is still frustrated by the relative lack of parent involvement, and parents still feel dissatisfied with their ignorance about ASC. The ASC staff has not yet found the solution for solving the problem of parent involvement.

Although our relationships with parents have been passive, relationships could have been worse. Many problems were avoided or solved by the ideas in ASC's proposal. First and most importantly, parent permission was required before a student could enter ASC. Any time during the school year a student could transfer back into regular school. This voluntary participation was essential to ASC's philosophy and to the best interests of those students who incorrectly selected ASC. Second, ASC required parents and students to attend an orientation meeting, during which we candidly explained both the risks and excitement of ASC, and described its philosophy, structure, and processes. When asked, "Will it work for my student?" we responded, "We cannot be sure. Our purpose is solely to provide you with information about the school." Any student whose parents attended the orientation meeting and gave signed permission to have their student in ASC was allowed in. These orientation meetings, sometimes supplemented by individual family conferences, helped insure ASC's success by letting the students and parents make the decision.

Reasons for ASC's Success

Most of ASC's successful processes, structures, and activities evolved through trauma and several mutations. Generally the evolution replaced vague and informal processes, structure, and activities with ones more formal and explicit. But the foundations for ASC's relationships and learning program were in place from the start. The later formal modifications were not "rules" or imposed procedures, and without the authentic listening, caring, trusting, and gentle advising, the more formalized processes and structures would not have worked.

One example of this blend between the formal and the "humanistic" process occurs when the curriculum for each ASC student is determined. Every student talks with each of his teachers, concluding the individual discussions with an agreement to do certain things: join or continue in an interesting seminar, accomplish an independent study project, work in the community, or participate in a tutorial. These tasks are usually accomplished in a day to a week, since longer term deadlines seem too distant to be meaningful. When the agreed-upon work or learning has been accomplished to the satisfaction of both the student and teachers, credit (identical to that in regular school) is given. The ASC teachers certify that the work has been accomplished. At a conference, the student and teacher determine the credit and grade.

During any part of this process, problems of communication or theory may occur between a staff person and a student. Because of these, ASC includes an ombudsman-advisor for each student, selected from the ASC staff by that student. The ombudsman-advisor performs several functions: he helps the student see possibilities the student may be ignoring, stays in touch with the student's overall feelings and activities, and protects the student if another ASC staffer becomes insensitive or arbitrary about developing or evaluating the student's learning program. The advisor-ombudsman system has evolved as one of our most valuable processes for helping students succeed and for keeping ASC student-centered.

Most of the structures and processes that have evolved in ASC—ombudsman, informal and frequent evaluations, and governing group, a scheduling process, a teacher peer-evaluation process, training in communication and group/team process skills—seem essential to our stability. But, as noted before, underlying the overt structure and procedures are the affection, caring, and the trust that govern day-to-day relationships. Trust, of course, cannot be manufactured.

Often informal recreational activities, occurring off-campus, broke down barriers between students and staff, allowed acquaintances to become friends, and helped young adult and adult become comrades. For example, the first two years one ASC volunteer—a self-professed "bored housewife" —frequently opened her house for dinners. As another example, different ASCers would frequently organize a sports-music-potluck dinner in the nearby city park. Each year one or two advisories (each "advisory" had about fifteen students and each student chose his or her own advisory) would organize a weekend retreat in the mountains, using a member's cabin or a YMCA camp. In addition to these numerous, often spontaneous, trust-building activities, each year ASC has gone off-campus to the mountains or somewhere else—so that ASCers could play together in different roles, make new friends, informally and formally talk about feelings, needs, and changes desired for ASC. Although such retreats are rarely preplanned at least one spontaneously occurs each year. The topics usually focus on how ASC can be changed to fulfill new dreams. Proposals and task forces generated during such weekend retreats are traditionally brought back to where they are debated, shared, voted upon, and often implemented into the evolving fabric of the school.

Typically, only a few of the many proposals become reality. A major proposal implemented this semester after one of these off-campus events was the inauguration of a "survival" class to teach new ASCers how to take the initiative, ask for help, and use ASC's resources. But everyone who has experienced one of those weekends has felt exhilarated afterwards—particularly because of the friendships that are made or deepened. People learn about one another in new ways, without interference from traditional school-related roles. This kind of activity is an essential method for collapsing roles and creating the trust and camaraderie that underlay the success of our processes and structures.

Despite the five and a half years of evolving a smooth process of change, decision making, and learning; despite the several successful things ASC models for others, the dominating memory of the past years is not intellectual, but emotional. The first two years were agonizing, frustrating, scary, ego-threatening, and, in short, hellish. In retrospect, we didn't know what we were really doing and we didn't know how to effect that dream the initial proposal described. Expectations were typically not realized.

Looking back I wonder sometimes how ASC flourished. But simultaneously I know. First, we had a supportive, flexible, encouraging principal. Second, despite our internal conflicts, we all wanted to effect that initial dream. We did learn to confront each other. We did learn the group process and communication skills. In times of near-despair, our students' excitement and resultant growth caused us to continue along the cutting edge between tradition and irresponsible innovation. We were absolutely determined to effect the proposal. And by the end of the third year we thought we had—perhaps in spite of us.

Third, after five years of trauma and renaissance, ASC has developed several patterns which help an alternative school work. Besides those already described—advisor-ombudsman, contract making, teacher-student evaluation, regular school relationships, and planning processes—there are three other unique processes which have helped our school succeed: the governing process, the scheduling process, and the peer-evaluation process.

The governing processes—the small decision-making group and the referendum—have continued for three and a half years and work smoothly. The election of the members has changed from election-at-large to election of one representative from each advisory group (ten to fifteen students and one staff). Budgetary and personnel decisions are now made differently. Budget decisions under $10 are made by the staff coordinator—an appeal to the governing group can be made if desired. Budget decisions over $10 are made by the governing group unless it chooses to use the referendum and have all ASCers vote. Personnel decisions follow a three-stage process: an interview by the ASC coordinator, an interview by an ad hoc group spawned by the governing group, and an interview by the ASC staff. A consensus is reached among all interviewers and given to the CHS principal, who in turn gives it to the district's personnel officer. As part of the school district, ASC has always had to comply with the district's rules and constraints on hiring or firing. And, as part of CHS, ASC is always subject to the principal's veto and authority, but in five years the principal has never exercised that kind of authority.

The scheduling method has worked moderately well for three years. It has several steps: (1) Anyone (teacher, student, volunteer) describes what he wants to learn and staples that description to a bulletin board any time during the year. (2) Those interested sign up. (3) The originator finds a person with sufficient expertise to teach that area of interest; and (4) announces (via notes in the mailboxes of those who signed up) a co-ordinating meeting during brunch or the beginning of lunch on a given day. (5) The activity coordinator conducts a meeting to determine when and where people can meet. The process is flexible. Changes in logistics or learning goals for the group can be made at any time by the learning group. Learning groups begin and end at all times during the year, according to student interest and the availability of a resource person.

The activity coordinator for each group also lists in the ASC scheduling book the learning group's name, meeting time, and meeting place. A group of different students who have previously accepted responsibility for managing the schedule book and for writing on the chalkboard the daily listing of ASC learning activities, copy the information from the scheduling book onto the blackboard. This serves two functions: advertising groups and reminding people of their responsibilities.

Finally, we have developed a staff-peer-evaluation process. Born out of an intrastaff conflict, and originally scheduled once a year in June, this process has worked so well to improve morale and to upgrade teaching performances that the staff elected to use the process semiyearly—at the end of the first and third quarters. Three meetings—with attendant home work—comprise the entire process. The content of all these meetings is strictly confidential.

Before the first meeting each staff member writes recommendations (implied criticisms) and commendations about each other staff person. During the first meeting each staffer listens to what others have to say. No one may respond to these perceptions until the second meeting which is held forty-eight hours later, thus allowing time for each staffer to reflect on what he has heard. During the second meeting all staffers may ask questions to gain understanding, ask questions for guidance, and add information. No one may discuss what was heard or thought about until the third meeting. Then each staffer brings to the meeting written commendations and recommendations for himself. Staffers then discuss what has been written until staffers feel they can sign, "I concur," below each staff member's self-evaluation. This formal process provides a structured opportunity for complete candor and helps to focus on strengths and weaknesses as well as what each staffer should do to improve.

As a result of these processes and structures, ASC is no longer an experiment, but an accepted organism enjoying a symbiotic relationship with the regular high school. ASC has established a variety of flexibly changing processes, roles, structures, and activities, and has also gained formal institutional recognition, insuring inclusion in CHS decision making about budget, personnel selection, and school policy.

In fact, the principal, at the end of our second year, declared ASC a department, with all the attendant rights and responsibilities. That clarity converted an unknown to a known and thus provided a certainty that comforted many inside and outside of ASC. Department status clarified areas of responsibility and accountability. And people seem to like clarity. We were accountable to the principal, not to another department. We were budgeted and staffed like any other department, no longer subject to the favor or disfavor of whoever was principal. The decision officially connected ASC laterally and horizontally with the school district's and with CHS's formal decision-making processes. ASC was now an institutional part of CHS, no longer an experimental project.

That fact is further buttressed by evaluation results. A parent conducted evaluation of ASC as perceived by parents produced 85 percent approval of ASC. Our students parallel the academic success of regular school students after high school, as determined by successful achievement at their chosen college. Standardized test scores show no significant differences in achievement between ASC students and regular school students. But attitudinal questionnaires show ASC students perceive themselves as having more influence on their life and circumstances, a more improved attitude toward school and learning, and closer personal relationships with teachers and students than do regular school students.

The Future

Although the original experiment has been stabilized and accepted as an integral institutional part of CHS, the changes within ASC continue. Next year we will be a major part of a RISE (California's Reform of Intermediate and Secondary Education) grant. We hope to develop several off-campus learning stations where students will stay anywhere from nine to eighteen weeks. We are continuing to develop instruments which measure specific cognitive achievement in English, science, and social studies. And we are searching for more teachers to replace two imminent vacancies.

It is this last concern that worries us most. We well know that an alternative school—even one as formalized as ASC—is person dependent. That is our greatest strength, but also our greatest vulnerability. When a single staff person leaves, the very life of a small alternative school is threatened because replacements are hard to find. It is an unusual combination of characteristics in a human being that causes him or her to be a successful alternative school teacher.

Enthusiasm and good intention alone will not work. One must be very psychologically stable, open, flexible, subject area competent, loving, and perceptive. One must recognize the delicate balance between the structured freedom healthy for a human being and too much freedom which causes a student to become discouraged and directionless, and thus negative. As this indicates, an alternative school teacher accepts much more responsibility for what happens, even though the students do too.

As I reflect upon our experience, a few major thoughts dominate. Ultimately the alternative school lives or dies according to just a few things: The psychological health and educational competence of the staff, the use of sound group process and communication skills, the support of the principal, a thorough process of educating all potential alternative school students about their choices, an inclusive explicit and yet caring process for making decisions about all important aspects of the school, a budget adequate to salary the staff and buy a few books, and a flexibility and spontaneity to relate, human being to human being, according to the needs and wants of those nearby—without losing one's individuality.

12
The Hoover Structured School
by Palo Alto Unified School District

The Beginning

Prior to the establishment of our traditionally structured alternative elementary school, Palo Alto had two other alternative elementary schools, an "open classroom" school and another progressive school based on the philosophy of Dr. William Glasser. Many parents felt that the district should balance its offering of elementary alternatives. Parents also discovered that the offering of different kinds of *public* elementary schools was a relatively new concept in education, one that was being implemented in various communities in the United States and Canada. The day after parents presented their original request to the Palo Alto School Board our local newspaper reported that parents of the nearby community of Cupertino had made a similar request of their district. Victoria, B. C., Canada had also just opened both its "more structured" and its "less structured" alternative public elementary schools. Later we learned of Pasadena, California's John Marshall Fundamental School. There are a number of other districts throughout the country which have established traditionally structured alternatives. Associated Press correspondent Terry Ryan has written several articles about these schools. Fred Hechinger has written articles about our school which appeared in the *Saturday Review World,* January 11, 1975, and May 3, 1975.

In early 1973, several Palo Alto parents were brought together through

---

*From a handout prepared for parents and visitors; Palo Alto Unified School District, Palo Alto, California, September 1976.

their similar concerns for the education of their children. They wrote a letter to the Palo Alto School Board which outlined their children's needs and requested that the district establish an elementary school with a consistent structured program which would stress the basic academic skills. What began as a letter from a few families developed into a petition with over eighty signatures as others heard about it and requested to sign. The parents then talked with the superintendent, showed him the letter, and asked his advice on how to proceed. Parents also spoke with school board members individually. Upon receipt of the letter the school board was very responsive. It placed the establishment of this school on its list of top priorities for the 1973–74 school year. Planning for new programs lay within the jurisdiction of the superintendent, and thus the board referred the matter to him. He met with his key administrators and decided to establish the Superintendent's Committee for a More Structured Alternative Elementary School. The committee was composed of five parents, three administrators, four teachers (one of whom is now our principal, Wallace Clark), an elementary school principal, a district psychologist, a special education teacher, and three high school students. The committee was charged with describing the school and making recommendations on the selection of student body, staff, and location. It met from October through March of 1973–74. The superintendent approved the committee's description of the school. A brochure containing this description and a questionnaire were sent to all parents of elementary school children in order to determine the number of children who might attend the school. During the spring of 1974 parents on the Superintendent's Advisory Committee visited schools and homes to inform parents about the school. The district also held a public meeting about the structured school.

Families of approximately 10 percent of the district's elementary children expressed interest in the school. The School Board then approved the establishment of the school, designated a site, and set a date for sign-ups on a first-come, first-served basis for 8 A.M. on a Saturday in May 1974. Parents began arriving very early, and most classes were filled soon after registration opened. Teachers were notified that they could apply to teach in the school, and they were selected from a list of volunteers. Our principal and teachers worked together to draw up a written list of behavior standards and specific academic goals for each grade level. (This list a reproduced in a following section.) Copies of these materials are given to parents at the beginning of the school year.

The main problem we encountered in the establishment of our school was the selection of a site. There were some families in each neighborhood school area who wanted their children to attend the structured school, but no neighborhood school contained a majority. Therefore each neighborhood school community had a sizeable number of families who opposed having the structured school at that site and thus causing their neighborhood school to change. The school board finally decided to open up part of a school (Hoover) that had been closed for two years. It limited the number of classrooms to six the first year with the idea that we would move to another location as other schools were closed due to the district's declining enrollment. Last year we shared our facility with administrators and storage of instructional materials. We are staying at the same location because our district hasn't yet decided which schools to close. The administrators are moving to allow us an additional four classrooms. We are making do without a multipurpose room and with limited library space until we are given a permanent location. It would have been much easier if one particular neighborhood school would have welcomed our program or if it had been decided early in the planning to house the school in an empty facility.

It really makes sense to offer parents (and teachers) a choice. We feel that our school has a built-in advantage: the principal, teachers, and parents are united in their support of the program and goals of the school. They have chosen it voluntarily. The principal, teachers, parents, and students all know the goals and work together to meet them.

Original Proposal for a More Structured Alternative to Elementary Education in the Palo Alto Unified School District

Primary Goal and Philosophy

The primary emphasis of this school will be on the basic academic skills and subject matter and the establishment of good study habits. The school will seek to build within each child a sense of responsibility, confidence, pride in accomplishment, and a positive self-image through proven academic achievement. The school will provide a quiet and orderly environment which many children need in order to learn.

The Instructional Program

The school will have a graded organizational plan, K through 6 (now K through 8), with self-contained classrooms. Classroom activities will be teacher initiated, directed, and supervised. Successful traditional and new methods of instruction will be used.

The curriculum will follow a definite progression, building on skills and abilities acquired at each level. At appropriate levels it will include reading, handwriting, spelling, composition, grammar, arithmetic, history, geography, government, science, art, and music. Such other "learning tools" as research, outlining, note-taking, and reporting (oral and written) will be introduced. A sequential program of physical education skills will be offered.

Priority will be given to the fundamental tools of learning as well as broad areas of knowledge. A majority of the school day will be devoted to the teaching of reading, writing, spelling, language, and arithmetic, using the district's written guidelines, "What We Teach in the Elementary Schools," as an instructional base.

Homework will be given on a regular basis to encourage independent work and good study habits. When appropriate, this work may be begun during periods of supervised study. Students will be informed of what is expected of them, and when, in order to learn to fulfill their responsibilities. Teachers will have the responsibility for correcting students' work and following through on assignments.

Students and teachers will enjoy the same support staff and special service programs (Educationally Handicapped, Mentally Gifted, Speech, Music, Guidance) available to other schools in the district. The use of qualified volunteers and resource persons will be left to the discretion of the staff.

Reporting Student Progress

The district curriculum guide will serve as the basis for the development of objective standards in terms of which student progress will be determined. On the basis of this progress report cards with letter grades will be issued regularly. At the beginning of the year, parents and students will be informed of the basis for grading. An academic performance grade will be given for each subject, followed by an effort grade, followed by a place for teacher comments. The academic performance grade will reflect scores on tests, homework, and the quality of daily participation. Effort grades will reflect the completion of work on time, attention in class, and participation in discussions. The staff will develop methods of rewarding superior work and effort.

Parent-teacher conferences will be held at least twice a year for each student. Teachers and principal will be available for informal communication regarding a student's progress, knowledge, and skill acquisition.

Standardized tests will be given at least once a year to evaluate student progress on a broader basis.

Role of Staff, Students, and Parents

Teachers will be selected from applicants who support the goals and program of the school. Fair and consistent methods of handling behavioral problems will be developed according to common sense guidelines established by the staff.

The principal will exert strong leadership in order to establish unity of purpose, based on the above stated goals and philosophy, among teachers, students, and parents.

Students will be expected to strive for excellence in their academic work, to respect the staff, to show consideration for others, and to demonstrate good manners.

It is important that the home provide positive support to the goals, philosophy, and program of the school.

Placement of Student

Each student will be placed in a grade according to the recommendation of his previous teacher and available test data. When a student has mastered grade level material, enrichment materials will be provided. When a student makes appropriate progress during the school year, he will be promoted at the end of that year. If the student fails to make progress sufficient to undertake the work of the next grade level, discussions will be continued between parents, teacher, and principal as to the best placement for the student.

What Will This School Emphasize?

This school will *consistently emphasize* the following priorities:
  —Acquisition of the basic academic skills in a sequential manner.
  —Establishment of good independent study habits.
  —Development of a quiet, orderly classroom atmosphere.
  —Quantitative measurement of student progress through testing and grades.

Implementation of the Structured School Philosophy

Fred Hechinger has stated in his article in the *Saturday Review* (January 11, 1975) "... it is possible to be traditional without being doctrinaire." Of course, the education at Hoover is free of political or religious emphasis. The implementation of the structured school's program is as important as the philosophy which guides it.

Classroom organization. Each class contains one grade only. In addition to language arts, reading, and mathematics, other subjects are presented to the class as a whole, and needs for enrichment and remedial work may be met in smaller groups or individually. There are articulated grade level skills and concepts in which the goal is for all students to reach grade level.

Measuring and reporting student progress. The Metropolitan Achievement Test is administered to students each spring to determine their progress over the past year. It is also administered at the end of the school year to next year's new students to assist in their placement. In our first year of operation our students averaged the equivalent of over a school year's growth in reading, language arts, and mathematics. The following are our grade equivalent increases from the 1974–75 school year as measured by the Metropolitan Achievement Test: Reading 1.2, Language Arts 1.3, Mathematics 1.8. Our 1975–76 grade equivalent increases were Reading 1.3, Language Arts 1.5, and Mathematics 1.4.

In addition to quarterly report cards and parent-teacher conferences which are mentioned in the school's description, weekly written reports on achievement, effort, and behavior are sent home for parents' signatures. These reports are forms with spaces after each subject for check marks under "satisfactory," "needs improvement," and "unsatisfactory." The homework and classwork for each subject area are evaluated separately on this form. Spaces are provided for teacher's comments and for indication of the child's general deportment in the classroom and on the playground. Our teachers say that the effort required to fill out one of these is well spent. Both teacher and child know that all times where the child stands. The parents are always informed of the student's strengths and weaknesses and can, if they wish, help the child where help is needed most. Weekly reports are required to be returned signed by a parent the next school day after receipt. Parents who fulfill this requirement set an example for their child.

Homework. In all grades except kindergarten, homework is given an average of four nights per week. This work requires about a half hour of time or less for primary students, a half hour to an hour for intermediate students, and up to an hour and a half for middle school students. The philosophy of homework at our school is to establish the practice of good study habits and to help children develop and reinforce the basic skills taught in the classroom. Homework can be regular class work that needs to be completed, enrichment work, or remedial work.

Honors. A system of honors and awards have been designed so that a high percentage of the student body can receive tangible recognition for its effort and achievement. It is possible for each child to receive an honor of some kind. There are two honor rolls for academic achievement: a "B" average is required for the Teacher's Honor Roll, and an "A" average is required for the Principal's Honor Roll. Honors are also given for effort, for good conduct, and for special service to the school. A list of those on the Principal's Honor Roll is posted in the school lobby, and lists of those receiving the other awards are posted in an inside corridor. Award ribbons for the Principal's Honor Roll and for the School Service Award are presented at assemblies of the entire school at the end of each quarter. Ribbons for the Teacher's Honor Roll, Effort, and Citizenship are awarded in the classrooms. Children in the kindergarten, first, and second grade who do not receive any other ribbon are given "trying" ribbons at the end of each quarter.

Discipline. Discipline is firm, fair, and consistent. Hoover School does not use corporal punishment. If a standard is violated, the reason for the standard is discussed with the student. Students are corrected for a first offense; they are not told that "something will be done next time." A sequential four-step procedure has been worked out for *persistent* discipline problems: (1) the student explains behavior (helped by principal) in a letter home; (2) parents, teacher, student, and principal meet and discuss difficulties; (3) student is sent home for a day; and (4) systematic suspension is used. A moderate, consistent approach has worked well so that extremes in discipline have seldom been necessary. Each successive step is required only if the preceding step has not solved the problem. The parents' support of the teacher and principal is indispensable to the success of the Hoover program.

Parent involvement. There is a recent trend in elementary school education to invite more parents to participate directly in classroom activities. Parent participation in the classroom is not permitted at Hoover because it often leads to erosion of the teacher's authority and runs counter to the standard that "classroom activities will be teacher initiated, directed, and supervised." At Hoover, classroom routines and program are maintained, and interruptions are kept to a minimum. Hoover parents are encouraged to help outside the classroom as library aids or as listeners for students who need extra help in developing reading skills. Of course, the best parent help can be given at home—by providing an atmosphere in which learning is obviously valued, by supporting the efforts of their child's teacher and principal, and by providing a time and a place for homework. Notes, lunches, and such are to be left at the school office and they will be taken to the classroom. If a parent wishes to visit a classroom, permission may be granted by the teacher or the principal and teacher.

Hoover Structured School Standards for Students

A. Students *will*:

1. Remain quiet and orderly in the classroom and be attentive to instruction.
2. Support their teacher, classmates, and school.
3. Behave courteously toward any adult or another student.
4. Use spoken expressions of consideration toward others (for example, pardon me, please, thank you).
5. Wear clothing of a neat and modest nature. Clothing should be appropriate for the P. E. program (light leather or tennis shoes and shorts under dress).[1]
6. Obey principal's directions for seating, conduct, and dismissal at assemblies.
7. Obey all student monitors.
8. Remove hats after entering the building.
9. Share any athletic equipment brought from home.
10. Move together to assemblies; stragglers will be considered tardy.
11. Keep open games played at recess and at noon.
12. (Primary students) line up quickly and quietly in the morning

---

1. Students may change normal wear to P. E. clothing before the P. E. period.

and after recesses and the lunch period to enter classes. Students who are late must go to the office for tardy slips.

13. (Intermediate students) line up after recesses and after the noon period. In the morning they may enter the classroom if the teacher is in the room. Students who are late must get a tardy slip.
14. Present a tardy slip to the teacher when late or an absent slip when absent for a day or longer in order to gain admission to the classroom. Teachers are to fill out tardy slips and return them to the secretary daily. Blank tardy slips are to be picked up by late students, and absentees will pick up blank absent slips.
15. (Ball monitors especially) make sure that all playground equipment is off the playground at the end of a recess, noon period, and P. E. period.
16. Stay out of the city park area.
17. Keep balls off the roof. They do not roll back off.
18. Stay only on the *red-top* when a *red flag* is displayed.
19. Stay only on the *black-top* and *red-top* and don't go onto the grassy areas when a *black flag* is displayed.

B. Students *will not*:

1. Leave the school grounds during school hours at any time without written permission.
2. Use profane language or gestures.
3. Engage in any type of fighting.
4. Intimidate, harass, or threaten other students.
5. Be disrespectful to another's property.
6. Engage in body contact sports on the playground unless authorized by a teacher.
7. Throw objects other than balls while under the school's supervision.
8. Bring toys, magazines, radios, or playground equipment to school without teacher's approval.
9. Eat during classtime or chew gum anywhere at school.
10. Run on the red-top.

Lunch Standards for Students

1. Students will be seated at tables assigned by class from 11:45 to 12:00 and will remain seated until they are excused.

2. Before the students are excused, the tables and the area around them must be neat and clean.
3. Talking is permitted, and good table manners are to be practiced.
4. Equipment is *not* to be brought to the lunch table.

Hoover Structured School Teacher Expectations

Teachers *will*:

1. Maintain neat, quiet, and orderly classrooms.
2. Stress reading, writing, and language arts in the learning experience.
3. Use weekly comprehensive teacher-made tests in basic subject areas.
4. Keep an accurate record of work completed and testing of each student in all subject areas.
5. Describe their methods of instruction, materials, and units of instruction for the year.
6. Assign a major biweekly writing assignment to students (Grades 4–7) of one to three pages in length.
7. Check completion of *all* homework assignments.
8. Establish homework as a routine by the second week of school.
9. Maintain class routine except for supplemental experiences (Speech, Learning Assistance, Music). Routines will not be broken for student volunteer duties (library aides, traffic patrol, and such).
10. Submit a short weekly report to parents concerning each student's progress, work habits, and completion of assignments.
11. Contribute to the formulation of uniform school standards.
12. Teach and encourage students to demonstrate good manners and language.
13. Consider all students their responsibility when on the playground whether on duty or off duty.
14. Contact principal immediately when a situation needs his attention. Final decisions in all cases will be made by the principal.
15. Encourage children's bulletin boards.
16. Not initiate rewards nor a system of points unless the entire school is involved.

Note: There is also a list of safety standards which is designed to meet the particular needs of our school.

13

A Student's View of the Successes and Failures of an Alternative School
by Kathy Gross

In the fall of 1970 I entered a reputably excellent public high school in a suburban New Jersey town. In the winter of that year I left Tenafly High School to attend an alternative school created by several students, some interested adults from the community, and myself. As a student deeply involved in an alternative school, this essay will explore some of the ways I was affected by its successes and its failures.

The first six months of organizing our activities and eventual operation were extremely stimulating and productive. But the next several months of the school were frustrating and draining. I left at the end of the first year disillusioned with what our school had become, and spent the next three years at a somewhat more conventional progressive school in New England. Our alternative school followed a familiar pattern. It began as a response to deep dissatisfaction felt by many students and adults, but it couldn't effectively provide answers to the questions it initially posed.

In one sense the school was a failure: we did not create the totally open atmosphere that we envisioned when we began. We did not succeed in creating a new way of socializing kids so that they'd remain curious and creative without becoming competitive. In another sense, however, the school was a success: the very act of examining our reasons for dissatisfaction and attempting to establish structures that would serve our needs, was probably the most worthwhile educational experience I've ever had. I felt bitterly disappointed when I left, not only because we failed to achieve our idealistic expectations, but also because the school did not evolve past its initial problems. Within months it was clear our perfect "learning environment" was not going to spring into existence. The issues were simply too complex for easy answers. Unfortunately, instead of going on to further develop and readjust our ideas, we sank into disillusionment. For me the school became a failure when the problems were no longer being creatively challenged.

My determination to discover some alternative way for my education was a direct reaction to the school that I was attending at the time. It was a typical, large suburban high school. I hadn't read *Crisis in the Classroom* but even then I knew that I was being bored by books I could have loved and material that could have been exciting. I did not enter high school expecting it to be totally "fun" but, through my family and some good teachers in earlier grades, I knew that learning could be challenging and satisfying. That potential was destroyed in my high school as predigested material was presented along with the expectation that I would cough it back in acceptable form. Literature, history, math were all taught as isolated meaningless units of information.

But, teaching methods were only part of the problem. I was also learning to hate school because learning was inseparable from a system of control which I found oppressive and humiliating. It was next to impossible to respect adults who took pink, blue, and white "slips" seriously. Even in classrooms where a teacher didn't condone the high school's pervasive atmosphere of concern over bathroom passes, saluting the flag in assembly and, attendance during study hall, it all seeped in somehow to destroy the positive aspects of the learning process. As adolescents we reduced the situation to black and white terms; schools were institutions designed to socialize adolescents into their roles as supporters of the larger political and social system.

That "either-or" assumption was not part of a sophisticated political analysis. It was part of a general attitude prevalent in 1970: societal institutions were considered repressive per se. We saw the educational system as an extension of a society which wanted to train its young people to accept the Vietnamese war and to leave ecology, the arms race, and other significant issues forgotten. This assumption about societal values did not lead to any overt political education in our school. As adolescents, we didn't favor Marxism, anarchism, or any ideology as such. We did emphasize questioning of traditional institutions as the most important skill we could learn in school.

Supporters of our current educational system often support its role in preparing the student for the world he or she will enter and passing on the culture and traditions of our society. But what disturbed me the most about my high school was that I, as far as I could see, was not being prepared for anything. Instead, the sedative effects of the school's structure was destroying my only resources—energy and enthusiasm.

Not only was high school failing to help me acquire sharp intellectual tools, it was killing my interest in obtaining them. When I realized what was happening to me I felt I had to leave the regular high school and find some other way to get my education. I was determined to find a school built on mutual respect and caring between students and teachers. I refused to believe it was impossible to have a sense of joy and satisfaction in doing challenging work. My hopes for the school were a combination of classical liberal arts ideals and John Dewey's "progressive philosophy." In public school the classes were a contest between students and teachers; how much of this meaningless information could we succeed in avoiding? I thought if subject material was approached differently, then literature, philosophy, science, whatever we studied would not be meaningless anymore. I believed that grappling with the concepts from any discipline would genuinely deepen my experience in the world. Basically I was looking for a revitalized liberal arts education where Dewey's education for "real life" would connect my education to my world and to help me discover, understand, and function more effectively in the society in which I lived. I had no firm plans for realizing those goals. I was ready and willing to try anything; from the Parkway Program "school without walls" approach, to work-study projects, or to Socratic seminars.

With vague goals in mind I looked for other students and adults who shared similar concerns. I took my first step after I read an article on the free school movement in the *Saturday Review*. It listed books, periodicals, and people influential in the movement. Among the publications listed was "The New School Exchange"—a clearinghouse for alternative education ideas from every region of the country. I wrote to the exchange and then addressed letters to every person in the North Eastern Region listed as interested in alternative education. I then wrote to alternative schools in the northeast asking for information on how they got started. I also put an advertisement in the *Village Voice* encouraging anyone interested in alternative schools to contact me.

Those who responded to the ads formed the nucleus of our school. Word of mouth was then the most effective way of getting people involved. People who were enthusiastic got their friends involved. Within two months momentum had gathered and the project had a self-sustaining energy.

There were about twenty people committed to investing time and energy in an educational experiment and about thirty more who were willing to be peripherally involved. After four months of discussion, argument, thought, and holding classes at night, forming a full-time school seemed like a natural step to take. We made ourselves a legal entity by drawing up a corporation contract. Fourteen kids dropped out of public school to attend our alternative school full-time.

Two types of students attended the school. Some were successful within the public school system but bored and turned-off. Others were severely alienated and found it impossible to function within the system. With a few exceptions the students were white and middle class. The adults involved were a more diverse group. College professors, professionals, artists, taught or helped in some capacity. The diversity of talent and expertise among the adults was one of the most successful aspects of the school.

Our "corporation" never considered attempting an alternative school within the public school system. It seemed to us that every one of our basic assumptions ran contrary to those of the established structure. Most of the people involved in our operation were radicals in that they didn't believe a worthwhile change was possible within the system. Although never explicitly stated these shared political assumptions helped shape our decision not to be connected with a system we identified as inherently repressive.

The first months of organizing and operating our school was most meaningful to me in three ways. First, being outside an accepted framework forced me to examine every value and goal that I previously held. The choice of what to do, when, and for how long, was completely my own. This was an incredible sensation. American history, math, foreign languages, and anything else were not to be taken for granted. I had to look behind the assumptions inherent to figure out where these subjects fit into my world. In what ways would these studies increase my skills or enrich my life? If they wouldn't, what would? In a fundamental way I had to confront what was meaningful to me. I couldn't answer most of the questions that arose. However, realizing these questions were there and attempting to confront them deepened my understanding of my own needs and capabilities.

During these initial months, I also learned a lot about making decisions and taking action in a group. Since we were "noninstitutionalized," the school consisted of a network of informal agreements, decisions, and commitments. All questions about administration, structure, and direction were decided by group discussion and consensus. Teachers, students, and parents had an equal voice in the general meetings that were held to discuss problems, suggestions, and ideas. Our school was predicated on the belief that everyone had a stake in the school and the right to help determine philosophy and direction.

We tried to define our aims and to agree on methods to realize our goals. How could the relationship between teachers and students be changed so that the student took a more active part in discovering and learning for him or herself? How much responsibility did we have for one another? If someone made the choice not to work for weeks on end, did anyone have the right to decide that that was a problem and approach the person about it?

As time passed I had an opportunity to see how groups reach an agreement and to observe the conditions under which decisions are implemented effectively or ineffectively. I came to realize that one can't ignore power structures in groups. A group can't function by pretending there are no differences in energy, ability, and interest. Instead, ways need to be discovered to channel abilities and energies into a workable structure. In our school this never happened.

I also observed and experienced the powerful kinds of influence which groups can have on their members. At times our commitment to each other and to the experiment was truly supportive and helpful. At other times, however, the group became an escape. Some people wanted unconditional love and acceptance without contributing anything.

I learned many organizational and administrative skills. Since the impulse to create the school originated in myself and some other students there was never any question that we were as responsible as the adults for getting the school going and keeping it going. This responsibility included everything from writing letters, proposals, and articles to dealing directly with the community. During the school's first stages, "public relations" were very important. Several of the kids who wanted to drop out and come to our school—myself included—were under the legal age. The local public school administration thus scrutinized the school carefully. Since it was not accredited, our school had to justify our existence so that minor students were not arrested for truancy.

To increase the school's legitimacy, we invited the local newspaper to see the school and made a concerted effort to explain our ideas and demonstrate our seriousness. As a result, we received sympathetic local press. Requests for interviews came from radio stations, public television, and even the *Christian Science Monitor*. We complied with requests in the hope of gaining community support and understanding. We were excited about our ideas and wanted to explore them with others. Our goal was more than increasing our school's legitimacy and support, however. Because we charged no tuition at first, we needed books, supplies, and space. We also wanted to increase people's awareness that there were serious problems with the traditional school system.

Once the school got started there was the job of coordinating students, parents, and teachers. At first the responsibility was everyone's. I got first hand experience in organizing the day-to-day function of the school: scheduling, answering correspondence, and handling particular problems as they came up. After several months it was decided that a full-time, salaried person was necessary to handle the paperwork.

One of the most important things that this involvement gave me was a sense of my own competency and control over my life. The school was instrumental in helping me understand what I wanted to do and giving me the assurance to do it. In a "Deweyesque" sense, I learned that I was capable of accomplishing certain things by doing them.

With time apathy and stagnation set in and everyone's energy was sapped by endless analyses of what was happening to the school. There were circular discussions of better ways to spend our energy without actual steps being taken to solve the problems. One reason for this was the total ideological confusion on the part of most people involved, plus disagreement between those who thought they knew what they wanted. Many people had no consistent ideas about their goals. It was the classic syndrome of everyone knowing what they wanted to avoid, but very few having much to replace it with. When goals were formulated, they were frustratingly vague. Free school rhetoric is great for expressing abstractions, but not much help in translating anything into reality. How do you help someone become "a whole person"?

A split developed between one group which considered itself "Summerhillian," and others who did not, or at least who did not agree with how "Summerhill" was being interpreted in this situation. Essentially, the Summerhill faction (for lack of a better title) maintained that emotional growth came first; a student would be ready to work when he or she had "gotten him or herself together." Therefore the school's priority should be to provide a supportive emotional base so that the student would reach that point. I felt, as did several others, that the school offered the opportunity to experiment with some new ways to set up the curriculum; like trying out apprenticeships, workshops, different kinds of problem-solving —and that that's where we should put our energies.

The Summerhillians accused everyone else of being uptight intellectuals who couldn't deal with emotions, while the other groups became angry and impatient with what was perceived as self-indulgence. My own experience was showing me that learning skills and being challenged was part of the "growth process." Splitting emotion from intellect was pointless.

Various responses evolved to some of these problems, which did little to actually solve anything, but did make everyone feel better because they gave us a sense that we were making progress. One such response was that rather than come up with any well-defined goals per se, the school should provide a structure in which people could discover their own goals. This sounded good, but it meant that the school should attempt to be all things to all people, which was not exactly a realistic aim. Another response was that the *process* of defining goals and working our priorities was in itself the most important part of the educational process. As I discussed above, that was a very productive process; but it came to be viewed as ultimately an end, rather than a means to an end. Another response was that any problem which kids were having in dealing with the freedom would be solved with time. Let the students alone and they would get the resentment towards school out of their systems. By doing nothing for a while, they would get bored and then be ready to work. This insight was also attributed to Neill, but I'm not sure he would have supported the way it was put into practice in this case. It was used as a blanket justification for inactivity.

Moreover, most people maintained a total relativism. There was a lot of resistance to applying anyone's decision which was not their own. It was assumed that it was impossible to make valid universal judgments. This relativism made itself felt in a number of ways. For one, it contributed to a general hostility towards anything that smacked of expectations, standards, or demands. In free school rhetoric, "expectations" mean an imposition of one value system upon another.

Since virtually everyone was reacting to structures they had found extremely limiting, there was a fear of dogma. In our attempt to avoid the mistakes of the past, we created a new dogma. With the refusal to approach things critically, openmindedness became mindlessness.

Our lack of structure was based on the assumption that kids have a natural curiosity which will assert itself if given the chance. How much meaning can that have for kids who have been taught to be passive and have not acquired the skills to help them deal with free choice? There was always a verbal recognition of this problem, but never an adequate response to it. The Summerhillian chorus recurred again: you have to give the students weeks or months to get the resentment and boredom out of his or her system and then they will be ready to handle the freedom. I did not believe that was a sufficient answer. In order to revive interest, you need a rich environment, full of choices, so that curiosity can be sparked.

Another problem which was never adequately dealt with was that students cannot completely determine what it is they want to know by following their own curiosity. There are fields and disciplines which will remain unknown without stimulus from somewhere. A free school cliché was that if you couldn't find the interest within yourself, it just wasn't there. I didn't believe that for myself. We've all had good teachers who have helped us see things we would have otherwise missed. In the same vein, students need help in understanding that sometimes you have to follow a sequence of studies that might not be fun or interesting in the beginning, in order to reach a level of expertise where you can do interesting things. It was assumed that somehow we would learn those truths on our own. If we didn't, that was alright. It just meant we weren't ready to work yet.

We wanted to be flexible, open, and respectful of individuality. But in our fear of repeating mistakes of traditional schools, we went to an extreme; flexibility and individuality became the only values. The emphasis on emotional growth and the reluctance to set down any standards or goals created an atmosphere in which it was acceptable to lie back and indulge oneself endlessly. Total self-involvement without any action was okay, because you were "getting yourself together." For a lot of kids this came to mean "I can sit around and think and talk about myself indefinitely and important growth will follow."

I was bitterly disappointed to see the school sink into narcissism and anti-intellectualism. The magical horizon-expanding atmosphere could not be sustained. At the end of the first year, I left the school. None-the-less, my involvement made a qualitative difference in how I approached my education from then on. I learned to keep examining my own motives and needs and to at least try to accomplish the things which make sense to me. I also learned to be critical of institutions, so as to be more aware of their strengths and weaknesses.

Somewhat ironically, I'm now attending a large, prestigious university. The analytical skills I learned from my free school experience have helped me to determine what aspects of Stanford University are meaningful to me and which are not. Also, if I had remained in my public high school for four years, I would have been so bitter and turned-off that it would have been difficult for me to do anything productive within a conventional framework, such as Stanford's. By examining those structures and rejecting them, I'm now able to accept and use those aspects which are meaningful to me.

Through the free school I saw that a range of different educational and lifestyle choices are possible. This has given me a very different perspective on Stanford from that of many students. For a lot of kids, Stanford or another university is like an entry point into the only world imaginable. There is very little questioning about other values or roles other than those of future doctor, corporate lawyer, or engineer. I'm glad that I perceive that world as one choice among many.

14

Great (and Dissimilar) Expectations: The Growth of the Albany Area Open School
by Daniel Linden Duke

Once upon a time there was a small alternative school where children of all ages played and worked amidst the serene surroundings only nature could provide. The young learned to be nonracist, nonsexist, and non-classist, while planting gardens, building geodosic domes, and exploring ant colonies. The teachers loved their students and spent hours patiently listening to what their youthful friends had to say. Cooperation replaced competition, organic foods replaced supermarket junk, and the honest expression of feelings replaced double-talk. Parents participated in the school's daily activities, finding in them affiliation and deep satisfaction. So pleasant were the interpersonal relations fostered by the little school that many families began to live communally, and there was talk of form-ing an alternative community, free of private property and nuclear families.

It is likely that the ten parents who first explored the idea of a non-public alternative school in Albany, New York, shared a fantasy similar to the fairy tale just described. Alternative schools with five families rarely survive, however. In an effort to recruit more parents, the shared vision became blurred, causing some to wonder whether survival might have been easier with the original group after all. The school fell heir to many of the problems that beset public schools. These problems seemed to center around conflicting parent expectations. Even in a relatively small-scale educational operation—one involving less than seventy children—the potential for disagreement was high.[1] It appears that schools—be they public or nonpublic, urban or rural, large or small—share a certain degree of complexity and what Decker Walker has called "problems of purpose."[2]

The Alternative School 'Movement'

While some debate lingers over the use of the word "movement" to describe the proliferation of alternative schools in the last decade, little dispute exists that the late sixties and early seventies witnessed an unprecedented growth of educational options. Schools-without-walls, schools-within-schools, street academies, free schools, community schools, parent coops, storefront schools, and ethnic schools were but a few of the lexicographer's smorgasbord served up during these ten years of educational innovation. Alternative schools, of course, were not new. American educational history abounded with examples of traditional-type alternatives, including parochial schools, military academies, and "prep" schools.[3] In addition, a few boarding schools based on the Summerhill model and a larger number of compensatory alternatives emerged over the past half century. It was a fourth "type" of alternative—which I prefer to call a contemporary alternative school—that lacked more than a handful of historical antecedents. Contemporary alternatives are optional public or nonpublic schools catering primarily to competent, white, middle-class youngsters—in other words, the very students for whom conventional public schools seem to have been designed. The Albany Area Open School exemplified the contemporary "type."

While a sizeable number of articles and books on alternative schools have been written in the past decade, most represent polemical statements in support of educational options or "do-it-yourself" manuals. The need exists for more of what Geraldine Clifford terms "narrowly institutional histories."[4] Educators need to be apprised of how contemporary alterna-

---

1. I found the same problem of conflicting expectations in a seemingly "trouble-free" rural high school. See Daniel L. Duke, *Life and Learning at Lewistown High* (forthcoming).

2. "Problems of Purpose" was the title of Professor Walker's Division B Vice Presidential address at the 1976 convention of the American Educational Research Association.

3. For a more in-depth discussion of various types of alternative schools, refer to Daniel L. Duke, *The Retransformation of the School* (Chicago: Nelson-Hall, in press).

4. Geraldine Joncich Clifford, "A History of the Impact of Research on Teaching" in Robert M. W. Travers (ed.), *Second Handbook of Research on Teaching* (Chicago: Rand McNally and Co., 1973), p. 4.

tive schools develop and how they differ from P.S. 127. In this spirit, I offer the following account of the genesis and formative months of the Albany Area Open School. To recapture some sense of chronological growth, I focus on a series of dates, pinpointing particular time-bound events and interpreting interevent developments. While stage theories can be useful, I prefer a chronological approach. The progress of the Albany Area Open School tended to defy discrete stages or developmental steps. At any given point in time, the developmental status of the school reflected the current moods of the parents, the quality of interpersonal relations, and the amount of work that needed to be done in the next week. One day the school might seem on the very brink of collapse. Several days later a visitor could be impressed by the atmosphere of enjoyment and productivity. If the Albany Area Open School is indicative, contemporary alternative schools can be very complex and confusing enterprises, despite their small size.

June 22, 1972

Approximately twenty-five parents crowd into the suburban home of Orrin and Cicely Einstein to learn more about the alternative school being advertised around local colleges and the state university. Many in attendance are professionals or professionals-in-training. Of the ten parents who originally began meeting and voicing dissatisfaction with the local school systems, seven are now on hand to welcome prospective members. All of the "core" parents are college educated. Orrin Einstein is an assistant professor of mathematics at the state university. Ruby Freud is a dean of an experimental college. Her husband, Eli Freud, practises psychiatry. Sigmund Swartz is a college professor at Ruby Freud's experimental college. Melvin Mason is a lawyer. Clarence Hoover is chief of security at the state university. Sabra Mason, Cicely Einstein, Bertha Swartz, and Alice Hoover are not employed. Perhaps for this reason, they are involved more actively than anyone else in the planning of the school. Each takes care of two preschool-age children. They have formed a "play-group." Three of them together with Ruby Freud participate in the same women's consciousness-raising group. Within two years, Sabra, Cicely, and Bertha will be back in college getting advanced professional training.

In addition to their relatively high socioeconomic statuses, college educations, and suburban residences, the "core" parents share another similarity. They all are recently moved to Albany. The origin of the school, in fact, can be traced directly to the efforts of Sigmund and Bertha Swartz, who, prior to their move from New Haven to Albany, explored the possibility of setting up an alternative school with the Freuds, who had moved from the same city previously. The Swartz children already had participated in an alternative preschool in New Haven and their parents were much enamored of parent-cooperatives.

It may be no coincidence that the "core" parents were recent arrivals in Albany. In past research on a random sample of forty alternative schools, I discovered that in many instances a majority of the parents were newcomers.[5] This finding prompted me to wonder whether many alternative schools established through parent initiative were not intended, consciously or otherwise, to meet parent needs as well as the needs of children. For groups of newcomers without local roots, alternative schools seemed to promise affiliation and an antidote to alienation.

Returning to the recruitment meeting at the Einsteins, each visitor receives a mimeographed description of the proposed school. The "core" parents insist the description is tentative, pending the expansion of membership. Among other things, the three-page handout says:

> We are a group of parents from the Albany area who are creating a new alternative open school and day care center. The open school will serve 25 children, age 5 through 13. The day care center will serve 25 pre-school children, especially siblings of the older school children, age 18 months through 4.9 years. Although physically discrete, both educational facilities will operate on the same philosophical principles: namely, that children are natural and individual learners, that children need opportunities to develop and express their own interests, that adults, materials and learning spaces must foster joyous, independent learning. Self-worth, self-evaluation, and an interpretive, non-competitive spirit are the goals of the entire school. . . .
>
> In each component there will be one paid, full-time master teacher and one paid, full-time assistant teacher. In the day care center adjustments of the adult-child ratio will be made as the need arises. . . . Teachers will have relative autonomy regarding curriculum planning and school activities. They will be aided by parents who will contribute time and skills on a regular, prearranged basis. . . .
>
> The parents of both the open school and day care components will make decisions for the school. A parent can sustain active, voting membership in the governing body by attending 3 "new people's meetings" and the regular monthly meetings. A board of directors will be elected by and from the general parent body. The board will have,

---

5. A thorough discussion of the factors influencing the emergence of contemporary alternative schools is contained in Duke, *The Retransformation of the School.*

essentially, an operational, administrative function. The ultimate decision-making power will reside in the entire parent-governing body. A school committee, directed by a school administrator, will serve as a liaison between parents, children and teachers.

My wife and I are two of the visitors this evening who are impressed by the "core" parents' intentions and their nine months of careful deliberations. We agree to attend two more meetings and then interview with a representative of the membership.

August 27, 1972

Paula, Joshua (almost two years old), and I are now full-fledged members of the Albany Area Open School. I also am completing a doctorate in education, while Paula finishes her pediatrics training. The school promises to provide Joshua with a pleasant atmosphere in which to interact with children his own age. Our monthly contribution has been set at $90, placing us in the middle-range of tuition-payers. Since at least one member of each "core" family earns a professional's salary, their payments are higher than most, ranging from $100 to $300 a month. Some of the younger parents pay as little as $20 a month. They either are full-time students or sworn to oaths of voluntary poverty, a peculiar offshoot of countercultural living.

This evening a meeting of all parents takes place. Several school meetings have been held previously to discuss the hiring of teachers and building facilities. Negotiations for space in a downtown Lutheran church have begun, signifying a victory for the group of parents who prefer contact with urban "reality" and shorter commuting distance to the bucolic serenity of a rural or suburban setting. The negotiations are going slowly, however, testifying to the fact that conservative elements in the church's Board of Trustees are leery about sheltering a "free school." The church has been burglarized several times, and elders worry that a steady stream of children in and out of the church's education wing will encourage more theft. The failure to conclude negotiations quickly, with school scheduled to open next week, confers an air of crisis on tonight's meeting.

Of the sixty-four adults (including four teachers) who are members of the school committee, more than half are present. There are three black parents, and several white families have adopted black children. Efforts to recruit minority parents and the decision to locate "downtown" have not produced the "mix" of students desired by many parents. Seven of the parents are separated or divorced.

The teachers have recently signed contracts drawn up by Melvin Mason. Sunshine and Peter Forrest, in their early twenties and fresh from the Mid-West, are in charge of the school. Dahlia Morgan, an experienced teacher from the South, and Gwen Forearm, a fiftyish woman attempting to complete an external degree in early childhood education and boasting plenty of childcare experience in England during World War II, are responsible for the day care center. Dahlia Morgan is in the process of finalizing a divorce. Her daughter is enrolled in the school.

So many pressing problems face the school that covering all of them in a single meeting is impossible. The lack of definite facilities has been mentioned. In addition, the State Education Department and the local superintendent must be notified of the elementary school's existence. Fortunately for the school, the State Education Department has not developed a set of guidelines governing elementary "alternative schools." As long as a school can indicate it provides an education "equivalent" to public elementary education, the state is satisfied. Likewise, the superintendent of Albany schools takes a "benign neglect" attitude toward the handful of alternative schools under his jurisdiction. The Social Services Department is less permissive, and they require that a long list of requirements be met. Tax-deductible forms must be filed. Bylaws must be drafted and corporate status sought. Instructional materials have to be ordered. The fire marshal has to inspect and approve the Lutheran church (though it is still unknown if the church board will approve the school).

Despite the great number of outstanding problems, the meeting never gets beyond mutual soul-bearing, philosophizing, complaining about the "air of crisis," and debating the relative merits of Pampers versus diapers and organic versus "junk" food for lunch. After considerable deliberation, consensus is declared (it is not achieved). The only two decisions to come out of the five-hour meeting are that the day care center will use diapers (since Pampers cannot be recycled) and that school lunches will be catered by "The Green Thumb," a nearby health foods restaurant. Within a month of tonight, however, both of these decisions will be reversed, as the youngsters get sick of black bean soup and yogurt and the teachers get sick of the smell of mellowing diapers.

Filing out of tonight's meeting somewhat bleary-eyed and less certain about the school's future than five hours before, the parents eloquently express by their silence the frustrations of trying to build a school among so diverse a group. Some doubt if a collection of middle-aged radicals, eccentric ecologists, old-fashioned do-gooders, blacks, college drop-outs, professionals, rich, and poor can fashion an educational enterprise to satisfy everyone. Some doubt if such a group can fashion an educational enterprise to satisfy anyone.

Tonight is a time for wondering. Will all the time, effort, and money be worth it? Do we really like the other parents with whom we shall have to work so close? Where were the discussions of curriculum and teaching strategies this evening? Will all the meetings center around egos and axes-to-grind? Maybe if the school actually opens, these concerns will evaporate.

October 25, 1972

The air of crisis that surrounded the August 27 meeting has not abated. The Lutheran church permitted the school to use its facilities, but after less than two months they are insisting that their premises be vacated. The Sunday school teachers dislike the condition in which they find the education wing each week. The Open School teachers resent having to spend more time protecting property than teaching (or, more accurately, facilitating learning). Negotiations with a nearby Unitarian church are in progress, but contingency plans have had to be developed in the event that no facility has been located by November 1. Parents are offering their garages and dens in case interim quarters are necessitated.

Several students have been injured as the result of accidents occurring while they were unsupervised. One child's parents threaten to sue the school for negligence. Six sets of parents have withdrawn their children, citing as reasons their unwillingness to tolerate the hostility of meetings, the ever-increasing amount of volunteer work expected, the poor quality of instruction, and the general atmosphere of crisis and chaos. Dissatisfaction with Sunshine and Peter Forrest mounts, as many parents question whether their children should be allowed to do whatever they want whenever they want. A few parents of preschoolers murmur that they dislike Dahlia Morgan's and Gwen Forearm's requests for more structure and less parent "advice."

Indicative of the feeling of a good idea gone bad is the children's decision—reached over the strenuous objections of some parents—to adopt the sober-sounding school title Albany Area Open School. Parents had favored clever, more *avant garde* names like Stonesoup. A school song was written, but, like the school title, it lacks the lighthearted, youth-is-fantasy quality so many had sought originally. The song goes

Song for the Open School
Tune: "76 Trombones"

Learning's a joy when children can ask and seek,
Learning's a joy when they're free to learn,
Learning's a joy when each can follow her own path
And discover worlds at every turn.

Each of our children has an intrinsic worth,
Each is accepted for what he is,
Each shall be helped to grow and surely come to know
That the future and the world are his.

We will reject all artificial labels,
Racist, sexist, authoritarian.
We'll nurture zest for life and love of learning,
And each shall become all she can.

And in this noncompetitive environment,
Sharing, caring, a true community,
We'll foster creativity, encourage curiosity,
Renew, revitalize society!

The parents who perform most of the volunteer work, committee assignments, and clean-up details grow more resentful of those who do little or nothing. Many of the latter have the time to assist, but they have lost the inclination. No matter what someone does, there always seems to be at least one person willing to say it was wrong. The dozen parents who plod along doing more than their share appear to have much more at stake than their children's educations. For them, the school has come to embody a dream—a hope for a better world, a promise for meaningful nondomestic involvement, and a chance to interact with kindred spirits. To give up the dream would mean most of these parents—in their late twenties and thirties—might never transcend "middle-classness" or have an opportunity to work closely with other adults to build something new and exciting. This almost desperate determination on the part of a few parents not to abandon their dream will carry the school through one crisis after another and eventually will result in the stabilization of the operation. In the process, most of the parents who joined the "core" group in September will leave.

November 26, 1972

The school now functions from the basement and second floor of the Unitarian church. Some talk circulated earlier about purchasing a building and a suitable structure actually was located, but when the time came to get firm commitments of money, only a few of the original parents plus several others indicated a willingness to contribute.

During the past month several changes have taken place. A decision was made to convene the entire school committee no more than once a month. Overcoming several people's stout opposition to anything less than "pure" democracy, executive committees for the day care center and elementary school were established. The opponents of this measure did secure a provision, however, that the committees would be reconstituted in January and that all executive meetings would be open. These compromises indicate the general lack of trust pervading school affairs.

Meeting weekly, the two committees make operational decisions and handle problem referrals. In part, the committees were necessitated because of the growing hostility and friction between teachers and several parents. These parents insisted on bringing a variety of personal gripes and philosophical concerns directly to the teachers, who in turn felt they had their hands full seeing that the church was not destroyed and the youngsters received some attention. A second impetus for the committee was the realization that most parents had no desire at all to be involved in routine decision making. Out of conscience they continued to attend meetings, but every unproductive school meeting generated greater disquiet and brought them closer to withdrawal. In fact, the frequent school meetings seemed to be in the worst interest of the school, since they served more as an opportunity for discord than consensus and they drew already overcommitted parents away from their homes and children.

Interestingly, a small group of parents seemed to find the meetings exhilarating. These parents eventually wound up on the executive committees. The fact that they did not seem to mind the meetings suggests a desire on their part to get away from home. Among this subgroup are young parents who find parenting a difficult and minimally satisfying task. Unemployed mothers make up the bulk of the subgroup.

Several parents now are noticing that the children do not seem very excited about "their" school. Their lack of enthusiasm is understandable. They have been evicted from one church, presently lack space that is truly their own to arrange and rearrange as they wish, and continually are saying goodby to friends whose parents withdraw them from school. Blame for the elementary school's state of affairs is placed on the Forrests. "Requests" are made for more structure. Peter Forrest, however, is gravely ill, and parents are reluctant to challenge him openly. Sunshine Forrest receives the brunt of the griping and grows more bitter. Plans soon will be afoot to relieve the teachers of their responsibilities and look for a replacement. Only one teacher will be needed due to the loss of students and tuitions. Within a month, all but one child over nine years of age will remain. From the outset, the school had little to offer older children. They had few peers from which to choose friends. They were exploited as volunteer tutors for younger children or as day care workers. Little in the way of structured learning was received.

February 2, 1973

Another year, another church. The Unitarians became concerned about wear-and-tear to their property and indicated that they had promised another group permission to use the facilities. A Methodist church, also in the downtown area, had been found. In need of revenue, it was willing to rent basement space.

The Forrests departed, disillusioned and resentful. A young woman from out-of-state was hired. Several concerned parents got to her before she began teaching and warned her to insist on more personal control over the school than the Forrests had been granted. Her first act as teacher was an intelligent one. She requested each parent to submit in writing a statement of expectations for the education of his or her child. Those parents who responded displayed a "mixed bag" of dreams and realistic goals.

A recruitment drive to obtain parents, particular parents who could pay substantial tuitions, was mounted in January. Several meetings were scheduled and advertisements written, but they netted no new families. The absence of new faces and new ideas is now beginning to be felt. Many of the parents who remain realize that they will never feel comfortable around the existing group of adults.

In short, the Albany Area Open School has survived the first semester, but few people are willing to wager it will last beyond the second.

Volunteer help currently is a major problem. Without adequate parent help in the day care center, much of the program must be cut. The day care center teachers express in private their intention to seek other employment after June. They cite growing frustration over the patronizing attitudes of a few parents, the openly critical attitudes of others, and the lack of supplies. Professionally, they are stifled; psychologically, they become more paranoid.

I have made an effort to procure volunteers from several local colleges in order to bolster the day care center program. In return for their assistance, I scheduled a dozen seminars on various topics in child development. Parents, as well as volunteers, were invited to attend. The seminars promised to be a unifying force within the school, a chance for discussions about children's problems rather than adults' problems, and an escape from crisis-oriented decision making. Unfortunately, a few parents criticized even this effort, finding the seminars too pedantic and too much the product of one person's initiative. For me, these gripes provided the final excuse to withdraw from the school. In order to retain any shred of idealism and positive regard for the notion of alternative schooling, it was essential that I sever my ties. Joshua was moved to a university-sponsored day care center, where he seemed to function as well as he had previously.

Fifteen children remain in the day care center and eighteen in the elementary school. Several parents admit they hang on because they cannot make other day care arrangements that are quite so convenient (the Open School's facilities stay open until five-thirty in the evening). One of the "core" families has dropped out. Other families and all of the teachers do not conceal their intentions to leave when summer comes.

September 1973

The Albany Area Open School begins its second year of operation. It is primarily a day care center now, but there are plans to "grow its own" elementary school as the preschoolers mature. The "core" parents plus several others who participated in the early days have contributed enough capital to purchase an aging row house in downtown Albany. The original teachers having departed, several parents who long had expressed a desire to teach at the school have been hired. The two families who have invested the most in the way of time, energy, and money have begun discussing the possibility of living together.

As of the beginning of its second year, the Albany Area Open School, or at least its day care center, has survived. The prognosis for the immediate future (as of 1973) is good. But once the original children have outgrown the day care center and elementary school needs to be reestablished it is doubtful if the enterprise will continue. Do-it-yourself projects such as the Open School rarely sustain the quality of support derived from the original members.

Organizational Problems in a Parent-Initiated Alternative

Trying to assess objectively an experience in which one has been involved personally is a challenging task. As one of the parents who contributed his time, money, energy, ego, and child to the Albany Area Open School, I perceive the school's development in one way. As an educational researcher, I have a somewhat different set of perceptions. In the latter role, I feel it is necessary to use a case study such as the foregoing one to unearth or illustrate generalizations about all parent-initiated alternative schools. I shall attempt to do this in the concluding section of the chapter. As a researcher, I also wonder whether alternatives share common problems. Why do they succeed or fail? How do they differ from conventional schools? For what reasons have they emerged in such profusion in the past decade?

As a parent, these questions and research concerns are much less important than the quality of the experience of working to establish an alternative school. I must admit that the planning and early development of the Albany Area Open School occasioned great personal expectations, not simply that my son would have a nice place to go to learn, but that a group of like-minded adults could work together to operationalize their ideals. When this cooperative venture turned out to involve the same pettiness and intolerance I hoped to escape, the resulting disillusionment was profound. My son was withdrawn from the school because I could no longer endure the unproductive meetings, bickering, and debilitating sense of lost opportunity, not because he disliked the school. It is difficult to determine whether he benefited from his experiences there or not.

Rather than discuss my reactions as a parent to the school, though, I prefer to focus on some of the general problems faced by the school during its early months—problems, no doubt, to which I periodically contributed. Following a review of these "growing pains" I shall consider the significance of the Albany Area Open School in the broader context of the contemporary alternative school movement.

The Albany Area Open School had problems, to be sure. Lengthy discussions with other people involved in alternative schools and considerable research on the subject suggest to me that most parent-initiated alternatives encounter similar pitfalls. The problems typically include (1) lack of group trust, (2) conflicting parent expectations, (3) early disillusionment, (4) the absence of adequate facilities, (5) financial instability, (6) teacher uneasiness, and (7) poor organization. Taken together, these problems create a general and continuing atmosphere of crisis that initially unites and eventually enervates members of the school community.

In retrospect, it might have been wiser to start the school in a more conventional manner, allowing it to stabilize before attempting to implement a host of radical and largely untried innovations. Simply starting a new school is taxing enough. As matters developed, so many problems arose from the very outset that parents never had an opportunity to interact casually. Each encounter centered around a crisis in need of resolution. In other words, parents had more opportunities to become adversaries than to become friends. As a result, an atmosphere of trust could not be established among all the members. The frank and honest interchanges at meetings served to undermine, rather than enhance, a feeling of community. Though usually intended otherwise, open expressions of disagreement with someone's cherished beliefs produced friction and discomfort. Eventually, a situation was reached in the meetings where no decision could be made unless everyone lost.

The absence of trust, in part, was a function of differing parental expectations. For many, the school was intended as much to meet parent needs as those of their children. Because lots of parents were newcomers to Albany and enamored of *avant garde* ideas and lifestyles, they were searching for sources of affiliation. The Open School was expected to replace the socialization traditionally offered by neighborhoods, churches, and clubs, groups with which most Open School parents had little dealing.

Some adults in the school were single parents or parents in the process of becoming single. Others saw the school as a surrogate commune, a first step toward an "intentional community."

Besides the parents who hoped the school would provide meaningful adult relations, there were those who expected the school to provide a creative, child-centered education for their children. This group's aims often ran counter to the parents who wanted academic enrichment and accelerated learning opportunities for their children. The latter group withdrew early. One group of mothers clearly viewed the school as a potential opportunity for satisfying, nondomestic involvement. A few other parents simply felt that an alternative school was the "revolutionary thing to do."

The various expectations, though often at odds with each other and many times having little to do with the needs of children, should not be regarded as shallow expressions of "radical chic" or "passing fancies." The need for affiliation, for example, is a very real and pressing concern in this age of rootlessness. The need for nondomestic involvement on the part of mothers cannot be ignored as a transient gripe derived from the women's rights movement. The question that must be addressed, though, is whether an alternative school is the appropriate agency to satisfy these noneducational needs.

Lack of trust and conflicting expectations produced widespread disillusionment early in the life of the Albany Area Open School. Parents' dreams of a warm, responsive environment failed to materialize. The lack of permanent facilities and monetary problems derived from constantly dwindling tuitions abetted feelings of frustration. Looking back, it is possible that the failure to secure permanent facilities alone might have undermined the future of the fledgling operation. As it was, a building was purchased only after most of the original families had withdrawn, an attrition process that also served to unify those who remained and eliminate conflicting expectations. A "we'll show them" attitude became the school's *raison d'etre.*

It is noteworthy that all of the teachers left after the first year and that parents were employed thereafter. Conflicting parent expectations took their toll and constituted a major source of uneasiness among the salaried staff. As Gertrude McPherson has observed, "The central expectation [of the teacher] is that she must teach (change) the pupil. . . ."[6] Some parents, though, had no desire for their children to be changed. Some saw the teacher more as a facilitator of learning. Some, notably those parents who had created learning environments at home, were content for the teachers to dwell on arts and crafts. Some parents wanted the teachers to spend time on group and individual awareness exercises. Unanimity of expectations was a commodity more scarce than volunteers for Friday clean-ups.

Despite their rhetoric of caring and cooperation, most parents manifested little sensitivity for the emotional and professional well-being of the teachers. Quite a few parents possessed greater training in education and the helping professions than the teachers, a fact which created a potentially threatening situation for the teachers. With mutual trust an elusive quality, the teachers were unable to separate constructive criticism from genuine dissatisfaction. To make matters worse, several parents openly

---

6. Gertrude H. McPherson, *Small Town Teacher* (Cambridge, Mass.: Harvard University Press, 1972), p. 83.

coveted teaching jobs. Others, particularly unemployed mothers who performed a lot of volunteer work at the school, resented it when the teachers complained that there were too many "cooks" for the soup. For the teachers, scheduling activities for volunteers and calling up replacements when volunteers failed to show up became a major task. Added to this problem was their inability to modify the instructional environment, the lack of supplies, and the steady withdrawal of children. It is easy to understand why the teachers needed encouragement. When support did come, it typically arrived too late or was accompanied by the ever-present "honest" opinions—opinions that generally came across as criticism.

The final problem faced by the school during the first year can best be described as a lack of organization. It is an important historical fact that the parents of the Open School were so suspicious of any form of organization that resembled the public schools. Hence, they were reluctant to appoint an administrator or outline a chain-of-command. In fact, they were more willing to endure traditional teaching than traditional administrative organization. Unfortunately, no viable substitute for traditional decision making emerged during the first year. Perhaps, had greater trust been permitted to build in the beginning, the executive committees or even the school meeting would have functioned more effectively. As it was, too many decisions were never made or else were made by default. Pressing problems were allowed to wait. When a parent administrator was finally appointed, she found herself inundated with scores of trifling matters most parents had wanted to unload since September. Throughout the early months the teachers sorely needed, but never obtained, an administrator-type individual to act as their advocate and liaison with the parents.

The Albany Area Open School
in the Context of Contemporary Alternatives

What is significant about the Albany Area Open School? The fact it survived the first year? The problems it encountered? I feel its historical significance, along with other parent-initiated schools, lies in the fact it was created in the first place. Never before in American educational history have so many alternative schools been founded by parents of competent, middle-class students—the very students for whom conventional public schools seem to have been designed.[7] That parents would undertake such ambitious projects suggests, in part, the low respect with which public

7. See the opening chapter of Duke, *The Re-transformation of the School.*

education had come to be regarded. Here is a grass-roots effort to innovate in a realm where most change trickles from the top downward.

That the Albany Area Open School eventually failed to meet the expectations of many of the original parents also is significant. Clearly, the venture had little to offer minority parents interested in a higher quality academic education for their children. Minority children became desired commodities for white parents concerned with providing their children with the "proper mix" of peers. This attitude infuriated the few blacks who decided initially to gamble on the school.

In light of the rhetoric about the United States being a child-centered society, it is also significant that the school seemed to be designed to satisfy parent needs as much as student needs. When the enterprise ceased to be a source of affiliation, satisfying volunteer work, and radical brotherhood, many parents left or lost interest. Whether or not their children were benefiting did not appear to be of critical importance to more than a few who withdrew. Actually, there never was much evidence that the children were benefiting to any substantial degree and certainly not to a degree commensurate with the time and energy expended.

It is significant that the Open School's parents eventually drove away the teachers, who then were replaced by parents. Conflicting parent expectations and indecisiveness over the purposes of a school presented too much confusion for professionals. Confusion was abetted by an unintentional disregard for the emotional needs of the teachers.

A final reason why the Albany Area Open School is significant historically is the fact that the instructional program—despite all the dreams and dialogue—was not qualitatively different from that found in most public schools. If one aspect of the school differed from conventional schooling, it would have to be the administrative organization (or lack of it). Many parents felt, consciously or otherwise, that the key to a better school lay in changing the process by which educational decisions are made. Too late they discovered that the conventional model had some merits also.

15

Casa de la Raza—An Alternative School for Chicano Students
by Francisco Hernandez

Introduction

Casa de la Raza was closed on June 13, 1973. The Office for Civil Rights of the Department of Health, Education, and Welfare had informed the Berkeley Unified School District that Casa de la Raza was in "probable noncompliance" with Title VI of the Civil Rights Act of 1964. It was the opinion of federal officials that the establishment of a Chicano school in Berkeley was a form of racial discrimination and thus in violation of the Civil Rights Act. When the Office for Civil Rights threatened to cut off federal funds to the Berkeley schools, the school board decided to close Casa rather than to lose this important source of funding. Thus ended an experiment by the Chicano community of Berkeley to operate a school designed for Chicano students—both elementary and secondary.

Casa de la Raza opened in September of 1971 after many months of political pressure and proposal writing. An ad hoc committee of Berkeley parents and teachers expressed the need to develop an alternative school for Chicano students. The proposal for Casa became part of a larger proposal to establish an Experimental Schools Program within the Berkeley Unified School District. When the grant was awarded to the Berkeley schools, the Chicano community was given the opportunity to establish its own school. But from its inception, Casa was surrounded by controversy.

Casa was challenged by those who felt that the establishment of a Chicano school represented a return to a policy of ethnic group segregation. Yet it was the ethnic orientation of Casa that made it unique and truly alternative school. The Chicano community argued that the most effective way to educate Chicano children was to use the students' culture and language as a medium for instruction, rather than to impose a foreign language and set of values, as is the case in most public schools. The underlying assumption for the development of Casa as an alternative program was the fact that the existing school system had failed to meet the educational and cultural needs of Chicano students.

The Casa experience is important because it provides an opportunity to examine an attempt by Chicanos as an ethnic minority group to establish and control their own school. Furthermore, the Casa experience raises the issue of whether alternative schools for minority groups are viable educational innovations or whether they represent just another form of racial discrimination. In this article, the Casa experience will be described to point out some advantages of Chicanos operating their own "alternative" school.

The changes which Casa de la Raza attempted to bring about fall into three areas: (1) the *language* of instruction—classes were held bilingually in English and Spanish, (2) the *content* of instruction—the materials and activities were specifically selected for their relevance to the Chicano experience; and (3) the *context* of instruction—the school's environment and the teaching strategies were closely related to the Chicano culture. In order to understand how these changes were institutionalized at Casa, it is necessary to review the school's curriculum and governance structure.

Casa's Curriculum

Casa's curriculum specifically relied on parent involvement and bilingual teaching as strategies for raising cultural awareness and for developing basic skills. In order to achieve a curriculum that was culturally relevant, Casa used the student's family and community as the focus of most instructional activities. One of the main tasks confronting both staff and parents was to create an environment for the students that provided continuity between school and home.

The environment of Casa is best explained by one of its graduates, Rita Guerrero:

> I like Casa very much, so much that I kinda wish I could flunk to stay here with all my close friends. The main reason I like it is that I feel good to be with my own Raza. It's just like my home. I've realized how it is to be put down by this society and how hard it is for us Chicanos to keep together without fighting each other. Here at Casa de la Raza we can communicate and usually will help each other

out in any way we can. To me, Casa is like one big family. If any one comes and asks what school I went to, I'll be ever so glad and proud to say, that I graduated from the "baddest" Chicano school, *Casa de la Raza,* where people really know you.

Rita Guerrero was describing a program which integrated traditional curriculum with the Chicano experience. For the sake of clarity in describing the program it is divided into areas familiar to those involved in public schools; however, in actual practice a deliberate effort was made to integrate these areas into a comprehensive learning experience for the Chicano students.

For primary students, the curriculum consisted of the following courses: *Raza Studies,* focusing on individual projects designed to portray history and social institutions from the perspective of La Raza, to develop a positive cultural consciousness, and to reinforce and maintain a positive self-image rooted in cultural tradition; *Language Arts,* teaching communications skills and emphasizing the development of functional bilingualism —oral and written—in both Spanish and English; *Mathematics,* emphasizing the practical use of mathematics through bilingual, individualized instruction; *Health and Science,* using student experiments and projects to guide students to discover practical applications of science and health practices within the Raza community; *Art,* emphasizing the development of cultural awareness and artistic exposure through different art media, including drama, murals, and ballet folklorico.

For secondary students the curriculum included the following courses: *Bilingual Communications Skills,* emphasizing oral and written skills for bilingual students through creative writing, reading, English, Spanish, Raza literature, and multicultural literature; *Mathematics,* emphasizing the development of mathematical logical and practical uses of mathematics; *Social Science,* emphasizing the perspective and contribution of La Raza as a way to develop skills needed for meaningful social action and community projects to teach students how to apply scientific principles in their daily lives—science instruction included biology, nutrition, first aid skills, and ecological studies.

Specific efforts were made to extend the local community as a site for learning and to use local community people as educational resources. The purpose in so doing was to increase students' awareness of the Chicano community. Students took field trips to museums, art centers, Chicano social services agencies, and various sites of historical significance to Chicanos. For example, in an effort to develop an understanding of the

Chicano movement and its effect on Chicano youth, the students of Casa visited the Juan Corona trial, the Farmworkers Service Center in Delano, and Escuela Tlaltelolco (1) in Denver, Colorado. Other activities took the students to hear speeches by Chicano leaders like Cesar Chavez and Rodolfo "Corky" Gonzalez.

Within the classroom teachers developed curriculum together and taught courses in a manner that reflected cooperative rather than competitive values. For example, in social studies and language classes the students participated in group work and peer-tutoring. In math and reading classes although each student's work reflected an individual student's skill level, the work was done in small groups. Grading as a form of evaluation was eliminated. Instead, the teachers evaluated the overall performance of each student, identified factors that contributed to achievement, and discussed these factors with parents and the other staff members who had contact with the student. Factors which inhibited achievement were reviewed and adjusted whenever the factors were within the control of either the staff, students, or parents. Most of the students who came to the Casa from the public high school were lacking in reading and math skills. Consequently, the staff designed the schedule so that all the students studied their basic skills in the morning, while the afternoon could be used for tutoring any students who had any special needs.

Casa's Governance Structure

Casa de la Raza was governed by a *Mesa Directiva*—which drew its membership from the staff, students, and parents. Initially the Mesa Directiva experimented with several different structures, including nine- and twelve-member boards. Ultimately, however, the decision was made to have all secondary students, staff, and parents serve on the Mesa Directiva. Policy was decided and monthly general meetings. The Mesa Directiva's function was to decide policy for Casa in these four areas: (1) staff hiring, (2) nonsalary expenditures, (3) curriculum focus, and (4) school organization.

An administration to implement the Mesa Directiva's decision consisted of a director, and an administrative secretary. In addition, the administrator disseminated information to all the participants of Casa. Other responsibilities were reconciling the differences between the "bureaucracy" of the regular school district and the community control model of Casa. The administration of Casa had to insure that the red tape of the school district did not interrupt the decision-making process of Casa.

In the Mesa Directiva students, staff, and parents had the right to initiate their own proposals and to vote on proposal policy. Theoretically, this provided the opportunity to review and weigh diverse points of view, to facilitate participation and cooperation in implementing policies of the Mesa Directiva's, once such policies were determined.

A Two-Year History

When Casa de la Raza started in the fall of 1971, most of the planning for the school had not been completed. The Chicano community was faced with combining both the planning and implementation phases of the project into a two-month period at the beginning of the fall semester. During the summer of 1971, most of the staff had been hired and a school site secured, but no supplies or curriculum materials had arrived.

One major problem facing Casa initially was the inadequacy of the school site. The buildings were converted barracks that had not been used previously for housing school children. They had no heating, no running water, no furniture, and improper lighting. In essence, Casa began its operation with teachers and pupils housed in an "unusable" building.

The inadequacy of the school site plagued Casa throughout most of its existence, and caused the Chicano community to spend countless hours in meetings focusing on the facilities or in efforts to improve them. In this campaign parents and staff of Casa met many times with officials of the Berkeley School District and once marched all the students to the district administration office to protest the lack of action. The official protest resulted only in the purchase of several portable heaters and portable water supplies. Consequently, Casa community members began themselves to improve Casa by organizing staff and parents to paint the building and to construct needed tables and benches.

It was not until February of 1973 that Casa was moved into what could be called an "adequate facility." For over eighteen months the staff and students had to suffer physical discomfort in an inadequate facility. The poor facility had a large negative impact on the morale of the school because the participants could not feel physically comfortable in such an inadequate environment. The second major issue that Casa faced initially was the problem of school organization. A twelve-member board called the Mesa Directiva was instituted as the first decision-making body. Three members each represented the students, staff, and parents. Problems arose because of the lack of participation by parents and students. After the initial struggle to get the school going, Casa felt that their task was done and that now the operation of the school could be left to the Mesa Directiva. Both the staff and students identified problem areas, but the Mesa Directiva could not respond either because it lacked participation of the important constituencies or lacked sufficient information. Even in those rare instances when the Mesa made decisions, no action resulted because of a lack of communication between the Mesa and the important constituencies. Thus, after many meetings and much controversy the Chicano community reorganized the Mesa Directiva so that everyone at Casa would have both a voice and a vote. This reorganization insured participation although it created additional problems of inordinate expenditure of time in debates and meetings. Moreover, this structure resulted in heavy participation only at times when controversial issues were considered and while almost no one participated in deciding mundane issues such as bus schedules or the purchase of paper and pencils.

At the end of the first year the Mesa Directive decided to institutionalize input from parents by creating an official office—parent assistant director —to insure that parents' viewpoint would be presented to the staff on a daily basis. The constant information flow between the parent assistant director and parents created a feeling of trust between parents and staff. Parents felt that they knew what was happening at the school and should voice their approval or disapproval by calling on the assistant director.

But, the issues of facilities and governance notwithstanding, the most controversial issue that confronted Casa during its initial year was around the prevailing "free school" philosophy. Initially, the Casa staff experimented with a "loose" structure so that the students could determine the learning experience in which they wanted to participate. Near the close of the first year, many parents complained about their children's lack of academic growth. The Mesa Directiva decided to abandon the "loose" structure of Casa and adopted tighter controls over student attendance at classes.

"Tightening the reins" at Casa led to the resignation of several members of the staff—including the director. Casa thus hired new staff for the second year, including a new director. The director was given the responsibilities of (1) translating the policies of the Mesa Directiva into a workable school plan, (2) coordinating the teaching schedule, and (3) facilitating the innovative efforts of the teaching staff. The parent assistant director was given the task of coordinating parent involvement, especially in the areas of tutoring and school decision making. The elimination of the former "free school" atmosphere saw the institutionalization of a structured grade configuration in which students at the primary level had self-contained classrooms and secondary students were scheduled for basic skills instruction during the morning sessions. This structure was designed to maximize instruction in reading and math skills.

Also during the first year, teachers became dissatisfied with the curriculum materials that the school had inherited. Casa teachers discovered that many bilingual materials were mere translation of old textbooks—with content and values unrelated to the Chicano experience. Much of the material was about Mexico or Spain. Although this material was useful for its historical significance, it became apparent that the curriculum was not relevant to the Chicano experience in the Southwest. Curriculum that would help Chicano students develop an understanding of their own lives and their role in society was almost nonexistent. It appeared that a massive curriculum development effort would be needed to provide culturally relevant learning for Chicano students. The Casa staff therefore hired a curriculum consultant to train some of the staff members in developing an articulated, sequential Raza Studies program for the elementary grades.

But this curriculum work and other projects were never finished because Casa was closed in June of 1973, by order of the Berkeley Unified School District. The school was closed because the Office for Civil Rights concluded that Casa's existence violated Title VI of the Civil Rights Act of 1964. The ethnic make-up of the school had been under consideration by the Office for Civil Rights since the initiation of the school. After considerable dialogue, the Office for Civil Rights notified the Berkeley Schools that Casa was "in probable noncompliance" with civil rights legislation. Following federal guidelines the next step was a series of negotiations and meetings. During this eighteen-month period the Berkeley Experimental Schools Program rewrote the Casa proposal several times in order to meet federal guidelines. However, the federal officials insisted that Casa should have the same ethnic mix as the public schools. Since the Berkeley schools are 5 percent Chicano, the Mesa Directiva felt that the inclusion of 90 percent non-Chicanos would make Casa useless as an alternative for Chicano students. Thus, Casa's activities were aborted before many of the underlying ideas received an adequate test.

The Casa Experience

The Casa experience illustrates the opposition experienced by those alternative schools designed for minority students. Because Casa was culturaly based, it used Chicano teachers, a culturally relevant curriculum, and bilingual instruction as a combined strategy to deliver basic skills to Chicano students. This idea is counter to the commonly held notion that an integrated setting would be of greater benefit to minority students. However, some Chicanos argue that educational change for the benefit of Chicano students can only come about when the Chicano community has control over the educational process. In some areas this means that the Chicano community should develop and run its own schools.

To those involved in Chicano alternative schools the separation of Chicano students does not represent segregation but rather an opportunity to avoid the racism and discrimination that Chicano students face in the public schools. Chicano alternative schools represent an opportunity for Chicano students to learn through their own culture and language as do white students in the public schools. Federal bureaucrats insisted that Casa represented reverse racism and thereby was contrary to the integration movement in education. Actually, Casa like other Chicano alternative schools represents a nationalistic effort toward community control by a minority community. Certainly Chicano alternative schools will continue to develop as long as the public schools fail to meet the educational and cultural needs for Chicano students.

Casa de la Raza was a viable alternative for Chicano students because it addressed itself to the specific needs of its students and their community. It attempted to develop curriculum materials and teaching strategies that would be most effective with Chicano students, plus to develop the school environment so that the students would not feel as if they were out of place. To the participants these issues were paramount to even the charge of segregation, because Casa was an effort to combat the effects of the past discrimination which Chicano students faced in the public schools. It is their opinion that Casa violated neither the letter nor the intent of laws against discrimination.

At the same time, Casa de la Raza experienced internal difficulties which it shared with many other alternative schools. Inadequate facilities, governance problems, channeling parental input, the struggle between the "loose" and the "tight" structuralists, and the need for curriculum material which related to new approaches to learning caused the Mesa Directiva and the administration more than their share of concerns. But unlike other alternative schools, Casa was denied the privilege of working through these internal problems to become a viable alternative for Chicano students.

Part III
GUIDELINES

Until very recently alternative schools have not been the subject of much serious analysis. This is due in part to the newness and diversity of the alternative school movement. But many inside and outside the "movement" are encouraging a more analytical approach by posing a number of important questions: How do alternative schools fit into the larger context of educational reform? How should alternative schools be evaluated? What patterns of governance and organization will help alternative schools achieve their goals? What changes, if any, do alternative schools produce in their students and staff? How can alternative schools be financed? The following articles (six of which were prepared especially for this book) are organized in terms of six important guidelines which should help alternative schools succeed.

First, alternative schools need to examine their past.

Lawrence A. Cremin, in "The Free School Movement: A Perspective," faults the alternative school movement for being atheoretical and ahistorical. Without looking to the past—especially to the philosophy and experiences of the progressive education movement—members of alternative schools end up wasting time and energy "reinventing the pedagogical wheel."

Second, alternative schools need more "hard-nosed" evaluation and research to provide a sound basis for improvement and test the criticisms of their opponents.

Many view alternative school students as antiintellectual malcontents and refugees from hard work. Brian McCauley and Sanford M. Dornbusch, in "Students Who Choose Alternative Public High Schools—Their Background, Their Education, and Their Academic Achievement: A Comparison of Matched Samples," refute this view. Moreover, McCauley and Dornbusch find that "the public alternative school did, in line with its ideology, provide an individualized and responsive learning environment." Contrary to the convictions of many alternative school critics, the evidence indicates that students attending an alternative school did not learn any less than students in the regular school and, in fact, in other areas showed superior progress.

No problem is of more concern to existing alternative schools than evaluation. Among other things, effective evaluation may be the key to continued funding. Jeff Amory and Tom Wolf, in "Evaluating Nontraditional Programs: A Handbook of Issues and Options," give a detailed, step-by-step guide to evaluating alternative schools. In "Walden III: An Alternative High School Survives Evaluation Quite Nicely, Thank You," David L. Johnson and Jackson V. Parker provide a concrete example of a complex evaluation program which was used successfully at one alternative school.

Third, because running an alternative school is a difficult, complex task, alternative school participants need to give careful attention to their decision-making procedures.

In "Innovative Governance Structures in Secondary Schools," Joan Chesler examines six innovative high schools which emphasize student participation in school governance. Chesler outlines a number of barriers to effective student participation but finds that a clear, formal governance mechanism when combined with open and honest informal relationships is most successful in running a school where the goal is the sharing of power by both students and adults. The Center for New Schools, in "Some Conclusions and Questions About Decision Making in Alternative Secondary Schools," summarizes the findings of a national conference on alternative school governance. These recommendations provide a checklist for those setting up an alternative school or for those having problems with an already existing program.

Fourth, alternative schools must recognize that teachers operate differently in alternative schools and that organizational patterns must be designed to support rather than hamper teachers as they carry out their complex tasks.

Robert R. Nolan and Helen Carey, in "In a System of Choice, Teachers' Roles Change," describe changes in the roles of teachers who participated in the Alum Rock Voucher Project, one of the first attempts to provide a districtwide system of educational options. Alternative school teachers will not always find the adjustment to these new roles and environments an easy one. Kathy Huguenin and Terrence E. Deal, in "Removing the Clouds from Sunshine School," employ an organizational perspective to examine the troubled staff relationships in one alternative high school. They describe a survey-feedback approach, which was used to help solve some fundamental organizational problems originally conceived by the staff as "intense interpersonal and philosophical differences."

Fifth, since teachers must teach and relate to one another and their students differently in alternative schools than in regular schools, their training must be redesigned accordingly.

J. Kelly Tonsmeire, in "Teacher Education for Alternative Schools," describes some new approaches to preservice and inservice training for alternative school teachers.

Sixth, alternative schools need external support to survive.

Contrary to the wishes of many alternative school participants, alternative schools cannot operate successfully in isolation from other organizations. Alternative schools must make a variety of demands on organizations and groups which, in turn, make demands on them. In "From Alternative Schools to Options in Public Education: The Alternative Schools Movement and State Education Agencies," Gary Natriello discusses the points at which alternative schools and state education agencies come into contact with one another. Natriello finds state education agencies as having either one of two general responses to alternative schools: ambivalence or encouragement and support. Natriello goes on to recommend some specific tactics to alternative school members for dealing with state education agencies, which can provide valuable assistance or almost insurmountable roadblocks. Finally, John Theroux, in "Financing Public Alternative Schools," provides a series of specific guidelines for getting the resources necessary for the successful operation of alternative schools.

16

The Free School Movement:
A Perspective
by Lawrence A. Cremin

About a decade ago, I published a study of the progressive education
movement of John Dewey's time—the movement that began around 1890,
peaked in the 1920's and 1930's, and then collapsed in the years after
World War II. I am often asked, is there any relation between that movement and the free school movement today? Is there anything to be learned
from a comparison? And if so, what? My answer is, we can learn a great
deal.

In my study of the progressive education movement, which I titled *The
Transformation of the School,* I put forward a number of arguments:

> *First,* that the movement was not an isolated phenomenon in
> American life, not the invention of a few crackpots and eccentrics,
> but rather the educational side of the broader progressive movement
> in American politics and social thought.

> *Second,* that the movement began in protest against the nar-
> rowness, the formalism, and the inequities of the late nineteenth-
> century public school.

> *Third,* that as the movement shifted from protest to reform, it
> cast the school in a new mold, viewing it as (1) a lever of continuing
> social improvement, (2) an instrument of individual self-realization,
> (3) an agency for the popularization of culture, and (4) an institu-
> tion for facilitating the adjustment of human beings to a society un-
> dergoing rapid transformation by the forces of democracy, science,
> and industrialism.

*From *Notes on Education* II (October 1973): 1–4.

Fourth, that the movement was exceedingly diverse, enrolling men and women as different as Theodore Roosevelt, Jane Addams, Booker T. Washington, and Samuel Gompers, but that one could discern at least three major thrusts: a child-centered thrust, which peaked in the 1920's; a social-reform thrust, which peaked in the 1930's, and a scientific thrust, which peaked in the 1940's.

Fifth, that John Dewey saw the movement whole and served as the chief articulator of its aspirations—recall his little book *The School and Society* (1899), in which the first essay ("The School and Social Progress") reflected the social reform thrust, the second essay ("The School and the Life of the Child") reflected the child-centered thrust, and the third essay ("Waste in Education") reflected the scientific thrust.

Sixth, that the movement enjoyed its heyday during the 1920's and 1930's, that it began to decline during the 1940's, and that it collapsed during the 1950's for all the usual reasons—internal factionalism, the erosion of political support, the rise of an articulate opposition associated with post-World War II conservatism, and the sort of ideological inflexibility that made it unable to contend with its own success.

In the original plan of my study, I included a final section addressed to the question, "Where do we go from here?" But when the time came to write it, my thoughts were not clear, so I decided to end on a "phoenix-in-the-ashes" note: If and when liberalism in politics and public affairs had a resurgence, progressive education would rise again.

Now, I did manage to work out that last section in 1965. I had a chance to give it initially as the Horace Mann Lecture at the University of Pittsburgh, and then published it in a little book called *The Genius of American Education.* I argued there that the reason progressive education had collapsed was that the progressives had missed the central point of the American educational experience in the twentieth century, namely, that an educational revolution had been going on outside the schools far more fundamental than any changes that had taken place inside—the revolution implicit in the rise of cinema, radio, and television and the simultaneous transformation of the American family under the conditions of industrialism and urbanization. The progressives had bet on the school as the crucial lever of social reform and individual self-realization at precisely the time when the whole configuration of educational power was shifting radically. And what was desperately needed, it seemed to me, was some new formulation that put the humane aspirations and social awareness of the progressive education movement together with a more realistic understanding of the fundamentally different situation in which all education was proceeding.

By the time I wrote *The Genius of American Education,* a new progressive education movement was already in the making. You are all familiar with it, so I shall describe it only in the roughest outline. I would date its beginning from precisely the time I was wrestling with that last section of *The Transformation of the School* that I found I could not write. I would date it from the publication of A. S. Neill's *Summerhill* in 1960. (Incidentally, the appearance of that book marked an extraordinary event in publishing. Nothing in it was new; Neill had published more than a dozen books on education; and most of what he recommended had been tried in the progressive schools of the 1920's and 1930's. When the original publisher, Harold H. Hart, first announced the title, not a single bookseller in the country ordered a single advance copy; ten years later, in 1970, the book was selling at over 200,000 copies a year.)

The new movement began slowly, with the organization of Summerhill societies and Summerhill schools in different parts of the country. It gathered momentum during the middle 1960's, fueled by the writings of John Holt, Herbert Kohl, George Dennison, James Herndon, and Jonathan Kozol (whose book *Death at an Early Age* won the National Book Award in 1968). And it manifested itself in the appearance of scores of new child-centered schools of every conceivable sort and variety.

Simultaneously, growing out of the civil rights movement, there arose the political programs of black and ethnic self-determination and the so-called community free schools associated with them—Harlem Prep in New York, the CAM Academy in Chicago, and the Nairobi Community School in East Palo Alto.

By the summer of 1971 Allen Graubard, whose book *Free the Children* (1972) is the most recent effort to state the history and theory of the movement, was able to identify some 350 such schools and in all likelihood there are more than 500 of them today. And these are what Graubard calls "outside-the-system" schools, so that we must add many more schools, schools within schools, and classrooms within schools that are part of the public school system and variously referred to as alternative schools or community schools or open schools.

Also, during the last five or six years, we have seen a fascinating interweaving of the child-centered and political-reform themes in the literature of the movement, so that open education is viewed as a lever of child liberation on the one hand and as a lever of radical social change on the other (the interweaving is beautifully illustrated in the early issues of the West coast quarterly *Socialist Revolution*).

At least two of the three themes of the first movement, then, the child-centered theme and the social-reform theme, have emerged full-blown in the present-day movement. Interestingly enough, however, the scientific theme of the first movement has been noticeably absent from the present version. In fact, there has been an active hostility on the part of many free school advocates toward present-day efforts to apply scientific principles to the techniques of instruction and evaluation. Whereas the progressive education movement reached a kind of culmination in the eight-year study, in which Ralph Tyler and his associates tried systematically to assess the outcomes of progressive methods, latter-day advocates of free schools have seemed on the whole uninterested in such assessment.

Interestingly, too, the radical side of the current movement has been much more sweeping in its radicalism than was earlier the case, culminating, I would suppose, in Ivan Illich's proposal that we deschool society completely. There were radicals in the 1890's who were fairly skeptical about educational roads to reform—one of them once told Jane Addams that using education to correct social injustice was about as effective as using rosewater to cure the plague. But I have yet to find a radical at that time who wanted to do away with schools entirely; it was rather the reactionaries of the 1890's who sought that.

What is most striking, perhaps, in any comparison of the two movements is the notoriously atheoretical, ahistorical character of the free school movement in our time. The present movement has been far less profound in the questions it has raised about the nature and character of education and in the debates it has pursued around those questions. The movement has produced no John Dewey, no Boyd Bode, no George Counts, no journal even approaching the quality of the old *Social Frontier*. And it has been far less willing to look to history for ideas. Those who have founded free schools have not read their Francis W. Parker or their Caroline Pratt or their Helen Parkhurst, with the result that boundless energy has been spent in countless classrooms reinventing the pedagogical wheel.

Further, the movement has had immense difficulty going from protest to reform, to the kinds of detailed alternative strategies that will give us better educational programs than we now have. Even Jonathan Kozol's *Free Schools,* which was written explicity to help people found alternative institutions, is egregiously thin in its programmatic suggestions; while Joseph Turner's *Making New Schools,* which pointedly proffered a rather well-developed reformist curriculum, has not even been noticed by the movement.

Finally, the current movement has remained as school-bound as the progressive education movement of an earlier time. Even Charles Silberman's *Crisis in the Classroom* (1970), surely the most learned and wide-ranging analysis to be associated with the present movement (though it did not emanate from the present movement), begins with a lengthy discussion of how television writers, film-makers, priests, rabbis, librarians, and museum directors all educate but then goes on to propose the open classroom as the keystone in the arch of educational reform. Ironically, the one book to come out of the movement that appears to have comprehended the educational revolution of our time is Ivan Illich's *Deschooling Society.* But the appearance is deceptive. Illich would like to abandon schooling in favor of what he calls educational networks, but he does not deal with the inevitable impact of the media and the market on those networks.

Now, it is easy enough to criticize, and my remarks should not be taken as a defense of the educational status quo. At the very least, the advocates of free schools have cared enough about human beings to try to make education more humane and that is to be prized. Where they have failed, it seems to me, is at the point of theory: they have not asked the right questions insistently enough, and as a result they have tended to come up with superficial and shop-worn answers.

Let me then put my question once again: What would an educational movement look like today that combined the humane aspirations and social awareness of the progressive education movement with a more realistic understanding of the nature of present-day education? What if free schools (and all other schools for that matter) were to take seriously the radically new situation in which all education inescapably proceeds? What would they do differently?

Let me venture three suggestions. First, viewing the situation from the schools outward, they would begin to contend with the fact that youngsters in the schools have been taught and are being taught by many curricula and that if they want to influence those youngsters they must be aware of those curricula. The Children's Television Workshop has a curriculum. The advertising departments of the Ideal Toy Company and Love's Lemon Cosmetics have curricula. The *Encyclopaedia Britannica* and the *World Book Encyclopedia* have curricula.

The Time-Life Science Program has a curriculum. The Boy Scouts and Girl Scouts have curricula. Our churches and synagogues have curricula —the Talmud has been a curriculum for centuries and so has the Book of Common Prayer. And each family has a curriculum, though in many instances that curriculum may do little more than leave youngsters to the fortunes of the other educators.

To understand this is to force educators to change fundamentally the way they think about education. It means, as James Coleman and Christopher Jencks—and one should probably add Plato—have pointed out, that the school never has *tabulae rasae* to begin with, that when children come to school they have already been educated and miseducated on the outside, and that the best the school can do in many realms is to complement, extend, accentuate, challenge, neutralize, or counter (though in so doing the school does crucially important work). It means that one of the most significant tasks any school can undertake is to try to develop in youngsters an awareness of these other curricula and an ability to criticize them. Young people desperately need the intellectual tools to deal critically with the values of a film like *The Clockwork Orange,* or with the human models in a television serial like *Marcus Welby, M.D.,* or with the aesthetic qualities of the music of Lawrence Welk. None of this can substitute for reading, writing, and arithmetic, to be sure; but reading, writing, and arithmetic are no longer enough.

Incidentally, if one accepts this line of argument, it is utter nonsense to think that by turning children loose in an unplanned and unstructured environment they can be freed in any significant way. Rather, they are thereby abandoned to the blind forces of the hucksters, whose primary concern is neither the children, nor the truth, nor the decent future of American society.

Second, looking beyond the school, once educators took seriously the fact that we are all taught by radio and television, peer groups and advertising agencies, libraries and museums, they would necessarily become interested not only in alternative schools but in alternative education of every kind. It may well be, for example, that the most important educational battle now being fought in the United States is over who will control cable television, who will award the franchises, and what will be the public requirements associated with a franchise. Once forty to fifty channels are readily available to every American home—some of them with the capacity for responsive interchange—then what comes over those channels in the form of education or miseducation will profoundly affect all teaching, in schools and everywhere else. There is simply no avoiding it, and educators had best face it.

Further, if educators were to take seriously what Urie Bronfenbrenner has been saying about the extraordinary power of the adolescent peer group in American society and the need for a greater variety of adult models in the life of every child, they would press for a host of innovations, both inside the school and out. They would be more interested than they seem, for example, in peer-mediated instruction, or in summer camps, or in arrangements under which children spend time in factories, businesses, offices, or shops, with real adults doing real work, along the lines of the experiment Bronfenbrenner carried out with David Goslin at the *Detroit Free Press.* You are doubtless familiar with the recent publication called *Yellow Pages of Learning Resources,* in which a whole city is seen as a potential learning environment and successive pages indicate what can be learned at an airport, a bakery, a bank, a butcher, a courtroom, a department store, and so on, all the way to a zoo. Once again, I might note that it does not take less planning and less structure to pursue these sorts of learning, it takes different plans and different structures. And without such plans and structures, there is simply no freedom.

Finally, focusing on the learner himself, once educators took seriously the fact that we are living through a revolution in which opportunities for education and miseducation are burgeoning throughout the society, they would give far more attention to the need to equip each youngster as early as possible to make his way purposefully and intelligently through the various configurations of education, with a view to the kind of person he would like to become and the relation of education to becoming that kind of person. In other words, they would do all they could to nurture an educationally autonomous individual.

I happen to think that kind of individual was at the heart of John Dewey's theory of education and central to his conception of a democratic society. And I find it not at all strange to be ending on such a note, for as critical as I have been of the progressive education movement of yesterday and the free school movement of today, I find myself much more in sympathy with the authentic aspirations of both movements—at least as articulated by Dewey—than I am opposed to them. In the last analysis, my critique is simply an effort to call the free school movement to the service of its own best ideals, and it can only learn what those ideals are by studying its own history.

17

Students Who Choose Alternative Public High Schools— Their Background, Their Education, and Their Academic Achievement: A Comparison of Matched Samples *by Brian McCauley and Sanford M. Dornbusch*

I. Introduction

The students and parents who choose to join alternative schools are "different." But different in what ways? And what happened to these students and parents as a result of alternative schooling? We sought to discover what characteristics led people to renounce regular public education and seek to participate in a different environment for learning within the public school system. We were also interested in the results of participation —for both students and parents.

Three separate studies are combined in this chapter to generate some answers to these questions.

The first study is a small one, in which some high school students (working closely with us) interviewed forty students in two alternative schools that operated as part of public high schools. To provide bases for comparison, they also interviewed forty students in the regular schools. This study permits us to examine differences in the characteristics of students and parents in alternative high schools and in traditional high schools.

The second study, which matches every student in an alternative high school with a student in the same regular high school, makes two comparisons. One compares again the characteristics of students and parents associated with a public alternative school with appropriate control groups in the regular high school. The other comparison uses the perceptions of the students and of the parents to contrast the educational processes in the two settings. Thus, in the second study we will be able to show both how the students and parents who entered the world of public alternative education viewed the educational process in the regular high school. By following the two groups through their first and second years, we can also see how these perceptions changed in response to the alternative school environment. The size of our sample of alternative school students was sixty-three in the first year and eighty-seven in the second year. Data were collected from control groups of fifty-two and fifty-six students, respectively.

In the third study, we will use the same groups of students, but this time compare their academic achievement. Do students in alternative schools learn less than those in schools with standard curricula?

Together, these studies present an integrated picture that helps us understand why some people reject traditional education organizations and seek to create new models for learning and teaching. Although separate groups of students and parents were compared, happily the findings were mutually consistent. The studies also permit us to compare alternative with traditional high schools in terms of both process and results. The findings are consistent with our study of the organization of alternative schools, particularly their evaluation processes (McCauley, Dornbusch, and Scott 1972).

II. The First Study:
How Do Students and Parents in Alternative Schools Differ from Students and Parents in Traditional Settings?

Student research project.   A student research project in a regular high school compared alternative school students in two public high schools to students in control groups. In the first public school which contained an alternative school, twenty randomly selected students in the alternative school were compared to twenty randomly selected students in the regular secondary school. In the second public school, we chose a control group to match on an individual basis the twenty students randomly selected from its alternative school. Matching was based on sex, race, academic aptitude, and achievement, and the number of course units taken for credit. We combined data from two samples.

Students in alternative schools.   The student researchers reported that a desire for independence was the most frequent reason given by students for entering alternative schools. The second most frequent reason was dislike for the regular school, either because "teachers push us around" or because "we get bad grades."

Among students in the control groups who, aware of the existence of the alternative school, chose to stay in the regular school, the main reason for that choice was fear that the new program would require too much self-control and self-motivation. Thus, both students inside and outside the alternative schools agreed that a desire for independence in learning was the key variable in determining participation in an alternative school program. Not everyone wants freedom, but those desiring independence and those liking their chains believed that freedom was more likely to be found in alternative schooling.

The students in the public alternative schools perceived a major difference between the alternative school and the regular school in the amount of individual attention they received. They thought, by a 3 to 1 ratio, that they did not receive sufficient individual attention in the regular school, and, by the same ratio, that they were now getting plenty of individual attention. It is interesting that many students who did not attend the alternative schools shared some of the same perceptions. About half of the students who remained in the regular programs said they did not get sufficient individual attention.

Parents of students in alternative schools. The student researchers also studied the political attitudes of parents. The students in the alternative schools were more likely to report that their parents were liberal politically than were the students in the regular schools. Students in alternative schools reported 69 percent of their fathers and 68 percent of their mothers as liberals, compared to 51 percent and 45 percent, respectively, reported by students in the control groups. The correlation between reported political liberalism of parents and attending an alternative school is expressed by gammas (see Costner, 1965) of 0.36 for mothers and 0.44 for fathers.[1] Obviously, these moderate relationships, on a scale from -1.00 to $+1.00$, might be a product of the environment of the alternative school creating students who wanted to perceive their parents as approved liberals. Yet they at least suggest that children of more conservative parents are less likely to attend schools.

Summary. The findings of the student researchers are consistent with some of our later results. We will present data which reinforce the importance of the image of the alternative school as a site for independent learn-

---

1. Costner, Herbert A., "Criteria for Measures of Association," *American Sociological Review* 30 (June 1965): 341–53.

ing. In addition, our results will also support the conclusion of the student researchers that even those who do not enter alternative schools are often dissatisfied with the level of individualized attention they receive in the regular school.

III.   The Second Study:
How Do the Perceptions of Students and Parents
in a Public Alternative School Differ from the Perceptions
of Students and Parents in a Traditional Setting?

Description of the study.   We took advantage of the existence of an alternative school within a regular public high school to examine ways in which students who were attracted to alternative education differ from those who did not heed its call. In the public high school we studied, we tried to match each student in the alternative school with a student who had roughly similar characteristics on the following variables: race, grade, sex, academic aptitude and achievement, and number of course units taken for credit. Using that student control group, we could then also compare the parents of students in public alternative schools with parents of students in the control group.

Nonrespondents among students, parents, and teachers in the alternative school and the regular school made our comparisons somewhat suspect. Yet, the consistency of our findings across groups and the ease of integration with our own observations make us fairly confident that we are indeed reporting on the major dimensions on which those attracted to the alternative school differed from those who were more satisfied with regular schooling.

Student perceptions.   We note with some concern that we had to ask students in the public alternative school and in the regular school to give us their images of the regular school during the previous year. Of course, this introduces the possibility of retrospective bias. Students who, having just entered an alternative school, want to portray the environment from which they have just escaped as evil will exaggerate its deficiencies and neglect its virtues. Therefore, we have examined carefully the responses of the two groups of students, both in the alternative school and in the control group, and note with pleasure the large number of questions for which there was considerable agreement about the nature of the regular school.

We will begin with those aspects of life in the previous year's regular school on which there was agreement between students in the alternative school and students who remained in the regular school. The most startling finding, surprising in that the other data we have reported would lead us to expect major differences, is that students who did not choose to join the alternative school were almost as negative as students in the alternative school with respect to their images of the degree of independence, personal responsibility, and initiative granted to students in the regular school. It is true that on these questions the students in the alternative school were slightly more negative, but the control group was also quite negative. For example, 13 percent of the students in the alternative school and 27 percent of the students in the regular high school reported they had been fairly often or more frequently engaged in independent work. For personal responsibility, 23 percent of students in the alternative school stated they had had "a sense of personal responsibility for your school learning activities," compared with 33 percent of the students who chose to remain in the regular school. Similarly, for initiative, 16 percent of the students in the alternative school reported "a sense of personal initiative in your school learning activities," compared with 27 percent of the students who did not go into the alternative school. It appears that students who were attracted to the alternative school had a greater desire for independence, responsibility, and initiative than did the control group, but both those students and the control group agreed that there was relatively little independence, responsibility, and initiative in the atmosphere of the regular school.

Both groups also agreed that they were not close to their teachers, did not "really exchange ideas about school" with their teachers, nor meet "with faculty members . . . in small informal groups to talk about matters of mutual concern or interest." The students who went into the alternative school perceived themselves as slightly more distant from teachers, only 11 percent reporting that when in the regular school they had fairly often or more frequently been close to their teachers, compared with 22 percent of the control group. On exchanging ideas with teachers, the students in the alternative school were slightly more positive, 21 percent to 18 percent reporting exchange of ideas fairly often or more frequently. Similarly, the proportion reporting that they had met with faculty in small informal groups was ludicrously low. Only 4 percent of the students in the alternative school and none of the students in the regular school reported that they fairly often or more frequently met in informal groups with teachers.

Students in both types of schools also agreed on the low level of student participation in governance of the regular school. The largest proportion in either group reporting that they fairly often or more frequently participated in governance, in decisions about educational matters or in the process of considering changes in the school, was 8 percent.

Students in the alternative school and control group agreed in reporting that parents seldom participated in discussions of educational matters with the staff and that parents seldom took part in the consideration of changes in the school. Four percent of the students in the alternative school said their parents fairly often or more frequently took "part in the process of considering changes," compared with none of the students in the regular school. Similarly, only 2 percent of the students in the alternative school believed that their parents "talked with members of the school staff about any educational matters which affect your education," compared with 10 percent of the students in the control group. Almost all students believed that parental participation in the regular school was infrequent.

Let us turn now to the major differences between those students who joined the alternative school and those who chose not to leave the regular school. The largest difference in perceptions was found for a question asking how frequently the regular school tried "to make you conform to a specific set of values other than your own." Seventy-eight percent of the students in the alternative school saw the regular school as fairly often or more frequently coercive, compared with only 27 percent in the control group. This was the largest difference for any item. The students in the alternative school were also less likely to report that they were "treated with sufficient respect by teachers" than were students in the regular school. Thirty-five percent of the students in the alternative school reported that they were fairly often or more frequently treated with respect, compared with 60 percent of the students in the control group. Yet this negative image of coercion and lack of respect for students was contradicted by responses to a question asking how often are you "free to state your honest opinions in school." An identical proportion of students in the alternative school and in the control group, 46 percent, fairly often or more frequently felt free to state their opinions. We do not know how to interpret this apparent conflict in the data.

As would be expected, students in the alternative school felt less satisfied with the educational program of the regular school than did students in the control group. When we compared the proportion who reported that they fairly often or more frequently felt their educational program was not responsive to individual needs, 57 percent of the students in the alternative school and only 21 percent of the students in the control group had that negative image. When we asked students whether they believed that they were receiving "an exceptional chance to get a high quality education," 22 percent of the students in the alternative school and 50 percent of the students in the regular school fairly often or more frequently had that belief. Students in the alternative school were obviously less satisfied with the regular program. Students in the alternative school, compared with students in the regular school, were also more likely to believe that school had little relationship to their lives after finishing school, less likely to believe that they were using "their school time for a worthwhile purpose," and less likely to believe that their school experiences were promoting "new and broadened personal awareness."

It is, of course, not surprising that 60 percent of the students in the alternative school reported that they fairly often or more frequently felt frustrated in the regular school, compared to 40 percent of the control group. When asked whether they were "happy and satisfied" with their school environment, only 11 percent of the students who later moved to the alternative school stated that they were fairly often or more frequently euphoric, compared to 37 percent of the students in the control group.

We will close with a disconcerting note. When asked how often they thought "methods used by your teachers are interesting and effective," we expected that the students in the alternative school would be much less likely to report favorably about the teachers in the regular school. They did in fact report negatively about their teachers' methods, but so did the students who remained in the regular school. Thirteen percent of the students in the alternative school, and a surprisingly low 23 percent of the students who remained in the regular school, reported that they fairly often or more frequently thought their teachers were interesting and effective. Few students, whether in the regular school or the alternative school, reported that their teachers in the regular school were interesting and effective. Since students are the people to whom classroom performances of teachers are most visible, this represents a serious indictment of traditional teaching.

In summary, the student responses indicated that those who were attracted to the public alternative school did indeed perceive school as a less favorable environment for learning and did feel less happy in school. In addition, our data showed that they were concerned about attempts to make them conform to the values of others. But, simultaneously, we note that students in both schools agreed that they did not have feelings of independence, responsibility, and initiative in the regular school; that students played only a small part in decision making in the regular school; that pa-

rents were unlikely to participate in school decisions; and that relations between students and teachers were rarely close and informal in the regular
school. Finally, they agreed that teaching in the regular school was seldom
interesting and effective, a sad finding.

Parent perceptions. Examination of the data for parents showed that on
every question parents of children who went into the alternative school
were more negative in their images of the regular school than were the parents of students in the control group. Often the differences were not great
between the two groups of parents. Only for four questions did parents of
students in the alternative school show markedly greater negative feeling
about the school environment. Their perceptions indicated that they had
been less likely to: participate in decisions affecting their child's education,
exchange ideas with their child during the previous year, believe teaching
methods were effective, and believe that the school administration was
flexible enough to meet their child's changing needs.

IV.   The Second Study:
Comparing Educational Processes
in an Alternative and Traditional High School

We will now compare the educational processes in the public alternative
school and the regular high school. Here we again present the perception of
students and parents of students in the alternative and regular schools. We
are comparing groups which are matched on numerous criteria. We can be
reasonably sure that the results we report are not the product of such traditional factors as age, sex, race, ability to perform on standardized tests,
and classroom performance. The consistency of findings makes it likely that
we are reporting accurately how a desire for a different kind of school creates differences in the educational process.

We will examine the impact of the public alternative school and the regular high school in four main categories: independence in learning, personal relationships, perceptions of schooling, and academic achievement.
The data are consistent and fit well with the findings we have reported
from 24 private alternative schools (McCauley, Dornbusch, and Scott,
1972).

Independent learning.   We asked a number of questions which focused on
student independence and found that student and parental responses were
mutually supportive.

We asked students in the alternative and traditional public school programs three questions on independent learning: How frequently do you: (1) "have learning experiences in school which require independent student work without close supervision by teachers?", (2) "feel a sense of responsibility for your school learning activities?", and (3) "feel a sense of personal initiative in your school learning?" Students who chose the alternative school, compared to the control group of students who remained in the regular school, when looking back at the regular program, reported less independent study, less sense of responsibility, and less personal initiative. However, at the end of their first year in the public alternative school, students reported that they did more independent study than was reported by students in the traditional school. Ninety-seven percent of the students in the alternative school compared to 57 percent of the regular students reported that they fairly often or more frequently engaged in independent study. The same pattern occurred in the responses for the other two questions. For responsibility, although students in the public alternative school initially reported that they felt lower levels of responsibility about their learning when in the regular school, at the end of the first year in the alternative school 94 percent reported that they fairly often or more frequently felt a sense of personal responsibility, compared with 51 percent of the students in the regular school. For personal initiative the percentages were, respectively, 94 and 48 percent.

Here is a comment one student in the public alternative school made about independent study:

> I think it's doing a lot of good for me because at the other school you just went to school every day and had the same teacher, almost the same thing every day, nothing new, never went on any field trips. Just the same old thing. In the alternative school there's a lot more time to do independent study on topics that you really like instead of topics that you are assigned to do. You can really get a lot more done that way.

Another student reported a new feeling of responsibility about his work after entering the alternative school:

> Like last year, I didn't do hardly any work and my grade point was 3.2. But it didn't really teach me how to study. I feel now like I am really working, like in the morning I work about 4 hours on one thing, and I can really get into it.

The new feeling of initiative has certainly helped some students:

> No one has told me what I have to do. Everything I've done has been what I chose to do. And that's great, because I do a better job.

> Last year you take a certain number of required subjects for college credits. The only thing I learned last year is how to cut class and get away with it. I didn't really care one way or the other.

The data from parents tell the same story. We asked parents of students in the public alternative school and parents of students in the control group two questions relating to students' independence and initiative. First we asked parents in both groups, "In general how frequently do you feel that your child is given a chance to make important decisions about his own education?" Parents of students who joined the alternative school were much less likely than the control group to report that their children had much chance to make decisions about their own education before participating in the alternative school. However, by the end of the first year in the public alternative school, an identical 88 percent of parents in both groups, parents of students in the alternative and regular programs, reported that their children fairly often or more frequently made decisions about their education.

One parent noted the importance of her child's independent decisions, noting that, "Doubt that she would finish high school otherwise."

The parent responses on initiative and responsibility, combined in one question, support the findings we have already reported for data from students and teachers. When we asked how frequently do "you think your child shows a sense of initiative and responsibility about his education," 80 percent of the parents of students in the public alternative school and 66 percent of the parents of students in the regular program responded that their children fairly often or more frequently showed initiative and responsibility.

One parent put it this way:

> The alternative school offers an excellent opportunity for expansion of the child's initiative and responsibility and also is a stimulus for creative learning.

Another said:

> Presently the alternative school is promoting interest and motivation toward our son's learning attitude. We feel that during the first three years of high school he merely went through the motions of being a student, and now we know he is out of the neutral gear.

The results of our analyses are clear. The public alternative school created an environment in which independent learning was encouraged. The students attracted to the alternative school had generally negative images of the regular school as a site for independent learning, but the alternative school successfully met their high standards. Students in the alternative school were perceived as having more independence, responsibility, and initiative than the matching control group.

Personal relationships. The pattern of data on interpersonal relations in the public alternative school and the regular public school was also consistent. Students who chose the alternative school reported they were less close to other students when in the regular school. But after a year in the alternative school, 65 percent of the students in the public alternative school reported that they were fairly often or more frequently "close to other students in the school." This percentage was almost as high as the 68 percent reported by the students in the regular high school. Here is how one student compared interaction among students before and after entering the public alternative school:

> You listen to other people's viewpoints more than you did in regular school. Like in government, we are doing a thing on justice, and we rap about what justice is, and everyone comes up with different ideas. Last year we just sat in class and listened to the teacher lecture and then had a test.

We have already noted that students in the public alternative school were less likely to report that they were "close to members of the teaching staff" in the regular school than were students who remained in the regular program. However, students in the public alternative school by the end of their first year were more likely than the control group in the traditional program, by percentages of 62 to 42, to report that they were fairly often or more frequently close to members of the teaching staff.

A student put it this way:

> The biggest thing is teachers, most definitely. Because you learn to relate to teachers as human beings and get to know them personally. It's not like when you are sitting in a class you can't approach them or anything. You get to know them and see them every day, and you have written out a contract with them, and it's not just something that is down on paper, it's something between you and him, and when you see him you kind of think, "Well, I better do my physics," or whatever. Like in class, I find that if I start getting behind, I come in and feel really bad when I walk into class.

Another said:

> I feel closer to the teachers because when I have a problem I can just go and tell them about it. I don't have to worry about it.

The same pattern again appeared when we asked students how frequently they felt that they were "treated with sufficient respect" by teachers. Initially, students in the alternative school were much less likely than were students in the regular program to report that teachers in the regular school treated them with sufficient respect. However, by the end of the first year in the alternative school, 94 percent of the students in the public alternative school, compared with 70 percent of the students in the regular high school, reported that they were fairly often or more frequently treated with respect by teachers.

For one student, the student-teacher relationship passed beyond mere respect:

> My teachers, I can call them by first names, and we are actually friends. It's a much more personal relationship. We respect them for knowing more than we do, but that doesn't mean we can't have a more personal relationship which is usually better for learning.

We asked a question about informal contacts between students and teachers. Students in the alternative school program and students who remained in the regular school both reported extremely low levels of informal contact with teachers in the regular school. At the end of the public alternative school's first year of operation, 62 percent of the students reported that they fairly often or more frequently "met with faculty members and students in small informal groups to talk about matters of mutual concern or interest." The corresponding percentage for students in the regular school program was 3 percent. This is a remarkable difference, 62 percent to 3 percent.

Two students made the following comments about their contacts with teachers:

> The teachers, we talk to each other and if I don't like something I can tell them. The teachers are more friends than teachers. You can get to know other students easier because you are all in the same meetings. It's a lot easier to learn from someone you like and whose attitudes don't completely turn you off the minute you walk into the classroom.

> (The alternative school) helps me form closer relationships with the teachers, because they seem more human, as opposed to regular school where they have 235 kids a day or something so you are just like another computer card to them, I guess. . . . This relationship helps with learning because it's not like you are sitting in a classroom with a computer up front giving out all this knowledge. When somebody you know is telling you, you are more interested.

In general, the alternative school produced a more informal climate for contacts between teachers and students. Students reported an interpersonal world of much greater intimacy, a direction of change that fits the ideology of the alternative school movement. The alternative school, by every measure, is a warmer social environment.

Perceptions of schooling. The perceptions of schooling by students and parents followed the same general pattern as we have described for independence and interpersonal relations. When we asked students in both schools how frequently: (1) "you feel satisfied with your school experiences?", (2) "you think the school you are now attending is providing you with an exceptional chance to get a high quality education?", and (3) "you think you are using your school time for a worthwhile purpose?", alternative students were in each case more likely to report that they fairly often or more frequently had these favorable perceptions of school. The percentages were, respectively, 71 to 54, 82 to 71, and 79 to 51. For each of the three questions, students in the alternative school had expressed more negative feelings about the regular school last year than did students in the control group.

One student in the public alternative school expressed satisfaction with the education he was receiving:

> I think it's at least as effective as the regular school, if not more so. I am more concerned about what I am actually learning, and about doing whatever I am supposed to do. Whereas in regular school you often get caught up doing whatever you're supposed to do, and if you are learning anything, okay, and if not, well you've done it. A lot of the time it's interesting. There's some subjects that didn't change that much. Now I at least don't have to go through long, intensive, boring periods.

We also asked both groups of students how frequently they "thought that their school tries to make you conform to a specific set of values other than your own?" Again the pattern repeated itself. Although 78 percent of the students in the public alternative school had thought the regular school was fairly often or more frequently forcing them to conform to a specific set of values, responses at the end of their first year in the public alternative school showed only 9 percent of the alternative school students perceived the same frequency of pressure to conform. Among students in the control group, 26 percent reported this level of forced conformity. The alternative school produced a remarkable impact on its students in causing them to perceive school as so much less coercive.

Next we asked students whether they thought that their "school experiences are likely to promote new and broadened personal interests and awareness?" Again we found that, although students in the alternative school had initially been less likely to report that the regular school was likely to broaden their interests and awareness, by the end of the year, students in the alternative school were more likely than students in the control group, by 91 percent to 38 percent, to respond that their school was stimulating new interests.

Here is how one student described his education in the public alternative school:

> Well, what the alternative school has done for me, is that I now have time to do the things that I have always been interested in. And for the first time I can go off and do what I want to do. They haven't exposed me to too many more opinions, but they have given me the time to look into things that I had always romantically thought of.

Data we collected about students' feelings of frustration in school also supported the favorable pattern in the alternative school. Students in the alternative school said that they had been more often "frustrated and unhappy about your school experiences" in the regular school than was reported by the control group. At the end of a year in the alternative school, students were less likely to report they fairly often or more frequently felt feelings of frustration and unhappiness than were students in the control group, by 15 to 26 percent.

One student put it very simply: "I'm happy with what's going on. I really like coming to school now."

The responses we collected from parents supported the data from students. Only 24 per cent of the parents of students in the public alternative school reported that they fairly often or more frequently felt that their child was frustrated or unhappy about his or her school experiences, while 45 percent of the parents of students in the control group reported this level of frustration and unhappiness. Once again this finding emphasizes the change in the feelings of parents of students in the public alternative school, since, before their children entered the alternative school, parents of alternative their children than the parents of children who remained in the regular school students had been more likely to report feelings of frustration for school program.

One parent states the change clearly:

> For the first time in years my child is motivated to study and also enjoys it. The staff and teachers have been very helpful. They have

treated my child as an individual and she has responded in a positive way.

We asked students and parents about the effectiveness of teaching methods. By the end of the year 85 percent of the students in the alternative school, compared to only 29 percent of the students in the regular secondary school, reported fairly often or more frequently that "the methods used by your teachers are interesting and effective." Yet the students in the alternative school had been more negative about the methods of teachers in the regular school than students remaining in the regular program had been.

The data we collected in teaching methods from parents supported the pattern reported by students. At the end of the first year, 86 percent of the parents of students in the alternative school and 71 percent of the parents of students in the control group reported that teaching methods in their respective schools were fairly often or more frequently interesting and effective. Again, parents of students in the alternative school had initially been more negative about teaching methods in the regular school than the parents of students in the control group had been.

One parent was convinced that the program in the public alternative school was of high quality:

> Education can and should be more flexible in these changing times, without sacrificing quality. My son (now in college), a graduate, is envious of his sister's opportunity. It would have been a godsend for him had the alternative school been possible a few years earlier. I hope the above sufficiently expressed my enthusiasm! I think Dr. X and the alternative school staff are to be heartily congratulated for their hard work, dedication, and understanding.

We asked students and parents whether their respective schools responded to the educational needs of students. At the beginning of the year, students who chose the public alternative school were more likely to report that the regular school did not respond to their needs than were students in the control group. However, at the end of the year, a slightly smaller percentage of students in the alternative school than students in the control group, 24 percent to 32 percent, reported that their school fairly often or more frequently did not respond to their own educational needs.

Responses from parents strongly supported the image of school responsiveness in the alternative school. At the end of the year of alternative schooling only 18 percent of the parents reported that the alternative school fairly often or more frequently did not respond to the needs of their child as an individual, while fully 64 percent of the parents of students in the regular program reported that level of unresponsiveness in their school. One parent argued forcefully for responsiveness to the individual needs of students:

> It's just plain necessary that there be different patterns of learning made available to kids with different conditioning, so that they may all ultimately achieve the same thing: an educated state.

We also asked students in both schools how frequently they "think that school has little or no relationship to your life after you finish school." Students in the public alternative school were more likely to report fairly often or more frequently that the regular school was not related to their later life than were students in the control group. The respective proportions were 49 percent to 25 percent. At the end of a year of alternative schooling, however, students in the alternative school were almost as likely as the control group to report that school was related to their later life. Only 12 percent of the students in the public alternative school and only 9 percent of students in the traditional school reported that school has fairly often or more frequently little relationship to life after school is finished. The low proportions for both groups are surprising although they may partially be a product of being one year older and close to the world of work.

One student put it this way:

> This year I am doing things that I am really interested in, and I must say that I am working harder this year than I ever have before in school. I think it will have an influence on what the future will be for me simply because I was really seeking something, and I found it through the alternative school. Had I not been admitted to the alternative school this year, I would have already graduated and would be working or something. And now I'm really finding out about myself.

Another said:

> Yes. It's giving me somewhat more of a direction, like I know what field I will probably end up going into. Before I didn't have any idea. I'll probably go into English or History. And in P.E. I get a chance to really do what interests me, like bicycling. A lot of kids in the alternative school would cut the classes in regular school, but here they don't.

We believe that the results reported show clear and important differences in the perceptions of the learning environments in the alternative school and the traditional school. The data from students and parents are mutually supportive. They were not just presenting a favorable image of the alternative school. For example, the data in our previous study (McCauley, Dornbusch, and Scott, 1972) on parent-teacher contact showed a failure of the ideology of the alternative school when viewed from the perspective of parents. Overall, we are convinced that the broad pattern of differences found truly represents a changed educational environment in the alternative school.

A replication. We have reported primarily on the data which we collected during the first year of operation of the public alternative school. We did this because we collected a wide range of data during this period from students, teachers, and parents. During its second year of operation we again collected data from students in the alternative school and from students in the control group. From these responses we were able to determine that the findings of the first year were essentially unchanged, although the differences between perceptions of the alternative school and regular school were somewhat reduced. We will not report these data here, for they merely repeat our previous findings and do not include responses from parents. But we can be sure that the results we have reported are not merely the fruits of novelty, a "Hawthorne effect" produced by change, any change.

V. The Third Study:
Comparing the Academic Achievement of Students in an Alternative School with Students in a Traditional High School

We have shown that the program of the public alternative school was significantly different from the regular school program. Our findings were that the students in the public alternative school had more independence in learning, had closer relationships with students and teachers, and generally had more positive images of their school than did the students in the control group. Although we understood that achievement on standardized tests was not a goal according to the ideology of the alternative school movement, we did feel that it was worthwhile to see the impact of the alternative school on standardized measures of ability. We knew that many who are interested in alternative schools suspect that more positive feelings about school are related to higher scores on standardized tests, while others think that the permissiveness associated with freedom in a learning environment leads to a decline in cognitive measures of performance on the standardized curriculum.

During the first year of the public alternative school, we used the Iowa Test of Educational Development to measure academic achievement. We administered the test in the early fall, 1971, and late spring, 1972, to students in the public alternative school and to students in the control group. There were subtests in four academic areas: science, language, reading in social studies, and mathematics. We used alternate forms of the test for pre- and post-tests.

We performed an analysis of covariance on the adjusted means for each subtest. We found no statistically significant differences for any subtest between the scores of students in the regular public school and those of students in the alternative school.

These results apparently support the view that the alternative school program did not result in any better or any worse performance on standardized tests. However, this was too easy. We had trouble in coaxing students in the public alternative school, and even those in the traditional high school, to show up for the testing sessions. Only approximately half the number of students in both groups who took the pretest in the fall took the posttest in the spring. Because of this possible sampling bias, we performed additional analyses to find the direction of that bias. We found that there were no substantial differences between those in the public alternative school or the traditional school who took both tests or only one test.

We now knew that the students in the alternative school who had taken only the test in the fall had been no different from those who took both tests. But that was in the fall. What if these students had changed over the year? Was there any way for us to make a guess about how they would have done *if* they had taken the tests in the spring? So we made a list of all the students in the public alternative school and gave it to the teachers in the alternative school. We asked the teachers to indicate the level of academic growth and responsibility for each of the students. We defined academic growth as "achievement you have observed in school work and other areas of cognitive growth; extent to which students have achieved measurable academic growth of any kind." Responsibility was: "comes to meetings previously scheduled; acts as if he/she understands the importance his/her actions have for others." For two of the four subtests on the Iowa Test, teachers in the alternative school perceived that students who took only the pretest were markedly higher in academic growth than students who took both the pretest and posttest. For the other two subtests and for responsibility, teachers in the public alternative school reported no difference between students who took only the pretest and those who took both tests. We believe, therefore, from these analyses that, if every student in the alternative school had taken both the pretest and posttest, the scores attained would not have been lower and might have been higher than those we found.

During the second year of the public alternative school, we again compared the scores of students in the alternative school and control group, this time using the Scholastic Aptitude Test and Preliminary Scholastic Aptitude Test. None of the comparisons revealed any major differences on any test between the scores obtained by students in the alternative school and the control group.

We well knew that many teachers, students, and parents associated with alternative education believe that performance on standardized tests and the comparisons between individuals which tests encourage are not goals of alternative education; instead, such testing is to be avoided. Yet we wanted to determine whether students who participate in alternative programs are likely to suffer when compared on standards used by the outside environment. We will then conclude by saying that we are not able to show that students in the public alternative school were able to perform better than the control group on standardized achievement tests as a result of their experiences in the public alternative school. But, on the other hand, it is encouraging to note that they did not do any worse than the control group, and that they were, while doing no worse, much happier in school.

VI. Conclusion

In general, this chapter has reported numerous successes of the public alternative school. We have previously noted organizational problems for the private alternative schools in areas in which the ideology was too extreme to provide guidance (McCauley, Dornbusch, and Scott, 1972). But the public alternative school did, in line with the ideology, provide an individualized and responsive learning environment. This made the students happier. Certainly we did not demonstrate that a warm and helping environment reduced the level of academic knowledge. The students in the alternative school did not learn more but they did not learn less than the control group. For some students, particularly those desiring more freedom and responsibility, the alternative school does provide a worthwhile alternative.

References

Costner, Herbert A. "Criteria for Measures of Association." *American Sociological Review* 30 (June 1965): 341–353.

McCauley, Brian L., Sanford M. Dornbusch, and W. Richard Scott. "Evaluation and Authority in Alternative Schools and Public Schools." (Stanford Center for Research and Development in Teaching, Technical Report No. 23) Stanford University, June 1972.

18

Evaluating Non-Traditional Programs: A Handbook of Issues and Options
by Jeff Amory and Tom Wolf

1.0 Introduction

1.1 Our Audience

This paper grows out of our experience working with and talking to people in alternative schools about evaluation. These practitioners have found themselves faced with the responsibility of evaluating their programs, often for the first time; and have found themselves without an *overview* of what is involved in the process of evaluation, the steps one might take, the issues that are important to consider. We will address this discussion directly to practitioners as though we were in an informal meeting to share with them our ideas of what might go in the process of evaluating their school or program.

1.2 The Organization of the Paper

The numbering system we are using to organize the paper reflects our desire to communicate the entire process in an understandable way. This linear rational approach does not mean we feel that these, and only these, steps have to be followed in this, and only this, order. It is simply that we have found this conceptual framework a helpful one for us in thinking about the process, and our experience has shown that the ground contained in this frame has to be considered and covered in some way. You may find that beginning somewhere in the middle and working out to both ends is more relevant to your own situation. Moreover, you may want to revise some of the steps or fashion new ones as you go along. Undoubtedly, some of your own specifics will differ from the ones we have used as examples. Hopefully, this frame will be helpful rather than constricting, and we would like you to view it with a healthy degree of irreverence.

1.3 Some Current Political Considerations about Evaluation

Much of the impetus for this paper grows out of a general philosophical struggle within the field of evaluation, the survival struggle of alternative schools, and the role evaluation plays in that struggle. It is not coincidental that these occur at the same time. The conflicts reflect the inevitable friction between the traditional or entrenched and the new or innovative processes of institutions.

Edwin House (1973) views the conflict in the technology of evaluation this way: As with other technologies, the technology of evaluation has shaped the minds of those who use it, the evaluators. Evaluation problems are automatically reduced to testing problems and to problems of measuring objectives. If the evaluator chances to cast the problem differently, he finds that his new formulation is perceived as illegitimate, uneconomical, and unacceptable. Even slight deviations in instrumentation are controlled by the norms of "reliability" and "validity." Powerful institutional forms have grown up around the technology as devices for maintaining the status quo. The governmental agencies accept only "hard" data. Phrases like "shaped the minds" and "automatically reduced to testing problems" make it clear that House feels that the technology that has developed over the last fifty years is outdated at the least and, at worst, an agent of control which effectively curtails innovation and creativity. However, House goes on to say that "during the last five years a crack has appeared in this carefully constructed measurement edifice." There are a number of authors who have stressed the need for new methodologies in evaluation, and House mentions some of them.

However, there are still a great many social scientists who espouse the "true" experimental design and all that it implies in the way of randomization of experimental and control groups and testing programs that yield statistically analyzable hard data. In a paper presented in 1969, Tom R. Houston, Jr., makes a very strong case for the true experimental design in what he calls the "Impact-Effectiveness Model" for evaluating social action programs. As part of his introduction he states that "to the skeptical ears of behavioral scientists, mere human testimony is less persuasive than the mathematical rhetoric of the impact effectiveness model which we will outline here."

The argument continues, escalates into a power struggle. Some of the more traditional behavioral scientists, like Houston, begin to say that their measurement techniques are not sophisticated enough to handle the social action programs of today with all their complex of variables and call on the discipline to review and update its practices. However, some of the more innovative ones counter by saying that this appeal to modernize the technology of measurement is merely an attempt to co-opt new values and techniques and represents no fundamental shift in the belief in the supremacy of the old way of doing things.

Many people find the conflict closely parallels the conflict that exists around alternative schools today. The people who believe in traditional schooling often find ways to belittle the concept of alternative schools, such as: accusing alternative schools as a dumping ground for students that don't "fit" in traditional schools; and, more recently, using the concept as a way to continue segregation and political control in urban areas. The people who believe in alternative schools counter by pointing to the wealth of material that has been written in the last ten years condemning much of American education as a wasteland and to the excitement that their alternative programs have generated in the community of people involved.

We see the conflicts over the technology of evaluation and alternative schools as highlighting two important concerns. First, although the traditional is an approach which prides itself on being rational, objective, and efficient, to a large measure it seems to deny the worth of the personal, subjective experience of real people. Second, the new technology and alternative schools feel themselves responsible and responsive to the community it serves and not only to some people or positions further up on the hierarchy.

Where this battle often gets fought in alternative schools is in evaluation. Much as been written about the highly explosive political nature of evaluating schools. It is our opinion that the process becomes even more controversial when evaluating alternative schools is the issue. Alternative schools may have to prove the worth of their programs, often before they are even off the drawing boards. Standards used to judge other schools or measurement techniques applicable to other programs may be insisted on, thus forcing the school into becoming more traditional or appearing a failure. A negative evaluation does not seem to mean that the School Board will vote to close the traditional school; but unfortunately, any negative evaluation may signal the end of the alternative program.

The political reality is, of course, that any new kid on the block will have to prove himself/herself. The irony is that the potential benefits of evaluation of alternative schools—program growth and continued dynamism, responsible study of the innovation, and ongoing communication of the nature of that innovation to the larger system—are often obscured by the politics of the process.

For most of this paper, the exception being Section 3.0, we are taking the political realities of the process for granted and do not focus directly on them. Hopefully, the preceeding discussion will serve to emphasize to you just how important we think they are; and we hope that you will keep the specifics of your own situation in mind as you design and conduct the evaluation of your program.

1.4 Bibliography and Resource Catalogue

This article can really be no more than an introduction to the evaluation process. Both an annotated bibliography and a catalogue of evaluations done by alternative schools that are available through the National Alternative Schools Program go into more theoretical depth and provide more specific examples than we can here. These may be obtained by writing to:

> The National Alternative Schools Program
> School of Education
> University of Massachusetts
> Amherst, Massachusetts 01002

2.0 Establishing a Purpose

2.1 Possible Purposes

Your evaluation may be system-wise, or it may focus on a particular school or program or on a subgroup within a group within a program, it may be concerned with the performance of individual teachers or students, or with input other members of the community have made. However, regardless of the particular level or constituency that is the *subject* of your evaluation, it can serve a number of possible purposes. Here are some examples of purposes; they are not necessarily mutually exclusive:

● to provide you with an overview of what is going on in your school or system.

- to provide information that will contribute to better understanding within the staff about what each is doing.
- to improve staff morale by helping to discriminate successes and to put hassles in proper perspective.
- to improve public relations by providing an organized information base which can be easily made available to "outsiders."
- to provide direction for program or individual improvement by discriminating continuing problems.
- to provide data on which fiscal decisions can be based.
- to establish a probable cause-and-effect relationship between programs and outcomes.
- to provide research data for projects involving other schools or systems.

The very fact that you are taking the initiative in this evaluation gives it a certain thrust and puts certain parameters on it, and the individuals you identify to help you in this process will, by their very presence, establish further limitations and directions for possible outcomes. Such successive "prenatal" developments in establishing a purpose for your evaluation are not something to be avoided, but it is important to be aware of their influence. In our minds, there is no such thing as a completely unbiased evaluation, and biases will begin to influence even in your contemplation of purpose.

2.2 Your Audience(s): Who Is the Evaluation For?

In order to help us pinpoint the purpose(s) of a particular evaluation, we have found it useful to start with the question, "Who is the evaluation for?" In our minds, this is readily broken down into two components: Who is asking for the evaluation, and who is going to use it? The answers to these last two questions are sometimes the same, but often those who might make use of the evaluation constitute a larger group than those explicitly asking for it. A superintendent, for example, might initiate an evaluation which he or she expects the staff of a program to use as a basis for improving the program, the School Board to use as part of its rationale for refunding the program, and parents to use as a guide in determining whether they want their children involved in that particular program. In such a case, the superintendent has explicitly asked for the evaluation but there are really four distinct audiences the evaluators have to take into account: the superintendent, the program staff, the School

Board, and the parents of present or potential student participants. We have found that the audiences most common to school-related evaluations are among the following; you may have others.

- the general public.
- parents.
- the local School Board.
- a private, State, or Federal funding agency.
- the central administrators of the system.
- the teaching staff and director of a particular school/program.
- students.
- other schools within or outside the system.
- an education research effort.
- a State or other accreditation agency.

2.3 What Do They Want or Need Information About?

This is a question you should ask about *each* of the audiences you expect will use the evaluation. The distinction between "want" and "need" is important to establish; neither should be neglected. You may determine that each audience has certain issues on their minds, and these issues have to be addressed if they are going to regard the evaluation as being of use to them. There will be, in addition, issues which you or those who commissioned the evaluation believe these audiences *ought* to be informed about. Both are legitimate concerns of any evaluation. How "wants" and "needs" line up will, of course, vary from one situation to the next. What follows are examples of the kinds of issues some of the audiences mentioned above are sometimes interested in. We do not regard this list as being all-inclusive.

Your School Board or outside funding agency:

- How does student achievement in this program compare with student performance elsewhere?
- What are the stated goals for the program and to what extent are they being met?
- What is the cost effectiveness of the program?

The staff of the school or program:

- What are the values that are really operative in this situation?
- What is the relationship of teacher behavior to the philosophy of the program?

- Are the goals of the program valid?
- To what extent are stated goals being met?

An educational research effort:

- What is happening in the program?
- To what extent is what exists a result of conscious input or design rather than something else?
- Are the goals of the program valid?
- To what extent are stated goals being met?

Parents:

- How does student achievement in this program compare with student performance elsewhere?
- How accurate are communications about this program?
- What is my child learning in this school?
- To what extent are the stated goals being met?

2.4 Prioritizing Purposes

Having generated a list of possible audiences and a list of the major concerns of each audience, you should then prioritize each of the above; i.e., the audiences should be ordered in terms of their importance to you and their concerns should be ordered in terms of their gravity and potential impact on the audience. This step is necessary because there are invariably constraints on evaluation: constraints of time, money, personnel, politics. With such constraints, you will have to make some decisions about limiting the audiences or issues dealt with. The prioritization indicated above provides guidelines for making such decisions.

At this stage in the development of an evaluation, we have found it useful to examine the values evident in the way we are initially inclined to prioritize audiences and concerns. The people you choose to address and the concerns you choose to examine say something very significant about your own values and priorities, and we feel it is important for you to be aware of this and to check to insure that the values you advertise in this way are those you want to advertise. A "values-check" of this sort also gives the evaluation planners as a group (assuming you have formed a group by this time) a better understanding of where each member of the group is coming from on questions of values. Clarifying these differences at this stage in the process will enable you to insure that your evaluation design accommodates them and to understand how they influence the complex processes of data collection and analysis.

3.0 Constraints

The best of all possible worlds might have an alternative school existing in a community that was wholeheartedly committed to the school's continued existence, that had more than enough money set aside for a thorough evaluation of the school, where there were people from a variety of constituencies who had a variety of expertise and evaluation experience interested in becoming involved in the evaluation process, and where there were no deadline that had to be met for the evaluation study. To date, we are not aware of any alternative school faced with evaluation that hasn't also been faced with political, time, money, and human resource constraints on the process. Because the evaluation will be limited, even shaped, by these constraints, it is important to understand them early in the process. The amount of time and energy available will determine just how thoroughly you will be able to study different aspects of the program. Political constraints may already have been a major factor in your prioritization of the purposes of the study. The following subsections present an elaboration of the constraints we have mentioned briefly here.

3.1 Political Constraints

There may be union objections to your school personnel policy. Alternative schools often use volunteers, practice teachers, community members, or union members who volunteer their time to teach. Unions may see these practices, and other non-traditional teacher-student interactions, as both threatening to the way their constituency operates and contrary to contractual agreement. A complicating feature of this constraint may be that the alternative school may find itself in the middle of a union-management struggle with each trying to use the school as a political weapon against the other.

State or school district policies may place additional constraints on the program. For example, if your alternative school is in a state that has mandated evaluation or accountability procedures, is your evaluation complying with the legislation, and what are the implications for the kind of information your evaluation has to supply or the kind of instrumentation you have to use to get that information? An example of district policy which may influence the evaluation study is the existence of a district commitment to individualized reading and math programs for students with specified sets of behavioral objectives for each grade level. The district may have a series of tests developed to measure student achievement for these objectives and may insist that the tests be a major part of your study.

The formation of the program and its history may have created factions within the community that are either opposed to or in favor of your program. For example, some people may be concerned about the amount of money that is siphoned off the regular program into yours, some angry about an elementary school that was closed in their neighborhood to make room for your program, others pleased that their children are in a program that they like and that gives them so much attention. If there has been a good deal of resistance to the school that resistance is often intensified rather than diffused during the formative months of the program, and evaluation may be seen as a way to crush the program by your opponents.

One other important issue to keep in mind here is the composition of the school board. It may change its political or philosophical nature between the time the program starts and the time the evaluation is planned for. There are examples of alternative schools that have been established by a close vote (3-2) of a school board that subsequently have been closed or put under pressure because new people have been elected to the board who disagreed with the philosophy of the program (often running on a platform of opposition to the alternative program).

Who do you consider to be the primary audience of the evaluation, what use they want to make of the study, and what use you want them to make of the study? Suppose you consider the central administration as the primary audience because you want them to use the evaluation to speak in your behalf for the continuation of the program. They may be primarily interested in controlling the system and maintaining rapport with the school board and want to use the evaluation as a means of establishing further control and cementing their position with the board. Thus the base of support you think you establish by providing the administration with information is illusory and will disappear as soon as the administration feels that supporting you is either no longer useful or potentially harmful to its relation with the board.

Finally, the necessity of providing information to your funding source will be important in determining who is your primary audience. There have been a variety of funding arrangements for alternative schools which may provide different political constraints on the evaluation study:

● local school district provides funds and the school must compete for funds with other schools or districts.

● local school district provides funds but your program receives additional funding from outside sources. This funding may make it seem elitist or favored and lead people to interpret a positive evaluation as natural, given "all the money it gets."

● the program has been funded by Title III which calls for a gradual phase-in into the local education system. Although your existence may be assured for three years, you will be gradually more accountable to the local district and more dependent upon it for existence.

● the program is privately funded. Here, too, your existence may be assured by funding outside the system. However, private funds will not continue to support an individual school indefinitely and your primary long-range audience may be the local district school board and administration.

3.2 People Constraints

Who has the time and skills to plan the evaluation study, collect and analyze data, and organize and disseminate the results? This question overlaps with who is to be involved and political constraints. For example, it may be unwise to use a heavy component of people involved in the program (staff and students) in the gathering of data if the school board is worried about the rigor of the program and the objectivity of the study. Here are four other questions which will have to be answered as you begin the process:

● Are the people available who can train others in the issues and techniques involved in evaluation studies?

● How much time, energy, and willingness do the subjects have to devote to giving data? You probably will design instruments that will disrupt people's normal schedules by requiring that they be interviewed, fill out questionnaires, take tests, attend extra meetings, or search through records to get information that you want. For example, how much time can you ask a staff member to devote to pro-

viding you with absentee records or figuring the percentage gain of students in reading tests?
● Are you asking for information that is available?

3.3 Money Constraints

Not only do you have to be clear how much money there is to spend, but if paid district staff, district supplies, or facilities are going to be used, you should be clear as to how much this "hidden" cost amounts to and its potential effect on services the program or district normally provides. Clarity about resources, as well as the priorities of the study, will help you allocate these resources to various materials or services, examples of which we listed below:

● visual documentation-money for films, tapes, etc.
● standardized tests
● clerical help
● format of the report
● outside consultant
● substitute time for staff
● supplies

3.4 Time Constraints

Different audiences may need different information at different times. The school board may need a preliminary report in February at it is making up the budget, but insist on a complete, summative report at a later date to help its long-range decision to continue the program after its trial period is up.

How much time between now and then—any particular due date for any report—is available to prepare the report? This task will include evaluation design, data collection and analysis, and preparation of the report. It is important to consider the time demands of each of these particular components in addition to the overall amount of time available. For example, you may decide that you want to develop your own instrumentation, but have to balance that expense of time against what would be saved for use elsewhere if you used already developed instrumentation. This instrumentation might not be as sensitive to your program as instrumentation you would develop but may be necessary given limitations of time.

4.0 Goals

4.1 Goal-based or Goal-free Evaluation

Most evaluations are goal-based. By this, we mean that the study is usually concerned with how well the school is achieving the goals and objectives it established for itself in the proposal or that have evolved from the interaction of the operation of the program with the originally established goals. However, some evaluation theorists, notably Michael Scriven, have advocated the concept of goal-free evaluation. This phrase refers to a process in which a person or group of people are asked to look at a program without prior knowledge of the goals and objectives, of what the people in the program are trying to accomplish.

4.2 Goal-based Evaluation

There are a variety of issues that should be considered in any goal-based evaluation. One of the first is the question of where these goals have come from. Depending upon the nature of the proposal for establishing your program, much of the work in goal-setting or deciding what it is you are looking for may already be done. In addition some proposals have evaluation components built into them which clearly establish which of the stated program goals or objectives will be looked at and the instrumentation that will be used in the study. In a great many instances, however, you will not be as locked in by your proposal. Even though you have stated goals and objectives, here are some ways that you might consider building flexibility into your evaluation:

● by choosing which of the stated goals and objectives you will study, given your constraints

● by choosing at what level of specificity you will look at your goals and objectives

● by working some flexibility into your original goals and objectives. One of the designs we have used is one in which we informally visit the school for the first year to see how the operation of the program has operationalized the goals it set for itself. The number, duration, and frequency of these visits should be determined by time and money constraints and kept to a level that maintains the informal tone of the procedure. This first stage of evaluation is informal and emphasizes the fact that any proposal cannot foresee all of the natural consequences that will happen as a program begins and grows through the first few months. As a result of this first stage of evaluation, a more formal second stage of evaluation is set up that is based upon a set of goals and objectives that are the result of the interaction of the actual program with the proposal.

In the previous paragraph, we mentioned the level of specificity of goals and objectives. People define these words differently and often refer to any of the sentences on the following two lists as a goal or an objective:

American schools should be a place where economic inequality is addressed	American schools should be a place where children learn self-respect
Program X is concerned with the level of student reading	Program X is concerned with the self-concept of students
Program X will work to improve student achievement in the area of reading	Program X will work to enhance its students' self-concept
Program X will improve student's ability to translate an abstraction, such as a general principle, by giving an example or illustration	Program X will improve the student attendance record at school (as it is an indicator or self-concept)
Program X students will be able to perform at least grade level on the Watson-Glaser Critical Thinking Appraisal: Test 4 by June of their second year in the program	Program X students' absentee rate will be equal to or lower than students' absentee rate at the district high school

These two sets of goals get progressively more specific. Whatever level you choose to operate on (you may have no choice) will be a determining factor in your choice of instrumentation, data collection, and analysis.

There is a good deal of politics that surrounds who sets the goals and what the goals look like. Your program can be controlled by others if they can influence either the degree of specificity of the goals or what outcomes the program should focus upon (as evidenced by the goals and objectives). Political realities or the funding situation may have made it difficult for you to have written program goals the way you wanted. In addition, you may not have been in on the process.

Goals that are stated as behavioral objectives may be an element of control and devitalization in your program. Control, in that you may feel forced to organize your program so that your evaluation shows you have lived up to them. Devitalization, in that you may find the school community focused systematically and unimaginatively on the step by step acquisition of these objectives with a minimal capacity for spontaneity and for making good use of the unexpected. Too heavy emphasis on goals and whether students are achieving them may interfere with your ability to see the side effects of your program, things that are happening that you hadn't expected or planned for.

However, there is a different kind of control that can be exercised in the goals that are more fuzzy. The lack of clarity may not allow you ever to convince your detractors that you are doing a good job and are not one of "those romantic do-gooders" who has no sense of reality.

In addition to the element of control that is inherent in focusing too intensively on goals in evaluation, such a focus can lead to simplistic conclusions that more often than not prove harmful to innovative programs. For example, if one of your goals is to improve student reading ability and your students score better than grade level in a test, you may be able to say that your program caused that positive outcome. However, if your students scored either about grade level or below, your program may be judged a failure or not worth the extra effort and/or money merely to produce the same scores the regular school did. The fallacy behind all the statements is the assumption that the program *caused* the scores. This may be true, but without any look at the process (the actual program and what went on) or some sort of attempt at a controlled experiment, it is merely speculation. Even when you conduct a goal-based evaluation, it is very important to study the nature of the program. Without it, your positive results might be due to anything—the expertise of the people who made up your program, the sensitivity of the people who work in it, the maturation of your students, an achievement test that is too easy, etc. Thus, we strongly suggest you consider two things, both of which we will emphasize elsewhere:

- investigate ways your evaluation can look at both process and outcomes
- use more than one instrument to measure outcomes; try not to stand or fall on the results of tests.

Finally, not meeting goals or meeting them may lead to judgments about the program that may not reflect its true worth, the range of unanticipated outcomes, or the quality of various parts of the process. Designing a study that has as its sole criterion of success whether or not the goals have been met may simply make it easier for people to make the judgments about the program they wanted to before the study was begun. Descriptive information about your program included in the study will both make it more difficult for others to exercise their own biases and make your own conclusions more substantial.

We do not mean to imply that goals are unimportant and should not be used in your study. However, an over-dependence upon them can trap your evaluation in too narrow an analysis of outcomes and the program itself in a pattern of behavior which doesn't allow for change and growth.

4.3 Goal-free Evaluation

Up to this point, we have discussed the problems that surround goal-based evaluation. Michael Scriven has coined the phrase "goal-free" evaluation for a process that presents an alternative to goal-based evaluation. Here, an evaluator deliberately avoids becoming familiar with the intentions of the program planners and looks directly at the program and the people in it. Knowing what is supposed to happen can only prejudice him/her from being able to judge the quality of what is happening. Knowing intentions may keep him/her from seeing unanticipated results.

It may be difficult for you to evaluate your program completely using the goal-free technique. People will want to know how well you are doing in relation to the goals and objectives that were established at the beginning of the program. However, it does have some advantages:

- it provides an independent point of view, inductively arrived at, by noninvolved observers
- it surfaces program effects that are not necessarily related to goals
- it has the effect of focusing upon process rather than outcome
- it may educate people about a more balanced, less restrictive use of program goals in the evaluation process

We see goal-free evaluation being used in two different situations:

- as a part of a goal-based study (despite the seeming contradiction, it is possible for you to stipulate in your evaluation proposal that an outside-consultant will be called in to conduct goal-free visits with his/her reports becoming an integral part of the final report)
- as the first stage of the two stage process that we referred to earlier in 4.2

5.0 Designing the Methodology

Having established your general purposes, identified the major constraints on your evaluation, and determined what it is you want to look at, the next step will be to map out a methodology for collecting the information you want. As has been the case with each of the major steps we have discussed so far, we suggest treating each phase of the process separately, generating a full range of possible responses at each step before you settle on anything. Particularly in instances where your evaluation is concerned with a number of issues, it will be helpful to have a variety of options on hand to deal with each issue.

5.1 Sources of Information

Legitimate sources of information or opinion on any given issue may represent a wide range of constituencies. For example, parents, other community people, program staff, district staff, other schools and/or their students, college records or other "outside" resources such as the Educational Testing Service or an independent observer may all have something unique to say about the reading program at your school.

- The students themselves can provide data about how fast they read, with what degree of comprehension, and at what level of difficulty; how they feel about reading; what they read, and how much they read.
- Program or district staff may have on hand students' scores on standardized reading tests they have taken before, which would give some indication of present or former speed, comprehension, and how they compare with their age group.
- The students, program staff, parents, and perhaps workers in the local public library or in a local book store may have some insight into how your students feel about books and what and how much they read on their own.
- An independent, goal-free evaluator may notice how much reading goes on during unscheduled time or on the variety of reading materials available to your students through the school.
- Staff and students will have information about what goes on in a special reading clinic you might have and how students feel about the teacher and the organization of the clinic.

● The teacher will have some opinions on the way in which other forces at the school impinge on the clinic's operation . . . or promote it.

Which source you choose to address in this kind of situation depends on what precisely you want to look at, the resources you have available, the politics of the situation, and your general purposes and audiences.

An important consideration is whether or not some of the sources who have the information you want will share it with you. You may, for example, wish to compare reading test scores of your students with those of another school in the district, but the other school may be unwilling to be singled out in that way and may have the political leverage to thwart you. In another situation, a source of information may simply feel "over evaluated" and refuse to become involved further: this often happens in situations where one source (students, for example) are hit at the same time with a variety of instruments relating to a variety of issues.

We also feel it is important to consider the effect of your merely asking any of these sources for the information you are looking for. It is possible (continuing with the reading clinic example) to undermine the progress of the clinic in helping students to feel comfortable with books by prematurely imposing a test of grade-level achievement on the students of the clinic. What they have come to regard as a privileged and pleasant activity may suddenly be cast as the same monster (a test-to-prove-I-am-dumb) that has been hounding them for years. It is equally possible for the recognition provided by an interview with the organizer of the clinic or observation of the clinic in operation may be just the boost a worthy, but uncertain, teacher needs in the way of reinforcement or of help in clarifying how much has been accomplished and what needs to be done. We do not advise a rigid set of "do's" and "don'ts" in this regard; however, we encourage you to consider the likely consequences before you determine which sources of information to approach with what kind of instrument.

In any case, our experience indicates that it is usually helpful to have more than one source of information on each issue. Additional sources may enable you to corroborate the impressions of your first source; they often help to identify more precisely strengths or possible problem areas (much like additional coordination in a mapping problem); and they sometimes make your conclusions more marketable to a skeptical audience. They are helpful even in situations where the conclusions you draw from one source contradict those of another: the contradiction may indicate shortcomings in either the instruments or the data collection process.

5.2 Choosing and Developing Instruments

As with everything else viewed in the abstract, there is a wide variety of possible instruments to consider for each situation. Certain purposes and certain audiences may combine to limit you to one category of instrumentation or another. To continue with the example of the reading clinic introduced above, your students' parents may be your principal audience, and the vast majority may be interested solely in how their children perform as compared to those in the school their children would have attended if they had not had your alternative. The parents may be suspicious of your school's pretentions and philosophy and may be likely to "buy" only data derived from comparative, so-called "objective" measures; that is, measures which produce information which is easily qualifiable and expressed in terms of numbers, percentages, or grade-level equivalents. With such parents as your principal audience, the situation may mandate a standardized test or an attitude questionnaire which is developed and administered by an "impartial" agency.

In many cases, however, you will not be locked in that tightly in advance and will have the options of (*a*) employing commercial or published yardsticks such as standardized tests, questionnaires, observation and interview protocols; (*b*) using yardsticks similar in format to the foregoing but designed particularly for your situation; and/or (*c*) presenting material as non-quantified data such as media documentation, anecdotal records prepared by subjects and/or observers, or a display of the products of the school's activities. With such a full range of options, you will want to consider the advantages and disadvantages of each.

The advantage of commercial or published measures is largely convenience: they have already been field-tested and there is almost invariably a substantial data base against which you can juxtapose the results derived from your program. In many instances, the agency that has produced the measure will tabulate the results for you. The main disadvantage is that because such measures are designed for wide distribution, they very often do not measure the nuances of your particular situation that you are most interested in assessing. There is often a fee connected with their use, too.

For examples and indices of the commercial measures and published protocols available to you, we refer you to the National Alternative Schools Program's annotated bibliography.

It is worth noting that the intrinsic value of commercial or published instruments is frequently overrated by professionals as well as lay people, and evaluators often feel some pressure to employ such instruments because of this rating. However, you should be aware that there are a substantial number of well-documented, scholarly studies which can be called on for support if you choose to resist political pressure to employ standardized scales in your evaluation. For example, a report of a joint effort of the Center for the Study of Evaluation (UCLA) and Research for Better Schools, Inc., pursuant to contracts with the U.S. Office of Education (1972) includes the results of an evaluation of about 2,600 scales and subscales in the Higher-Order Cognitive, Affective, and Interpersonal domains. It reads in part:

The quality of the instruments, as expressed by their VENTURE evaluations, is predominantly poor to fair. . . . The average ratings for Validity, Normed Excellence, Teaching Feedback, and Retest potential are uniformly poor, while the ratings for Examinee Appropriateness and Usability are predominately fair, with good ratings on these two criteria occurring most frequently in the Interpersonal domain and less frequently in the Higher-Order Cognitive domain. In short, much work remains to be done, both in developing, instruments where none now exist, and in improving the quality of these instruments which have already been developed.

Original tests and questionnaires and your own observation and interview protocols are not intrinsically "better" than commercial fare, but they are not particularly difficult to design either, and are often more to the point of your special concerns. However, they take time and energy to develop, and need to be carefully field-tested.

If you have not had much experience with evaluation, the prospect of designing your own instruments and protocols may appear to be a large task. Your first glance at the literature is likely to turn up an enormous range of possible formats for questionnaires, tests, observations, interviews, and for presenting non-qualified data, each of which has its own claim to potential validity and reliability. To discuss the particular advantages and disadvantages of each format is beyond the scope of this paper. As long as you take care to describe accurately any instrument or protocol you use, how it was developed and field-tested—in short, as long as you do not represent it as being more than it is—we do not think you can go very far wrong.

In the absence of a clear sense on your part of where to begin in developing an instrument or protocol of your own, we suggest the following general procedure:

- Identify what information you want
- Identify who has it
- Make your own best guess as to how the information can effectively be obtained from them. The most common options are:
  - (a) by direct questioning where there are no "right" answers (an questionaire, interview, or attitude test);
  - (b) by direct questioning in which there are "right" answers (an achievement test)
  - (c) by observation of activities (these may be activities especially designed for the evaluation or they may be activities that those you will observe are ordinarily involved in);
  - (d) by an examination of the products of activities.
- Find a general model or models (from sources identified in the appended bibliography, if you have no others in mind) which, in your best judgment, you understand and feel you can adapt to your purposes;
- Develop a draft instrument or protocol which seems to get at the specific issues you want to deal with, using whatever form you have chosen for a general guide;
- Field-test your instrument or protocol, and modify as necessary.

Field testing is important when using original instruments and procedures, and is sometimes necessary even with established protocols: a field test is a dry run not only for the questions in your instrument but also for your presentation of those questions and the means you use for recording answers. Interviews, for example, whether they are of your own or someone else's design, should be practiced. In our work together we usually first role-play an interview we are planning to conduct—one of us playing the interviewer and the other playing a "difficult" respondent. This helps us to determine whether the questions as designed are clear, whether the order makes sense, and how much time we need to allocate for the interview. It also gives us an opportunity to try several approaches to questions and various ways of recording responses. But even such role-playing must be regarded as only the first part of the field test. In our own situation, one of us usually follows up on the role-playing by conducting the interview with several real respondents while the other observes. This second phase of the field test allows for further refinement of the interview procedures and an opportunity to develop a recording procedure which will make our notes easily understandable to each other when we are ready to pull our data together. It is only after this second step that we separate and proceed with interviews independent of a monitor.

Likewise, observation protocols need to be checked first by a team observing in the same situation. Do several people observing the same situation and following the same set of guidelines come up with similar pictures of the situation in question? In unstructured observation, of course, these issues are not as significant because the observers may be looking at different aspects of the situation. However, even with unstructured observation, we have found it useful to compare notes, if only to establish some sense of what may be useful to look at.

Questionnaires and tests should be tried out on a sample of real subjects to determine if the directions and questions are clear and the optional answers, if they are spelled out, are seen as real options.

Non-quantified data (e.g. photographs of activities, anecdotal records, product displays) constitute the third general category of "instruments" which we have mentioned above. Through such means it is possible to reflect the quality of an environment in a way that t-scores and tabulated questionnaire responses cannot match. Such data are generally presented without extensive comment, and the evaluator's "statement" grows from his/her selection of material and their juxtaposition. The main disadvantage is that such data are often difficult or expensive to reproduce for wide circulation. Alas, some audiences are inclined to regard "non-objective" data as being unworthy of a rigorous evaluation. We do not agree, but we do not advise speaking to your audience in a language they will not comprehend.

At the beginning of this section on methodology, we suggested that you seek information on each issue from more than one source. Among other advantages, this enables you to corroborate the conclusions you arrived at from your first source. We also feel it is important to collect data through more than one type of instrument. This provides a different kind of check on the reliability of your data and sometimes allows you to appeal directly to audiences with different prejudices about evaluation methodology with the same evaluation.

One final note on instruments: the determination to use certain instruments never precludes your noting "incidental fallout" which comes to your attention during the process of collecting data but which is not directly related to the instruments or issues in question at the time. "Incidental fallout" in this case means observations not directly a part of your formal evaluation strategy; it does not necessarily mean observations that are unimportant to your program. These observations can provide important reinforcement for other conclusions, as well as underscore successes and/or problems that your planned instruments do not get at.

5.3 Who Should Be Involved and At What Point?

The question of who should be involved is germane not only to the design of the methodology but also to a number of other steps in the development of an evaluation. Establishing a purpose, identifying constraints, and determining what specifically to look at are all steps in which people besides yourself can be effectively involved. But it is during the design of the methodology and the data collection that the implications of who is actively involved in the process begins to be felt. (We are speaking now of who is involved in the development of the evaluation rather than those involved merely as sources of information.)

The implications are often political, to a large extent. You must consider whether or not your audiences will question the validity of so-called "non-objective" data collected by insiders and, if so, to what extent might this hinder your credibility or the use to which you plan to put the evaluation. You should also weigh the probable impact an "outside" evaluation might have on staff and students in your school or program: if they feel undermined by the whole process, then they might effectively boycott it and thwart whatever benefit you hope will accrue from the process. Because alternative schools and programs are often politically "hot" issues, such uncompromising reactions need to be *considered,* even if in the end you determine that the political climate will accommodate an evaluation effort that is planned and/or executed with conspicuous "inside" or "outside" control.

Another consideration in the question of "outside" participation in the evaluation is directly rooted in the purposes of the evaluation. If you have determined that it is important to have a goal-free evaluation, it will necessarily be conducted by someone or a group unfamiliar with the school's specific purposes and programs. In this kind of situation, the evaluator's task is to describe what they see happening at the school, without reference to what has been singled out by you or your staff. The advantage of this approach is that very often unanticipated benefits as well as consequences are observed when the observers are not initially blinkered and obliged to focus on what you or the staff think is supposed to be happening.

We also recommend that you take into account the training possibilities an evaluation effort represents. You might wish to take advantage of the opportunity by involving a cross-section or one or more of the different constituencies related to your school community. In one school we have worked with as outside consultants, we designed the overall methodology in consultation with the staff as well as most of the instruments we needed to complete the evaluation. However, one component of the evaluation (which involved designing an interview protocol or questionnaire for parents, field testing it, collecting and analyzing data) was the responsibility of a committee of two parents, two students, and one staff member, whom we were available to help as needed. Given the time press, this one instrument or component was all they felt they could handle during this particular formal evaluation effort, but this group came to form the nucleus of an on-going evaluation team for the school. Given enough time and other resources, the role of such a committee could well have been expanded to include more or even all of the design and implementation of the methodology.

From our experience, we have identified three general categories of potential evaluators whom you might draw on:

- "Insiders" directly connected with your school or program (the staff, students, perhaps parents).
- "Outsiders" indirectly connected with the school (parents, community or board members, district staff members, representatives of a state or regional education bureau).
- "Outsiders" not connected with your school (people associated with an alternative school in another district, college or university-based personnel, other consultants).

All might be useful and all should be considered. Your choice will, of course, depend on who is available and what you want to accomplish.

5.4 A Final Note About "Outside" People

We would like to emphasize one final thing here. As a director, you will probably be the initial contact for any outside evaluators that you use in your evaluation. Time and again the whole process of entry is emphasized as crucial in the outsider's ability to achieve an effective level of acceptance. Thus, your introduction of the process, of the outside people to the school community becomes very important. Here are some things to keep in mind:

- Be clear with the outside people just what is expected, what their roles will be, what is expected of the school, etc.
- Be sure that whatever introduction to the school that is agreed upon (introductions to key people, a simple announcement, a general introduction at an all school meeting) is done through you.
- Follow-up to see that the entry procedures you have agreed upon are happening and that undue resistance has not occurred.

5.5 Timing

When developing your own instruments and protocols you should keep in mind the general rule that the more time you invest in their design and refinement, the less time is required for actual data collection and analysis. An open-ended interview, for example, takes relatively less time to develop than a questionnaire with multiple-choice responses, but the responses to the interview will take much more time to collect and codify.

There are two other dimensions to the time issue. First, there is the question of how much time the methodology design and data collection itself will consume; second, there is the question of when the data collection takes place in the history of your school. If the evaluation is goal-based, i.e., if it is designed to determine to what extent the school has achieved goals set of it, you will need to take into account the amount of time that has passed since the beginning of the program or since the last evaluation. Has enough time lapsed to expect change and to justify attributing it to the influence of the school or program? Also, is there enough data available regarding where things stood at the beginning to make a pre/post comparison? If not, you might want to build that into your timetable.

As a general rule, we recommend small-scale, formative evaluations that occur at regular intervals throughout the school year. Each does not necessarily deal with the same issues, although over time any given issue should be addressed more than once. There are two advantages to this kind of pattern: it makes evaluation a regular event rather than an isolated experience, and it precludes your school community's being overwhelmed by demands for a lot of data at any one time.

5.6 Communicating the Evaluation Design

This is the final but equally necessary step in the designing of an evaluation methodology. In essence, it involves asking those who have participated in the design as well as those who are going to make use of it to review your design systematically. Have you focused where you wanted to focus? Has anything important been left out? Most evaluation designs will be less complete than you would like them to be, but, even given the constraints discussed above, it should touch the bases you want touched.

In addition to testing for completeness, you will want to test for clarity. Do people perceive that the pieces fall together sensibly? Do they understand it to be a responsible evaluation? If not, it may be too haphazard ... or it may be inadequately described: in either case, now is the time to work this through.

We have found that charting the overall evaluation design not only helps you to communicate your plan clearly to others but also serves as a valuable tool in your test for completeness. We have included two sample charts on the following pages. The first is more informal, but both will help you get a picture of the entire process.

Goal Area/Objective		Paper/Pencil	Observation	Interview/ Questionnaire	Unobtrusive documentation	Logs/other documents
Instrumentation	1					
Sampling	2					
Data acquisition	3					
Data analysis	4					

6.0 Data Collection

6.1 Are the Conditions Right/Conductive for Data Collection?

Data collection techniques depend to a large extent upon the specific instrumentation you choose for the study and the nature of the setting and subjects. For example, if you choose to administer a standardized test, then the manual for the test will have a set of directions which usually include the amount of time allowed, the directions to give students, and the way in which the test should be monitored. If you design an interview,

Performance Objective	Measurement Instruments			Data Collection Procedures				Data Analysis Presentation				Dissemination of Evaluation Results for Overall Projects
	Name/Type of Instrument	Data Instrument to be completed	Baseline Data	Target Group	Scheduled Date(s)	Person Responsible	Data Analysis Techniques	Evaluator's Report Date	Person Responsible	Method	Schedule	Recipient Audiences
1	2	3	4	5	6	7	8	9	10	11	12	13

256

you may want to specify the conditions under which the interview is conducted so that you can have some confidence in the consistency of your results. (It is just as important to maintain these conditions as it is to specify them.) For example, we designed a structured mini-interview for all 50 students in a school which required them to reflect on their experience. Our conditions were that we would individually sit down with one student during the student's free time in a quiet place in the school. On the one occasion, one of us tried to hold the interview in the office at the beginning of school when people were moving in and out; the student could not focus on the questions. In retrospect, we recognized how these conditions had markedly influenced the student and felt that we had to discount the interview.

The nature of your setting should also be considered in data collection. A question like, "When should data be collected?" is an issue which will depend upon the established rhythms of your school. Here are some possible questions, which reflect conditions that may influence the information you get:

- Does the mood of your school and the expectations of your students depend upon where you are in a semester (learning cycle)?
- Is your schedule significantly different at different times of the day? Are different students in school at different times?
- Are the semesters (learning cycles) all fairly similar, or are they different in style and content?
- Do you see the school cycling through a phase where there is a strong sense of community and feeling of excitement? Has the school recently undergone an interpersonal crisis?

Even the data you get from standardized tests with their very specific directions will reflect the conditions under which they are collected.

Where the data are collected will also influence the results. Once again, if you choose to interview students, there is a range of possibilities— at home, on site at some kind of field experience, in an office unfamiliar to the student, or at the school. The last option once again breaks down into a series of possibilities which depend upon your building and how people use it. For example, there may be established territories for students and teachers. The function of some places or their size or mood may interfere with the process of interviewing.

Finally, it is important to consider who gathers the data—both in terms of how the subject will respond and how your audiences will treat the validity of the information. For example, you may have to balance the possible strengths and weaknesses of using inside people (staff, parents, students) or outside people in interviewing students. Will the inside people be too familiar with the subjects or will some of the staff be too scary for some of the students? On the other hand, will the outside people generate too much hostility and defensiveness or will lack of familiarity with the program lead them to represent fact and fiction equally? If you decide to use students as interviewers and observers, there will be some people who will impugn the validity of the information, despite the fact that these detractors would be guilty of as much or more bias if only of a different kind.

We have used the interview as the major example in this section on conditions. However, we feel that a set of roughly similar questions exist to be considered for any data collection techniques. The point we want to emphasize is that you should keep them in mind and answer them in light of the specifics of your program as you begin the process of data collection.

6.2 *Are the Conditions Stable or Changing?*

In a sense, this question is rhetorical because your school is not a laboratory and always changes. The issue then becomes to determine how much the process of data collection is responsible for that change. A great deal of writing about evaluation and research emphasizes the "obtrusiveness" of various instrumentation and its possible effect on the subjects (the extent to which an instrument or data collection procedure interferes with the natural process of events in a setting). Two common ones are the practice effect of a pre-test which will influence the results on future post-tests and what we will call the focus effect of a question which alerts the subject to the fact that you are paying attention to his/her behavior or attitude in a particular area. A commonly held opinion is that instrumentation and data collection should be as "unobstrusive" as possible, and we agree with this opinion. However, we also feel that you should not approach the process of data collection with the expectations that your evaluation can be completely unobtrusive. It might be possible to design a methodology of "document search" (reading records that already exist or accumulate naturally in the life of the program) or "trace analysis" (studying the changes in the setting without the subjects being aware you are doing it, i.e., counting the cigarette butts in different parts of the building to determine where people felt comfortable or noting the amount of vandalism that occurs in a building over a period of time). However, if you plan to really look at your program, then you have already chosen instrumentation that will get you into much more direct interaction with the program than document search and trace analysis can ever do. Evaluation of social setting is much different than evaluation in medical situation. It is interactive, two-way, and the issue becomes being aware of the ways in which your data collection is obtrusive in some way, working to minimize the obstrusiveness, and being honest about it when you analyze and report data later in the process.

6.3 Debriefing Procedures

The classical way of discovering how reactive (the degree to which you and data-collection techniques influence your results) your methodology is and minimizing it is to employ a true evaluation design—randomization, control groups, and statistical procedures. However, for a variety of reasons listed below, you may decide not to use this technique:

- you may feel that your program cannot be organized or managed in a way that would allow it to fulfill the conditions necessary for the design.
- you may feel that your program is philosophically or politically opposed to such a design.
- constraints of one kind or another may make it difficult or impossible for you to fulfill the design.
- your choice of instrumentation and the number of people involved in data collection may make it important for you to get more immediate information about the data-collection process than is available through the experiment design. This is especially true when a number and variety of people are interacting with the program as they gather data (observation and interview, for example).

We strongly recommend some sort of debriefing procedures be built into the collection process, especially if you are not using a "true" experimental design and if you are using the kinds of instrumentation mentioned above. By debriefing, we mean some sort of procedure which enables you and the data collectors to focus on the data-collection process —the role played in it, how the subjects reacted, the effect of the instrument, and how their feelings may have influenced the data they collected. In the absence of true experimental design, debriefing becomes an important part of a responsible, reflective approach to evaluation which enables you to both regularize your methodology and present your findings with a sense of perspective and confidence. We have used all the following debriefing techniques in varying combinations:

- begin the data collection in pairs or groups and have these pairs or groups compare their behavior and their observations and tentative conclusions.
- schedule regular meetings of data collectors to exchange their experience of the process.
- design a form for the data-collectors to fill out or have some other way for them to maintain a written record of the process.
- design some way to get feedback from the subjects on the process. (This may be tricky in that involving subjects in a formalized way here may make the collection process even more reactive than it already is. Perhaps trying to become informally more sensitive to the subjects' responses may be the more effective thing to do.

6.4   Mid-Stream Corrections

Debriefing procedures will hopefully highlight not only the ways in which the data collectors and instruments are impacting on the system, but also some emerging data which may or may not look like the results you anticipated. You may decide that mid-stream corrections in either the instrumentation or the data collection (the people or the process) are advisable as a result of the debriefing. Here are some things to consider in deciding whether to make some changes or not.

If the data-collectors become too involved in the program or are misusing the instrumentation, it is clear that more training or different people are needed. For example, if you have designed an observation protocol to measure the amount and kind of student response in a classroom and some of the observers are consistently at variance with the rest of the team because they do not fill in the protocol at the correct intervals or confuse the different response categories, then additional training or dialogue is necessary. Another solution to this problem is to modify the instrument.

You may also find that, despite field testing, the instrument, or specific parts of it, has proven inadequate:

- It may be vague and provide information that really isn't useful for people. For example, an observation protocol may be designed to catalogue the kinds of verbal responses between a teacher and students at given intervals; but several of the classes observed are laboratories where the students work primarily on their own and the bulk of the interaction is quiet conversation between the teacher and individual students.

- It may be vague and provide information that really isn't useful for people. For example, a question on an interview that elicits student opinion about your program might provide an overwhelmingly positive response. Without some elaboration—some qualification, some specific reasons—the data really won't be useful to you for planning purposes, and may appear either sloppy or misleading to your detractors.
- It may ask for information your subjects can't provide.
- It may either take more time or be more complicated to use than you anticipated.

For all these instances, it is a relatively easy decision to make either to modify the instrumentation, or to eliminate it from the overall design. However, we have found other instances, specifically in the nature of the emerging data, where it may not be advisable to make mid-stream corrections:

- The first occurs if you notice an unusual pattern of responses. While it is possible that this unusual pattern might be attributable to some of the causes mentioned above, it is also possible that you may be getting some valuable "fall-out." By fall-out, we mean that the instrument and collection process may be surfacing unanticipated outcomes of the program or may be measuring characteristics of your program other than (or in addition to) the ones it was designed to assess.
- In addition, and this may be true especially where you are interviewing or observing, there may be a natural selection process at work which will influence the order in which you get your data. For example, we were interviewing all the students in a small school over the period of two months. Toward the end of the process, we began to get our first negative opinions of the school. One conclusion might have been that student attitude was changing. As we looked more closely at the phenomenon, we realized that our casual (by design) approach to students had made it probable that we would get to interview the most visible, active, and positive students first.

6.5 Preliminary Negative Data, Some Political Implications

What happens if preliminary data seems to be presenting a negative picture of an aspect of your program or seems to be presenting evidence contrary to a hypothesis you have advanced? This is a difficult issue, especially if your political situation is problematical in any way—if, for example, the survival of your program depends upon the study. Evaluation has traditionally been an adversary proceeding in education, with those in inferior positions (you, in this case) feeling the need to justify themselves to the others higher up in the structure. Your political environment may be another example of this proceeding. It would be nice to think that the politics of every situation made it possible to use emerging data as process evaluation which you would then be able to feed back into your program in a continuing process of change and growth and to think of evaluation design with that kind of flexibility in mind. However, the best of all possible worlds does not often exist, and you may be faced with this difficulty. One of the ways to protect yourself is to design the overall evaluation so that preliminary data are not published.

7.0   Tabulation and Analysis

Somewhere between the mass of undifferentiated numbers and notes and the final report lies a series of activities which may be a great part of the mystery which surrounds the evaluation process. Numbers, scores, and responses must be tabulated. The results must be analyzed. Finally, conclusions have to be drawn, recommendations made. How do you begin to deal with the mountain of numbers and transform it into data? How do you go about seeing patterns in the data? What confidence can you have in the patterns that you see? How should you state the conclusions you finally made? What are they worth anyway? All are difficult but essential questions to answer.

7.1   Tabulation

There are a variety of ways to begin. You might consider tabulating the scores or responses from one instrument, analyzing the tabulated data, and then moving on to another. You may decide to follow the process of tabulation, analysis, and drawing conclusions/recommendations for all the instruments used to assess a particular program goal and then move on to another goal.

Our own bias is to do all the tabulation first, before we attempt much analysis. This way of organizing the process seems to be more open, an attempt to avoid interpretations of early data biasing our interpretations of subsequent data, especially those for which we are using the techniques of inductive categorization.

7.2 Fail-Safe Tabulation

We strongly recommend that you tabulate in pairs and that the tabulation is double-checked in some way. Here are some fail-safe techniques we have used:

- allow for a lapse of time between tabulation and checking.
- get a third party to double-check your results.
- don't hesitate to follow up any uneasy hunches you have about the tabulation.
- switch operations if you are working in pairs or find some other way of breaking the routine.
- if you think you've made a mistake, do the whole process again. This is especially true for complicated mathematical computation.

7.3 First Things First

Each of the instruments you have used in the study was chosen or designed to look at a particular process, outcome, attitude, etc. It is important that you use the data generated by each instrument for those purposes first. However, we have found that fall-out from the data may often occur if you can look at the data in new ways or if you combine information from two or more data sources. There is no guarantee that either interesting or useful insights into your program will result from this process; but, if nothing else, it will be a double check of your initial processing of the information.

7.4 Statistics and Analysis

Using statistics often persuades people that you are reporting the truth. Arrays of figures, impressive mathematical operations and their equations, and the mathematical certainty of a number probably all contribute to the sense of inadequacy that many people feel in the presence of statistics, which in turn encourages their deference to them. Statistics are really no more than a way of organizing numbers. In your study these numbers will be the result of one or more observations (broadly defined as any way you have looked at or measured your program) of your school. All data are simply that—the record of observation—and *not* the thing or process observed.

We do not mean that hard data which can be quantified in some sort of statistical analysis are no good but that they are only one effective way of looking at those aspects of your program.

Broadly speaking, there are two kinds of statistics—descriptive and inferential. Descriptive statistics are used for describing the characteristics of the sample (population) that was tested. Thus, you would use descriptive statistics to characterize the population of your school—how your students did on a reading test, their self-concept, or their perception of the school environment as measured by a particular scale. Inferential statistics is the process of making educated guesses about a total population based upon the results of your particular sample. For example, if your study compares the changes in reading ability of a selected group of students in your program with a selected sample of students in another school you would be using inferential statistics if you used those results to generalize about all the students in both programs and predict how students in both programs would do next year.

In using statistic, we have found the following helpful to keep in mind:

- if you have used commercial publishers' instruments use their computer programs or tables for converting raw scores into statistical information.
- do not interpret these statistics more specifically or more powerfully than they are designed for. For example, many reading scores are reported in percentile bands rather than points. Do not convert these bands to points even though it may appear to be a simpler form to assimilate or a way to make your program appear more favorable.
- use the right statistics. For example, t-scores are computations used to measure whether there is a significant difference between different test scores; (whether or not a person's reading scores have improved significantly from one test date to another). There are different formulas for t-scores depending upon whether your interest is comparing individuals or groups;—there are reputable methodologies for dealing with soft data, non-quantifiable responses. It is not a good idea to sell your data for what they are not. First, if you do, you leave your report open to damaging questions. Second, you may give the reader the impression that you are defensive about non-quantifiable information, that you think soft data are not really a legitimate way of looking at your program.
- be clear about your use of descriptive and inferential statistics.

Commercially available instruments use inferential statistics in their norms. They have the benefit of continued testing in a variety of settings. It may be wise not to attempt to use inferential statistics, especially if your conclusions may be comparing your school with another one.

7.5 Classification Methodologies for Soft Data

It is important to remember that simply counting responses to a questionnaire and presenting the results is not statistical analysis. This process is a form of classification. For example, if we were assessing student attitudes in a survey we might get the following responses to one question which we classify, according to which school the students attend.

Degree to which students feel they
control what courses they take

	strongly disagree	disagree	agree	strongly agree	no opinion
alternative school students	0	4	16	16	8
high school students	22	6	10	2	10

This question might be one of a series that assesses student attitudes toward their school environment. The classification occurs in the degree to which the students agree with the statement and the school that they attend. However, classification schemes are not always easy. You may have decided to use a self-reporting form, an interview form, or an observation form that is open-ended. Thus, the data will not be in already existing categories that you simply have to tally but will be written statements from people, notes or transcriptions of interviews, or reports of observations. Dealing with this kind of free-form data takes time and energy; and you should keep this in mind as you sort out your priorities.

At the risk of over-simplifying the classification process, we will say that there are basically two ways of proceeding—deductively and inductively. The deductive method occurs when you develop your categories beforehand and then read your data looking for examples of these categories. The inductive method occurs when you read all the responses you have, gradually grouping these responses in increasingly larger pools and increasingly higher levels of abstraction. We have tried to include examples of both these processes in the bibliography.

Which of these methods you choose to use will depend upon your particular situation. Variables such as when in the instrument design, data collection, and analyses processes you have the most time, the experience and expertise of the people to be involved, whether you have definite hypotheses to be looked at or performance objectives to be assessed—all will play into your choice. When you do use one of these soft-data-processing methods, it is very important to be clear, responsible, and "scientific" in showing your particular methodology to others. If the potentially skeptical can see a method, clearly outlined step-by-step, then you increase the chances of "evaluating" the process in their minds to the methodological status of statistics. For those who believe in the worth of non-statistical information, your responsible approach will begin useful dialogue.

We hope that this section has made clear that there are reputable methodologies for dealing with soft data. It is not a good idea to sell your data for what they are not. First, if you do, you leave your report open to damaging questions. Second, you may give the reader the impression that you are defensive about non-statistical information, that you think soft data are not really legitimate to use in looking at your program.

7.6 *Conclusions and Recommendations*

We have found the following things helpful to remember in drawing conclusions and making recommendations:

- do not confuse the process of drawing conclusions with the process of establishing cause and effect relationships between parts of the program and outcomes. Unless you have very clearly set up an experimental design and controlled for variables, direct cause and effect will be hard to prove.
- if you are using correlation equations to measure the relationship of one variable to another, be clear about the surrounding variables that may have influenced your study and be responsible about reporting results.
- However, do not be afraid of juxtaposing outcomes and processes and making conjectures about the characteristics of your program or the part your program has played in student change. It is the degree of absoluteness with which you make your claims, the degree of responsibility with which you look at how you arrived at

these claims, and the amount of descriptive data you marshal in support of these claims that will establish the strength of your conclusions. You can cut down on the absoluteness of your statements:

- if you include both strengths and weaknesses of your program. In talking about weaknesses, you may want to talk about areas for continued growth. The euphemism is not dishonest. Most programs we know of are already focused upon the areas they feel need strengthening, and yours is probably no different.
- where you have made conjectures, you may want to surface issues for continued investigation, perhaps posing them in terms specific enough to be researched with a "true" experimental or quasi-experimental design.
- if you do not shy away from drawing "no conclusions" from a particular data source or sources. The no conclusion may be the result of inconclusive evidence—t-score computations on a reading test may prove to be inconclusive—or your analysis of an instrument and its collection process may lead you to decide that a particular data source was not sufficiently discriminating.
- if you do present your evidence descriptively, in unloaded language, letting the numbers and observations speak for themselves in addition to your moving beyond them to your conclusions and recommendations.

8.0   Presenting Your Report

8.1   *Summary and Full Reports*

In every evaluation situation we have worked in we have found it advisable to report out in summary as well as full form, and the only situation we can imagine in which this two-level response might be usefully bypassed is when the scope of the evaluation is so narrow that the full report amounts to a few pages more.

A main function of the summary is to get information to your audience(s) very soon after the data collection process is completed. That is when people are usually most ripe for getting a handle on your findings. A second function of the summary is to have documentation in a form available for wider circulation (summaries are generally less expensive to reproduce) and for those in your audience(s) who have a low tolerance for length and detail. A full report, on the other hand, amounts to a complete record of the evaluation and will serve as a reference to anyone who follows up on your findings. If you hire a consultant to participate in your evaluation, it will be important for you to insure that the expectation of a full written report is provided for in your contract.

8.2 *Components of the Report*

Whether you are dealing with a full report or a summary, we recommend that your report touch base with each of the following components. It is not necessary to be equally elaborate with each component. Nor is it necessary to identify each with a separate subtitle; the components might be addressed in a number of combinations. We see them as elements of the whole, however, regardless of the particular shape of the final product.

- A context for reading the evaluation which might include descriptive information about the system which is being evaluated (for example, characteristics of the school system and the school itself), how the evaluation came about, and/or information about the evaluators themselves.
- A description of the methodology used in identifying issues: the process used in developing instruments, collecting and analyzing data. It is helpful to include evaluative comments about the methodology as it looks in retrospect.
- For each specific goal or objective of the evaluation, a description of each instrument used, an analysis of strengths and weaknesses of the instrument, presentation of the data generated, analysis of the data, and conclusions you see in them.
- A description of the full reporting and feedback process. This is simply an indication of how the information collected in the evaluation has been or will be disseminated. The distinction we make between reporting and feedback is noted below in 8.4
- Summary of conclusions and recommendations: This should not be confused with the summary report, which touches all of the bases mentioned above. We envision this as a quick-reference mechanism for those who have already reviewed the report and need a recapitulation for determining next steps. Such a summary might be represented by underlined or italicized portions of other sections of the report, which are easily identified and returned to. In some cases, a recommendation may follow on a single conclusion statement, but in most cases, recommendations will probably grow as conclusions cluster and point collectively towards changes.

We believe it is important to differentiate in any report, full or summary, between observations or conclusions that are essentially descriptions of what you see happening and judgments about what you see regarding cause or benefit. Neither, however, should be left to stand alone, they go hand in hand. This is true when you are basing a go/no-go decision on the evaluation as when you see it as a routine, mid-course check. It seems to us to be misleading to state judgments without describing the basis of your judgments. (It can also be damaging: you make it easy for your detractors to take negative judgments out of context if they are not closely aligned with a description that puts them into a healthy perspective.) On the other hand, we feel it is something of a cop-out for an evaluator to describe a situation without expressing whatever judgments he/she derives from that description.

8.3   Format of the Report

The format of the report, whether summary or full, will depend on a number of factors. Here are what we see as the major ones:

Your audience(s):   Every audience will have a format they will find easier to handle and you will need to balance your sense of integrity with what your audience(s) will digest. One audience, for example, may respond efficiently to a report which is dominated by graphs and tables and contains a minimum of commentary and description beyond the presentation of raw data organized in this way. Another, however, may feel overwhelmed by what seems to be a blur of numbers, and you may be well advised to keep your tabulations to a minimum and housed in the appendices. Still another may be most at home with a little flash: pictures, color-coded sections, glossy paper, foldouts. The important consideration here is what you have to say about the school and what format will resist a stereotype you want to avoid.

The instrumentation you used: Some instruments lend themselves to charts and graphs, others to t-scores and notions of statistical significance, and others (excerpts from student logs, for instance, or media documentation) to presentation without extensive commentary.

The money available to be invested in presentation of your report: This needs to be taken into consideration when you are dealing with financial constraints on the evaluation.

In general, we would encourage you to seriously consider a "multiple bias" format which contains *something* for a variety of audiences, for basically the same reasons we earlier recommended to you the use of more than one instrument for gathering data on any one issue. Media documentation and "hard" statistics, for instance, which together support the same conclusion—or even when they refine each other's conclusions—are much more powerful than either one by itself.

8.4 Public Reporting vs. Feedback

We think of feedback as observations shared with individuals in the settings which pertain to those individuals but are not necessarily an integral part of the report contracted for. In collecting data on student initiative, for example, you may observe several classes in operation. In your report you may use this information to develop a composite picture of opportunities for, and incidents of, student initiative in the school. It would probably also be helpful if you discussed with each individual staff member you observed what you saw him/her doing to promote or hinder the development of student initiative. The latter is feedback and is most useful if given as part of a dialogue with the individuals concerned.

9.0 Follow-up

9.1 Why Follow-up?

Except in instances of terminal evaluation (a retrospective look at what happened in a school or program that has been discontinued), ongoing, formative evaluation seems to us to be essential to the health and well-being of any school or program. Even in situations where an initial evaluation indicates that the program is accomplishing its goals and meeting the needs of clients, it will be advisable to regularly reassess what is happening: staff and client changes as well as a subtle hardening of procedural arteries influence the definition of needs and accomplishment of goals, and as with any organism, a program's resilience and vitality may depend on periodic checks.

It is, of course, *not necessary* to repeat the *same* evaluation procedure each time. For any given follow-up, your audience(s) and their biases may be different than they were the first time, the constraints on the evaluation may have changed, your sophistication as an evaluator will have developed, and the goals of your program may be realigned as a result of the earlier round. Although in some cases you will want to check to see if the specific recommendations that grew out of an earlier evaluation were implemented and in what ways and with what success, in others you may simply want to note your program's general growth since the earlier evaluation. You may want to do both: they are not necessarily mutually exclusive objectives. If your initial evaluation has been a concentrated effort and a sig-

The Organization	The Progress			
	1. tabulate, analyze, draw con- clusions/ recommen- dations	2. tabulate and analyze	3. draw con- clusions/ recommen- dations	4. tabulate, analyze and draw con- clusions/ recommen- dations
1. by general pro- gram goals				
2. by performance objectives (within general program goals)				
3. by type of instru- mentation (all inter- views looked at to- gether)				
4. by date of ad- ministration randomly				

nificant one-time drain on your resources, you may decide to deal with subsequent evaluation in smaller packages spread more evenly over time.

9.2   Who Should Follow up?

Any decision about who is chosen to conduct a return evaluation carries with it certain implications. If the follow-up is conducted by the outside person who was responsible for the initial evaluation, it is likely to be completed relatively quickly, but it may also reflect the biases of the first evaluation. A different outside person would be able to add a goal-free dimension to a follow-up, but he or she would also need more time. A program which provides its own ongoing evaluation provides for its own revitalization; in some circumstances, however, this arrangement might appear to be self-serving and one which would undermine the "objectivity" of the evaluation.

We do not necessarily feel that any one of the above is better able to conduct a follow-up to an evaluation than the others. It depends entirely on your particular situation and what you want to accomplish with the return. A review of Sections 2 and 3 of this paper, with an eye to the special circumstances of your return evaluation, should help you to decide on this issue.

19

Walden III: An Alternative High School Survives Evaluation Quite Nicely, Thank You
by David L. Johnson and Jackson V. Parker

As alternative schools are adopted in the public sector, the problem of evaluation rears its head. The alternative schools movement, which has never been strong on evaluation and indeed is often philosophically at odds with conventional means of evaluation, may be colliding head-on with the accountability movement. Now, with a polarity strongly established between traditional and open education,† a simple-minded dichotomy has been created. Open or nontraditional education is seen as automatically meaning a sacrifice in academic achievement in order to gain certain affective results. This article provides evidence that this is a false conclusion. It presents evaluation results for one alternative public high school, Walden III of Unified School District No. 1 in Racine, Wisconsin. We feel these results may serve as a sign to evaluation advocates and critics alike that alternative schools do work in the ways that adherents of traditional education would want them to. At the same time, they fulfill their own specific purposes. For those interested in starting alternatives, our results may serve to convince gatekeepers that alternatives need not sacrifice conventional education outcomes.

The current "state of the art" in evaluation of alternatives schools is best summed up in a statement by Mike Hickey, one-time director of Seattle's alternative programs: "(1) An art it is not, and (2) the only state it is in is a state of general chaos."[1]

---

*From *Phi Delta Kappan* LIV, 9 (May 1975): 624–28.
†*Newsweek,* October 21, 1974, describes this polarity.
1. Mike Hickey, *Evaluating Alternative Schools,* position paper prepared by the National Consortium on Educational Alternatives, 1972, 1.

Four factors account for this state of chaotic non-art. One is the perception of those developing and working in alternatives that evaluations based on the theories of behavioral science have no application to the outcomes sought in alternative public schools. Another is the practical fear that conventional school evaluation procedures may not be used as tools for program improvement, but as weapons to close alternative schools. Moreover, alternative school programs and students provide difficulties in administering conventional evaluation designs. And finally, alternative and traditional pedagogies are based on conflicting theories of pedagogy and knowledge. Yet most educational evaluation is based on traditional pedagogy and its theory of knowledge: therefore, it is not suited to evaluation of alternative program outcomes.

Despite these difficulties, one of the things we want to communicate to those advocating alternatives is *act* rather than *react* when it comes to evaluation. If we don't initiate reasonable evaluations, we may be trapped by unreasonable ones. Public alternatives will be evaluated, and it behooves those involved in them to initiate and exercise control over such evaluations rather than have them imposed from outside.

Therefore a relatively traditional evaluation was part of the proposal that created Walden III. The proposal was adopted by the Racine Board of Education in May, 1972. As designers of the proposal, we felt that evaluation was part of the game, and we wanted to play in the public education ballpark.

The Walden III plan was implemented in the 1972–73 school year, serving 155 eleventh- and twelfth-graders. Enrollment reached 230 in 1973–74 and 1974–75. The school is located in a large old elementary school building in downtown Racine. Enrollment is open to any district student on a first-come, first-served basis. The Racine Unified School District has about 7,000 high school students drawn from its 99-square-mile area. In many ways, the district is a microcosm of the United States, showing much the same racial balance, extremes of wealth, and rural-urban division.

The Walden III plan has features found in alternative high schools across the country. Student involvement in curriculum, school policy, and environmental decisions are emphasized, as is use of the community for learning experiences. Personal choice, freedom, and responsibility are maximized. Affective as well as cognitive outcomes are sought, and interdisciplinary studies are encouraged. The schedule is flexible and personal, the atmosphere open and informal. The college-format schedule can be altered, interrupted, or canceled to meet the needs of individuals, groups, or the entire school.

Evaluation of the first year centered on achievement, ability, certain affective traits, and attitudes. The students were administered published instruments on a pre/post basis. Additional data were obtained through student and parent questionnaires, as well as student record searches. All data, including significance tests, were processed by the school district's research and development staff. The use of R & D staff monitored the administration of instruments by the school staff. Local instruments were jointly designed by the Walden III co-directors and the R & D staff. This design was essentially replicated for the second (1973–74) year's evaluation.

The group used in the first year's evaluation was socioeconomically heterogeneous, but blacks were not present in percentages equal to district averages, a situation corrected in the 1973–74 and 1974–75 groups. Persons involved in the first year's evaluation were categorized ethnically, by sex and grade level. The ethnic breakdown was 145 whites, four blacks, and six Chicanos. By grade level there were 88 seniors and 67 juniors. Eighty-two females and 73 males made up the group.

The Hollingshead Index was used to characterize the group as middle class to lower-middle class. Mean IQ was 106, slightly above the district average of 102. However, the group had a past course failure rate significantly higher than the district averages, and a combined GPA of 2.15 on a four-point scale. The students came from all three of the district's public high schools, from two of the three private schools, and from schools outside the Racine district. Expecting this heterogeneity, we also generally expected that achievement and ability could be enhanced or at least maintained by the Walden III plan, along with significant gains in affective areas.

The evaluation supported our expectations:

1. *Achievement*—The instrument used was the Iowa Test of Educational Development (ITED). The ITED has subtests that yield a reading score, a math score, a composite score, and scores on three background tests. After the pre-test was given, an expected gain score was computed, representing the amount of improvement needed to maintain the same percentile rank. Eleventh-graders generally exceeded their expected gain scores, but the differences were not significant. However, in reading, their actual gain

was significantly greater than the expected gain.[2] Twelfth-graders exceeded all of their expected gain scores, but in no case was this increase statistically significant.

We can offer two explanations of the reading gains. First, at Walden III people are expected to read as though reading were a process as natural as breathing. No special reading programs were created. Second, the informal and open schedule allowed time for reading—time to read something to its conclusion, not waiting for some future study hall, open lab, or free moment at home.

2. *Learning Ability*—The testing instrument was the Analysis of Learning Potential (ALP). ALP measures general capacity or potential for school learning. It correlates with the Metropolitan and Stanford Achievement Tests (.70 to .85, depending on the subtests), as well as with the Lorge-Thorndike IQ tests (.83). Its nine subtests yield a reading composite score, a mathematics composite score, an index of learning potential which compares students with others their own age, and a general composite standard score which compares students with others in their own grade. Though the test was not developed within a framework of mental ability or intelligence (rather, it tests ability to perform tasks related to school learning, i.e., it predicts school success), it would appear in theory that for a given individual this score would be relatively unalterable. However, the Walden III group increased on all four composite scores, and the increases were all statistically significant.

These findings were not hypothesized by the program developers, though we had a hope that the so-called Rosenthal Effect might work to our benefit.† Treating students personally, humanely, and expecting that

---

2. "Significant" or "statistically significant" refers to t-tests at the .05 level

†Or Pygmalion Effect. Robert Rosenthal and Lenore Jacobson first presented this concept in their *Pygmalion in the Classroom: Teacher Expectation and Pupils' Intellectual Development* (Holt, Rinehart, and Winston, 1968). Their research supported the idea that students will achieve at the level teachers expect them to—a version of the self-fulfilling prophecy. Furthermore, they said students' ability would be directly influenced by such expectations. The effect has been difficult to replicate, and the work of Rosenthal and Jacobson has been criticized by none other than Arthur Jansen, among others. Rosenthal defends himself in "The Pygmalion Effect Lives," *Psychology Today,* September, 1973, 56–63. At Walden III we felt that treating students as though they were mature, expecting them to think and be concerned about things of the mind, and offering a new start where there was little emphasis on the students' past history might constitute an ideal situation to stimulate the effect. Others might argue that the Hawthorne Effect explains our results.

they would learn appear to be contributory causes. It may be that the combination of feeling more comfortable and personally challenged "unblocked" existing potentials in students. In addition, providing a place where students could achieve individual identity in a small school no doubt contributed to the results.

3. *Attitude-affective Outcomes*—Instruments used included the Maslow Security-Insecurity Inventory (SI), Rotter Internal-External Scale (IE), and Intellectual Achievement Responsibility Scale (IAR). We had hypothesized that, in a personalized setting, students should become more secure, more internally motivated, and more willing to take responsibility for their own academic successes and failures. The hypothesis was borne out. In one case, we had a local norm group. The Rotter IE had been given in 1970–71 to a random sample of tenth-, eleventh-, and twelfth-graders in the district. Walden III students started out more externally motived than the norm group and ended more internally motivated. The amount of change was statistically significant, though the post-score difference between the norm group and the Walden III group was not.

Similar results were achieved on the Intellectual Achievement Responsibility questionnaire. The instrument yields three scores: One related to responsibility for school success, one to school failure, and one is a composite. All changes were statistically significant in the direction of taking personal responsibility for academic successes and failures. Students were less willing to ascribe personal academic success or failure to "luck," "fate," or "powerful others." According to the Maslow Security-Insecurity Inventory, Walden III students tended to be insecure at the beginning of the year. They were significantly more insecure than the national norm group. By year's end, however, they were as secure as the national norm group, and the change was statistically significant.

The locally constructed instruments produced some interesting results. As could be expected, students were extremely positive about the school and its staff. Thus no changes occurred pre- to post-test, except that the quality of the staff was seen as an even more important reason for staying at the school than it was for coming in the first place. There was a significant change in a positive direction in response to the item, "The school stimulates students to think." In addition, students were significantly more satisfied with their own "ability to be happy most of the time," with their "ability to keep going when (their) feelings are hurt," and their "ability to handle worries." Naturally, some of the changes would be attributed to normal maturation.

"Finding personal happiness" became significantly more important as a life goal from pre- to post-test, but "living my life my own way" became significantly less important. The most important values for the students, both before and after, were "being independent and original" and "standing up for your rights." Nearly half of the responses were located there.

In regard to feelings about the future of society, Walden III students became significantly more positive. Their feelings about the local community also improved significantly. However, in the end they still felt better about the school and their own personal futures than they did about the community and society.

Contrary to the image many hold of alternative schools, Walden III students agreed strongly that the school was not "easier" than their previous school. Both the academic content and the need for growth in self-awareness and self-discipline required in the Walden III program were the causes of this perception. Almost no one came to the school because he thought he could get better grades without working for them. The strongest reasons for going to Walden III were that it was small and friendly, the teachers were good, it would help intellectual and social growth, it would provide a wide variety of interesting courses, it would provide a chance to pursue interests in depth, and it would help one to learn responsibility.

Parental response on a questionnaire was overwhelmingly supportive. "Better than 80 percent of the responding parents (116 families out of 155 responded) were glad their child was attending Walden III, felt that Walden III had less of a problem with student discipline than other schools, were satisfied with Walden III methods of communicating pupil achievement, felt Walden III had changed the attitude of their child for the better, that teachers had been more cooperative than in previous years, and that their children were less tense about going to school since attending Walden III."[3]

Negative responses ("somewhat dissatisfied" or "very dissatisfied") on the 22 items of the questionnaire averaged about 10 percent. Positive parent response in the areas of academic rigor of the program, basic skills, student/parent communication about the school, increased self-discipline, improved attendance, student happiness, improved family relations, lack of school boredom, community learning opportunities, and staff

---

3. Unified School District No. 1 of Racine County, Department of Research and Development, *R & D, Walden III*, 1972-1973, 62.

concern for others ranged from 52 percent to 80 percent. Parents did express some concern about the loose structure and "lack of control," which appears to be at odds with their feelings about discipline.

Thus, from this relatively traditional evaluation, it can be seen that some of the fears regarding traditional educational outcomes in alternative situations are groundless. Conversely, achievement gains needn't inhibit affective growth; rather, they appear to be intertwined. It can also be seen that alternative schools perhaps needn't fear undertaking such an evaluation.

However, the tentativeness of this evaluation must also be underscored. It is, after all, a one-year evaluation, the first year at that. Results could be attributed in part to the Hawthorne Effect.

It is also important to emphasize that this was not experimental research. The lack of control groups suggests this. The kind of tight laboratory controls such research requires would have been too intrusive, indeed would have shaped our school's program. This would have been antithetical to a program that had as one of its goals evolution in unknown directions dictated by the character of the people and their immediate life and times. We do not feel that this evaluation got clearly and cleanly at the essence of what Walden III was about and what important successes we achieved, though it revealed important aspects of our work. A more total anthropological-novelistic approach is probably required. Nevertheless, the results speak for themselves.

We must also indicate that the second year's results, which are just now being written up in final form, seem to replicate those of the first year. This appears to be so even though the second-year population differs in some critical variables. For instance, the second-year group's IQ is closer to the district average. The base-line established by the pre-tests in achievement (ITED) and ability (ALP) indicates significantly lower scores than the first-year group's. Nevertheless, substantially the same growth results as reported above for the first-year group are revealed in this group's post-test scores on the two instruments. Eleventh-graders met all of their expected gain scores. Twelfth-graders exceeded their expected gain scores in all four areas, and in three (total language, total math, and total composite) the excess was significant.

Results on the ALP were virtual duplicates of the 1972–73 results. Results on the affective instruments also duplicate the first-year group's, as do the parent's responses. The questionnaire on students' feelings about school was modified, and a comparison group from two of the three traditional schools was selected. On 50 out of 57 total items, Walden III students were significantly more positive about their school experience than the comparison group. This same comparison group was also used on the affective and achievement instruments. At the end of the year, Walden III students were significantly more secure and more internally motivated than the comparison group. There were no significant differences in academic achievement.

Naturally we would like to see our results replicated in other alternative settings. This would add further credence to our school, and would provide support for other alternatives. However, we are not endorsing all types of evaluation, and it would be against our wishes to have such evaluations "laid on" alternative programs from above. The kind of evaluation was important, and we wanted a hand in designing it. We believed we could succeed—which may be the ultimate example of the Rosenthal Effect—and felt comfortable with the evaluation process.

It is tempting for alternative schools to remain insular, as long as things go well. We at Walden III realize the danger of insularity and the resultant false sense of security. We try not to be to lulled by it, so that it inhibits our growth. Given the milieu we must operate in, we hope the Walden III evaluations will help others to either maintain the luxury of insularity, feel more comfortable about coming out of it, or be able to establish more firmly the value of alternative programs for districts considering their adoption. In one sense, the evaluation process was important to our program. In another sense, it was secondary to the stuff of life, the daily excitement of being in the school. This excitement was so consuming that we hardly thought about the evaluation except when we were planning it and administering the pre- and post-tests. Even then, the excitement tempted us to lose sight of the fact that we did have an obligation to do more than revel in the struggle with our minute-by-minute joys and frustrations, that we did have to do the evaluation properly (even if we quarreled with portions of its philosophical base) in order to make a significant statement for the alternative schools.

We feel the statement has been made.

20

Innovative Governance Structures in Secondary Schools
by Joan Chesler

As high schools increasingly become the loci of intergenerational and interracial tensions and crises, their members seek new institutional forms. Students and teachers are demanding more influence and power in determining policies, programs, and curricula, and many are finding traditional formal and informal patterns of interactions unsatisfactory.

There is convincing data that one of the more critical causes of student dissension and unrest—particularly among blacks, Chicanos, poor whites, and other minority persons—is their systematic exclusion from participation in school policy making. Members of the Educational Change Team (ECT)[1] have amassed significant data linking school unrest with student perception of racism and youth oppression.

Schools comprise heterogeneous groups of people, among whom conflict is normal and natural; yet schools are most often administered as though a single set of procedures, policies, and regulations benefit all persons, who are perceived as essentially alike and interested in similar goals. An alternative to this alienating and stress-producing form of governance

*From *The Journal of Applied Behavioral Science* IX, 2/3 (1973): 261–79. Reprinted by permission. This research was conducted while the author was a research associate with the Educational Change Team, University of Michigan. The author is indebted to Ms. Glorianna Wittes and Ms. Dale Crowfoot, from whose collaborative writing this article is extracted.

1. The Educational Change Team, located in the School of Education at the University of Michigan, was a multidisciplinary, multiracial group of scholars engaged in action-research conflict in schools.

is decision-making structures that include students, teachers, administrators, community members, and representatives of significant minority groups present in the school. Legitimate influence by students and minority persons may counteract some of the ill effects of youth oppression and racism, in that the policies and procedures of a heterogeneous decision-making group may be more appropriate to a wider range of interests and styles.

To document, understand, and discover collaborative governance models for schools, a group of us at the ECT investigated six high schools with innovative decision-making structures. Although there was a wide range of experimental schools and programs which we might have studied, certain limitations narrowed the field. First, since the focus of our study was on participatory forms of school governance and curriculum that heavily involved students, we focused on schools with student rather than community participation and control. Second, the study was designed to provide models for middle- and long-range change in secondary public schools. We thus selected models that were already operative and seemed applicable to public schools. Third, we focused on white and interracial schools, and did not investigate alternatives in the black community. It was our feeling that this task would be more appropriate for a group of black scholars.

Research teams of three to six adults and students, with a racial composition appropriate to the specific schools, spent five days in May of 1971 at each site. We used a variety of methods to collect data, including (1) individual and group interviews, for which some people were selected at random and others because of their experience in the program's development or current operation; (2) a questionnaire administered to school participants; (3) observation of classes, activities in the halls, lounges, and so on; (4) analysis of documents and records, such as minutes of meetings and program proposals, and evaluations and articles as well.

Our study confirmed our hypothesis that student power and participation in school governance and curriculum can benefit all members of a school community in many ways:

1. Students and other institutionally and socially oppressed groups can make school policies and programs more directly responsive to their own perception of their needs—the clients—rather than to (primarily white) educators' ideas of their needs.

2. Students, teachers, and administrators can establish relationships that hold them mutually accountable, not unilaterally accountable from student to teacher to administrator, as is usually the case.

3. Students and others improve in academic and behavioral skills, gain experience in independent and self-assertive styles of thought and action, and increase their self-esteem and sense of potency.

4. In view of the emergence of differing styles, needs, and opinions, school members are forced to confront conflict and to some extent legitimate and accommodate these differences, a process which serves as a stepping stone toward a pluralistically operated school system.

5. All school members learn how to make their institution more humane and how to cope with similar bureaucratic institutions.

6. If youth, blacks, Chicanos, and others are able to participate meaningfully and powerfully, their schools will move toward the eradication of youth oppression and racism.

The extent to which students and members of oppressed minorities are able to participate with power determines the degree in which the above changes occur. If students control only student activities, if blacks determine the curricula of only black studies programs, their limited power and participation will realize only limited benefits. If however, students also serve on councils that, for example, determine hiring policies, curriculum, and evaluation policies and procedures, their influence will be broader and more significant.

Descriptions of the Six Innovative Schools

Franklin High School

Franklin is a multiracial inner-city high school in Seattle, Washington. In May 1971, it had 1,550 students: 46 percent were white, 26 percent were black, 24 percent Oriental, 3 percent Filipino, and 1 percent native American. There were 88 teachers, including 70 whites, 11 blacks, 5 Orientals, 1 Filipino, and 1 Chicano. In addition, the staff included three administrators and five counselors, two of whom were black and none of whom were Oriental. Although it is a comprehensive school, its curriculum is geared largely toward academics, since 62 percent of the recent graduates have gone on to college.

In 1969–70 school members who had participated in various workshops on school problems and skills in communication and problem solving began to plan for a representative school Senate. This mechanism was designed as a response to student and faculty feelings of impotence and a need to have a say in school decisions and changes. One year later its constitution was approved and elections were held. In February 1971 the Franklin High School Senate began its work. Between then and May 1971 the Senate had dealt with the following issues: (1) smoking rules and areas for students and adults, (2) narcotics agents in the school, (3) extortion, (4) organizing support for the school levy, (5) planning for a restructured day, and (6) desegregation by participation in a voluntary racial transfer program.

The Senate was the school's official policy-making body. Although the Senate did not formally abridge any of the principal's stated powers, there was an informal working agreement between him and its members, and he actively supported the Senate. Although the principal retained the power to veto any of its decisions, in the first semester of operation no issues arose that pitted the Senate against the administration.

The Senate was composed of 33 members, including membership of the principal ex officio. Half the remaining members were students (16), while others included nine teachers, five parents, and two representatives of noncertificated personnel. Senators participated by indirect representation: they had no specific parties or constituencies within their role groups, nor did members of their role group try to influence their votes. The main sources of information about the Senate's activities were the school newspaper and the Senate minutes, which were distributed weekly. Communication was nonetheless limited, and few members of the school considered themselves well informed about the Senate.

In May 1971 many Senators were pleased with their accomplishments in real and important areas of school decisions. But many were discouraged by their low visibility and impact. They had encountered little or no resistance after each decision had been reached and so had not yet tested the extent and limits of their power. Senators also were wrestling with how to extend participation to a larger number as well as to a more racially and culturally representative mix of staff, students, and parents in their school.

Metro High School

Metro High School had 350 students, drawn by lottery from metropolitan Chicago. One-half of the student body was black. There were 21 staff members, of whom approximately one-third were black and Puerto Rican. Most staff were under 30 years old, with highly libertarian or New Left perspectives and values, and were deeply committed to Metro.

Metro is part of the Chicago public school system, but was financed in part by participating organizations in its School-Without-Walls structure. The curriculum was heavily oriented to community need, with a few of the nearly 300 courses taught by Metro staff and many by cooperating agencies in the city. The flexible curriculum was developed in large part through interests of students as well as availability of resources. In May 1971 problems in curriculum revolved around (1) the lack of continuity of courses—there was no required progression of courses toward skill development in one or more areas; and (2) teaching or reading skills were inadequate for students with minimal skill level or motivation.

Informality in class was the rule, and most instruction was highly individualized and rooted in practical, real-life problem solving rather than in highly theoretical or abstract efforts. Attempts were made to reach and motivate all students, but the organization of learning at Metro was highly problematic for some students. Those who were benefiting from Metro's loose structure and permissiveness tended to be white or middle class blacks who were heavily socialized into the mainstream of white work and life style. Staff placed high value on their relationships with students (warm, relaxed, informal), and were afraid to "rock the boat" by imposing rules, policy, and discipline on them. Many black parents objected to this looseness and were hostile to staff, whom they saw trying to protect their own jobs, and to students, who they felt were abusing their freedom. Both staff and students were unanimous in wanting parents to stay *out* of their territory, for they feared many parents' ignorance about the goals and philosophy of Metro.

Metro was organized around small counseling groups that were representative of a cross section of the student body and were to be stable over the four years of a student's Metro career. Attendance at weekly counseling group sessions was compulsory—the only compulsory feature of Metro. However, the counseling groups were considered a failure by all; students used them as little more than a homeroom base, and most teachers were uncomfortable or felt inadequate to the loosely defined task of creating a "community" with their counseling groups.

Committed to sharing power with students, Metro's members had not yet evolved a *formal* structure for achieving it. Neither students nor staff trusted a delegated system; so representative structures had all failed. Total school meetings for decision making also had failed on a continuing basis, except during various crises when active and full participation of students complemented that of staff in dealing with the crisis. In 1970–71 most governance matters were dealt with by the faculty in after-school committee meetings that students were encouraged to attend; however, few did. Agenda setting was not done before the meetings, so students were not aware of what would be discussed. The principal attended some of these meetings but left a tremendous amount of the day-to-day governance of the school in the hands of faculty, since he was engrossed in external liaison work with the creaky bureaucracy of the larger school system. Despite the lack of a formal faculty-student-body to govern the school, Metro students felt they had a great deal of personal power in the school. They also felt tremendous trust in the faculty to make decisions in their behalf. Personal influence and the humanistic values were seen by students as better guarantors of shared power than a formal internal governance structure.

A formal structure was emerging, however, for external governance. The participating community organizations formed a council to receive and distribute monies directly to Metro, bypassing the Board of Education. A Policy Board was developed as the official negotiating agency and liaison with the Board of Education, accountable directly to the General Superintendent rather than to central staff, with whom the principal had to deal. This Board was representative of staff, students, parents, administration, and participating organizations and it may serve a valuable function in dealing with the public school system.

Milwaukee Independent School

Milwaukee Independent School (MIS) is a small private high school located in a downtown office building. When we visited in April 1971, we found it an informal, relaxed, friendly place. There was a high degree of acceptance and "do-your-own-thing" flavor among the 43 students. People spoke only for themselves, they rarely generalized in order to protect themselves. White middle class students began the school, and the current staff and student body remain all-white. After being accepted by the school, students must earn $300 ($25 per month); parents are encouraged to pay an additional $300. Many fund-raising drives have been conducted. In late spring of 1971, a crafts and rummage shop was opened to help defray tuition costs for those who worked in it.

MIS was started in February 1970 by two key students, others who planned to quit school and attend MIS, and a few selected adults. A Board of Directors (with the two initiating students as members) was created for legal reasons, but as time progressed it exerted more and more actual control. In 1970 a professional director of the school was hired and was held responsible to the Board of Directors until a student-adult coalition forced him from power. Students, who worked throughout the summer of 1970, planned the next year, hired staff members, and selected students from a waiting list. By April 1971 professional leadership more closely resembled the original values of the school.

The staff offered courses based on their own interests or on requests from students. People in Milwaukee, many from the University of Wisconsin at Milwaukee, offered their services for classes, discussions, and apprenticeships. Most students planned a program of individual study. There was a list of "minimum expectations," which suggested that a student do an individual project, take two group courses, attend the general meetings, have periodic discussion/progress checks with a staff member, and so on; but it stated that students would not be held to this if they did not choose to be. This ambivalent instruction represented differences among students; those who felt some requirements were necessary, and those who believed requirements were a violation of their learning rights. Evaluation of student progress was conducted jointly by students and teachers; the same feedback process was used in evaluating teachers. Both academic growth and social relationships were used as criteria.

Decisions were most often reached through a consensus of those attending the weekly General Meeting, its key governing mechanism—an open forum for student and adult discussions, disagreements, and proposals. Sometimes, "depending on time and temperament," a vote was called for and ¾ of the students and staff present would pass something. In 1970 the staff did not have votes; in 1971 they did. Small groups met regularly to plan or debrief those weekly meetings, to have personal discussions, and to integrate personal and political activities.

Survival of the school was a critical issue in the winter of 1971, when many students did not pay their tuition. The staff was forced to put pressure on students, and this raised the issue of where responsibility lay at MIS. After much discussion, the school's one rule was determined: PAY TUITION! However, a review board of three students and one staff member was established to hear appeals. By April, two of six appeals for tuition release were accepted. The locus of responsibility in a student-controlled school was also expressed in student decisions around curriculum, the role of weekly staff meetings, and the criteria for graduation.

Community High School

Berkeley Community High is an alternative or mini-high school now in its fourth year of functioning. It is the first of a series of alternative high schools within the Berkeley school system and has served as a working model for the development of two more alternative schools within Berkeley High.

Community High began with 100 students as an outgrowth of a summer drama program developed by a group of Berkeley staff members. Teachers developed this experience into a full-time school program, and it began in 1968 as a school-within-a-school. Since they wanted to give students meaningful responsibility and control, teachers worked actively with the student body to generate a new program and attempted to develop a student-oriented curriculum providing a good deal of freedom for individual work. Pressure from other local students and parents served as an impetus for the creation of two additional alternative schools in February 1971. Each of these programs responded to the Community High experience by attempting to explore other kinds of structures for alternative learning experiences. At the same time, Community High divided into small tribal units as a response to its increased size. In 1971 there were 300 students in the program. One of the tribes, Black House, split off from Community High, becoming responsible to the school district administration rather than to Berkeley High's principal. Black House recently opened admissions to all black students in the larger Berkeley High School.

In May 1971, the following issues were seen as major sources of conflict within the school: (1) staying small and homogeneous (primarily white, middle class) vs. increasing size to get additional staff positions funded in order to hire black or Chicano staff to attract a broader range of students; (2) building a strong sense of community within the program vs. "doing your own thing in the community," seeking individual apprenticeships, and more stimulating real-world learning experiences; (3) being defined in relation to Berkeley High ("we are a destroyer of standards," . . . "we are only the lesser of two evils") vs. building a positive, viable educational alternative and providing relevant, often nonacademic, learning experiences.

At that time Community High's governance structure centered on the

Intertribal Council, which consisted of two students, one staff member, and one parent (recently added) from each of the five tribes. There was no administrative veto; in fact, the school administrator was selected by the student body. The Council had jurisdiction over all school activities, including curriculum, budget, and planning. Students generally felt that the staff had the most power by virtue of their expertise, experience, and longer tenure in the school; however, students had a sense of themselves as a powerful group. Thus they felt that if they really cared about an issue, they had the power to outvote the staff. This proved true regarding the choice of a director, when the underlying issue was whether the school should devote energy to becoming truly multiracial. This would have meant altering the curriculum and increasing the amount of structure to meet the needs of black students. Most students felt this would restrict their freedom considerably and preferred to support a separatist solution to educating blacks, thus supporting the work of Black House. The school was still committed to "multiracial" educational goals, but students clearly felt this was not the major priority. Hence, on this occasion, students voted for a candidate who would not push for a multiracial school. The students were successful in outvoting the staff and getting as director the candidate who advocated their position.

Sudbury Valley

Sudbury Valley is a private day school located on a large rural estate approximately 40 miles west of Boston. It has 70 students, ranging in age from four to 45. Tuition is $950 a year for elementary and high school, and $2,400 for a college degree program. The college program is in a developmental stage (with only one student). There are 10 staff members, ranging in age from 24 to 55, some part time and some without pay. The staff is generally heavily credentialed with MAs and Ph.D.s, and those without advanced degrees are well traveled. Currently the staff and students are all white.

The focus of a great deal of energy in the school has been its democratic structure, which has been evolving for three years. The school was founded by several adults, some of whom are now on the teaching staff. Governance was originally lodged in these founders and was then shared with a group composed of all trustees, staff, and parents. In December 1970, all students were given votes in the Assembly, which met biannually. By May 1971 the school was run by a weekly School Meeting, where all students and staff made all decisions about budget, discipline, staff hirings, firings, and salaries, and so on. The functions of the School Assembly had decreased considerably when the School Meeting took over budgetary responsibility. The School Assembly still voted to approve individual students' graduation, but was essentially a legal "rubber stamp." One of the predominant features of this school was its concept of "pure democracy," which had been built into a highly bureaucratic and legalistic system of committees, hearings, appeal bodies, et cetera. One major purpose of these procedures was to provide legitimacy and space for work on political activities in ways that encouraged open learning activities and trusting personal relationships.

The curriculum was open, with individualized learning defined by student interest. There were very few classes, and persons were free to actively pursue their own interests. Students taught some classes, and also held jobs in an apprentice fashion. The younger students in the school went on many field trips in small groups, and there were positive norms supporting cross-age sharing. There was an impressively high energy level for academics. Sudbury's desire to be a model for public education opened it up to at least 12 visitors a day. This had a "cooling" and disrupting effect on the school and raised a continual dilemma of whether it existed mainly to be a model for others or a school responsible only to itself.

When we visited, several critical issues for the school were: the effect of having entire families participating in the school in student, staff, or trustee roles; finances; its heavy denial of the tone and importance of interpersonal relationships and conflicts in the school; the difficulty in running a school servicing elementary, high school, and college ages. Further, the process of graduation had come under severe criticism, and changes were under consideration.

Dillington High School[2]

Dillington High School is situated in a small town of 30,000 in Dillington, Massachusetts. The town is multi-ethnic and multiracial, composed largely of working class and university people. Dillington High has 560 students, of whom 54 are in the SIAS (School in a School) program. SIAS is located off-campus in a private apartment and operates autonomously from the parent school.

---

2. The principal of this school requested that its actual name, program title, and location not be revealed, because he and a number of the faculty members disagreed with our report. The previous schools described gave permission for their real names and locations to be used; "Dillington" is the only fictitious name in the report.

The idea of SIAS was generated by seven teachers who had formed a seminar on "affective education." This group carried out the political tasks necessary for the establishment of the program, despite resistance and minimal cooperation from the larger school. Five of the seven original teachers are now the core staff of the SIAS program. Through a lottery, 50 students were selected to be involved in the program for the 1970–71 school year. Over the summer of 1970 ten of these students volunteered to work with the core staff and parents to plan for the coming year. By September 1970, they had decided to set up a curriculum in which students had a substantial say in the course offerings and content. It was also decided that there would be five evaluation periods, one after each curriculum component was completed, in order to make changes quickly for the next component. In May 1971 the agreed-upon curriculum was very broad and fairly well structured. Classes were rather informal, and students as well as the faculty taught.

Originally, all governing of the SIAS program was to be done by two teachers, two parents, and two students. The six representatives of their respective role groups were to rotate every two months. By December 1970, that was replaced by an open forum, run on a "one-man-one-vote basis." In May 1971, the open forum was still in operation.

At the time the ECT retrieval team visited SIAS, there was an enormous amount of community life going on. Teachers became friends to the students, and the general atmosphere was overt friendship. Students were very concerned about one another; however, this warmth did not extend to relations between black and white students. The seven black students maintained a strong clique and preferred to seek out relationship with the black students in the traditional school. Most members of SIAS, white and black, saw this as a problem. Another subtle problem in SIAS related to the traditional pattern of school administration. One could feel that the principal was considering "tightening up the reins," especially in regard to problems arising from the differences between SIAS and the parent school. His previous policies on attendance and behavior had been lenient, almost to the point of allowing complete autonomy. The direct cause of his shift in attitude had not yet been determined, but pressure from the parent administration was widely suspected.

Forms of Student Power and Autonomy

Following analysis of our data, several issues emerged as crucial: the meanings of power and autonomy in innovative programs, the formal and

informal governance processes used by school members, and the relationships between a school's instructional process and student power. We have
chosen to highlight and exemplify these issues as they cut across the
schools in our sample rather than to compare the organizations with one
another.

In traditional schools, students frequently have enough personal power
to make decisions on some issues that affect their individual school careers:
for example, what to study, when, how, and with whom. Less often, however, are students collectively able to make the formal institutional decisions that affect the fundamental nature of their group life in that institution: curriculum, rules and regulations, budget financing, teacher hiring
and firing, principal hiring and firing, student population, student activities,
and special programs. That MIS students were able to make decisions in
all these areas is most unusual.

School members are often confused and deceived by the different forms
autonomy and power may take. *Autonomy* is the individual student's freedom to chose his courses and select his teachers; i.e., his freedom to determine issues that affect him personally. *Power* is the students' collective
ability to influence not only curriculum decisions but also school policy
and management issues. At Sudbury Valley School, students had a great
deal of autonomy but little power. But because their need for individual
freedom was met they did not organize into a collective and push for a
different form of power. It is our view that if students are to gain any real
control of their lives at school, they must have significant and legitimate
influence over both the individual and the institutional decisions that shape
their school careers.

Student Power: Structures of Expression

In each school, we studied the forms, patterns, and degrees of student
power as expressed through formal structures and informal influence patterns. Formal power involves known, testable channels for influence, such
as votes and representatives. Informal influence relies heavily on subtle,
fluid interpersonal understandings. In our view, the ideal governance structure offers formal and informal means for influence, with each supporting
and enlivening the other.

Each innovative program was developed from a commitment to involve
students in school policies and programs. Yet frequently the initial design
did not allow for students' *formal* participation. When no formal mechanisms were developed, ad hoc gatherings served the total school body when

issues arose and vital decisions had to be made. The innovators at Metro, Community High, and SIAS were adults who believed that people, not necessarily structures, direct an active democracy. Student power was expected to be an organic outgrowth of the informal and unstructured environment where, it was hoped, the open atmosphere of autonomy would generate active student participation in all phases of school decision making and planning.

However, most students did not readily participate in school governance, which we interpret as the result of several factors. First, socialization fosters dependence on adult authorities, who make and enforce rules for the young. At school, youngsters are taught to trust adults. They are concomitantly taught to deny whatever power they do have: Teacher control of large groups of students results in students' learning to be controllable and thus dependent. Second, experience has taught students to distrust student councils and collaboration with teachers in school government, and some students distrust any formal regulations or government at all. Third, students are not skilled in the political process, nor are they taught problem-solving and political skills.

To counteract these effects of socialization, school innovators can facilitate student involvement in decision making by building formal mechanisms and processes that engage participation and make it less threatening. Initial creation of a *formal* structure with clearly delineated roles, responsibilities, and channels offers participants the greatest possibilities for active involvement in governance. This was done at SV and Franklin High School. Students at SV knew very clearly how to participate and exert influence—informal structures are neither as easily recognized nor controlled as are formal ones.

Power in informal settings is a delicate matter, depending on face-to-face interaction and access to information. If interaction and communication can be controlled by any one group, that group will obtain and retain the power in their school. The structure of traditional, authoritarian, adult-controlled high schools assures that information and communication will be one-way—from adults to students. Student power is minimal because there are no formal shared governance structures and because informal structures are adult-controlled.

Our findings strongly suggest that power is most successfully shared with students in a setting whose formal governance processes are clearly delineated, known, and understood; where informal communication between youth and adults is open, trusting, and honest; where students are organized as a collectivity of separate interests; and where information is freely and appropriately shared between school members. Using these four criteria, we will discuss some formal and informal aspects of student power in three of the schools.

At Franklin High School, most students and staff felt they had more freedom than at most other public schools. Faculty attitudes generally favored student participation in school life. However, participation is not power, it is far removed from control, and the Senate apparatus at Franklin was designed more to share power with many groups than to achieve student control.

Although its formal structure was clearly delineated, not many students outside the Senate understood how it might benefit them or how it operated. Thus, despite student access to power through their representatives, their influence was limited. Nor did the system, by its very structure, help students actualize their potential power: it had no sanctioned channels for student organization, caucuses, nor meeting times or places for Senators to meet with their constituencies. Although the 16 students composed half the Senate's voting members, never once had they voted as a bloc or even grouped to caucus. Nor had the black or Oriental Senators caucused, as far as we knew.

The informal means of information sharing also were underdeveloped. Senators did not communicate directly with their constituencies, nor did they know which sector of their constituency to represent. Members of Franklin High School were keenly aware of this problem and were trying to improve the flow of information and opinion in and out of the Senate.

Students' lack of information and feelings of disunity made them even more accessible to adult influence, but the Senate was adult-dominated for other reasons too. First, because adults had more time and expertise and felt more influential in and responsible for the Senate, they communicated more openly and regularly with one another. Second, informal encounters left students less powerful than teachers because their classroom interactions were dominated by adult expectations and teacher norms. And, finally, the school was adult-controlled because the administration controlled most of the information, partly by determining which items to refer to the Senate and which problems to handle administratively or through the Faculty Instruction Council.

At MIS, governance relied heavily on informal processes and active interaction among school members. The emphasis on informality and intense individualism discouraged use of the formal structure, and the "do-your-own-thing" ethos mitigated against many rules. Most policies (other than the tuition stipulation) left breadth for individual choices, yet, paradoxically, the "minimum expectations" encouraged students to attend the weekly General Meetings. Most students did attend, and many were active in discussions and committees. Students who were not active fought for the right to be uninvolved and were respected for it. The legitimation of this right gave students tremendous autonomy without relinquishing their influence. Furthermore, sanctioning students' rights not to participate reduced some of the staff's usual influence over students, in that they had less control of which students had power on which issues; in this situation, teachers found it more difficult to urge only the "good" students to participation in school governance activities, depending on their own schedules and interests and the agenda issues up for discussion. However, when issues became critical, governance and program planning took priority and frequently became the curriculum for all students.

MIS combined both formal and informal processes in its communication structure. Before General Meetings there was a good deal of informal communication about decisions to be made, but ultimately, decisions were made by the school body through the formal governance structure of the General Meeting. Occasionally, informally planned responses to issues were reversed because of broader and more open discussions at these meetings.

We found the greatest amount of student power at MIS: its formal and informal channels for decision making operated to the students' benefits. In addition, because students had started and maintained control of the school, information was shared among them and was not withheld. And, finally, because students intended to maintain control of the school, they were very conscious of the need to protect themselves as a group from co-optation by adults. MIS students allowed no one to advocate for them, nor did they give adults more power than students.

In comparison, student power was fairly low at Metro. The Metro faculty never managed to circulate the agenda for their meetings prior to meeting time. Many students failed to show up at meetings where important decisions were being made because they did not know in advance that these issues were up for discussion and decision. "We don't know our agenda ourselves, before our meetings," explained a teacher; "it's not that we deliberately withhold it." This was undoubtedly true, but a message had unwittingly been communicated to students that teachers did not really want students involved in school governance or that information discussed in faculty meetings was of a different order than information shared between students and staff in close personal interactions. So it was through the latter form of communication that Metro students made their interests known to teachers, who then used their own power to respond to them—a benevolent form of paternalism.

Although students at Metro (and SIAS) were not active in a formal sense in school decision making, they nonetheless were informally involved in school governance through their counseling group sessions and informal "raps." School governance was treated as a legitimate educational activity, and in a sense was part of the curriculum; however, it clearly was not valued to the extent that it was at Sudbury Valley or at MIS.

Our data indicate that if students are to function meaningfully in the daily operation of their schools, governance must be built into the school's ongoing curriculum and philosophy. Governance was integral to the regular functioning and educational philosophy of MIS, Sudbury, and CHS; in other schools, such as Franklin, policy making was a feature added on to the curriculum and available only to a few. Not coincidentally we believe, in May 1971, students had the most actual power at MIS; the least, at Franklin. Metro and SIAS students were drawn into decision making only periodically, either at time of crisis or regular periods of evaluation; routine maintenance decisions were made by the teachers.

The Instructional Process as It Relates to Student Power

If students are to feel powerful in a school's governance, they must have influence in the classroom and over the range of curricular offerings: but they will have significant control of the curriculum only when student power extends to the managerial and instructional processes. MIS and SVS illustrate this conclusion. At MIS, student power was supported and maintained by student control of the school's management as well as of their own individual educational programs. Because MIS students were free to choose what, when, how, and from whom to learn, and because evaluations were a matter of mutual feedback between students and staff the students and staff enjoyed more or less equal power.

In contrast, SVS students enjoyed a highly individualized, open curriculum, but informal processes in governance and curriculum supported much deference to adult authority and expertise. In governance meetings, for example, few students spoke. Furthermore, the learning settings were highly individualized and dominated by adult norms, expectations, and expertise; peer learning in groups was rare. Even though students there were encouraged to be active and influential in governance and curriculum, the interpersonal and student-teacher norms produced an adult-dominated learning setting.

Student power is strengthened when students can influence their course selections and requirements. At MIS, students determined their "minimum expectations," but Franklin standards were set by the public school system. While adhering to course requirements for accreditation, Metro offered a diversity of unorthodox and orthodox selections (but not teaching styles) by which students could fulfill these requirements. SIAS and Berkeley CHS also offered considerable choice to their students, along with certain requirements. Nevertheless, student choice of staff-developed options is very different from the structural power to decide and implement personal and collective concerns.

If students are to influence their own learning styles and directions, teachers must actively offer an appropriate amount of help. In several of the schools we studied, and most outstandingly at CH, teachers were reluctant to offer guidance to students. To do so, they feared, was to infringe on student control and self-responsibility. However, if a teacher works with him to develop his own guidelines and a programmatic *gestalt* to his curriculum choices, this does not mean that the individual student is dominated. Individual students can make unwise choices for themselves; their power is not diminished when they are assisted by someone of equal power, but perhaps more educational expertise, to consider appropriate choices.

Periodic evaluations of the curriculum, when the data are shared with students as well as with teachers, develop, support, and implement student power. Evaluation procedures can do more than provide feedback about student performance; they also can give feedback about teacher performance and the school program itself. For example, one of Metro's goals was to offer courses particularly suited to black students' interests and needs. Data from many black students and some white students indicated their satisfaction with the range of course content offerings, but also indicated their dissatisfaction with their teachers' pedagogical styles. This information allows these students and teachers to design methods more appropriate to their own needs and learning styles.

Skilled teachers or special consultants are useful in teaching school members effective communication, problem-solving, and political skills. Only at Franklin were there workshops, but these involved very few people in proportion to the total school population. All too often adults believe that their work is done once they have built a structure in which young people can be involved. This abdication of their teaching roles is one reason many forms of student government fail. All participants in a system which relies on member participation need to learn communication, problem-solving skills, and political skills such as organizing, caucusing, defining issues, planning strategy, negotiating, collaborating, and compromising. When no such training is available, the students suffer most, due to their inexperience. Unfortunately, when unskilled and inexperienced students do participate ineffectively, adults then blame them personally or collectively, instead of realizing their co-responsibility for that inadequacy. Yet, if teachers and administrators were to teach students political skills, they might find themselves outmaneuvered and outvoted by coalitions of students and other adults. This may account for the "hands off" rationale held by some teachers.

Teachers may also need to teach students to be involved and concerned about issues relating not only to personal interests but also to those of the larger social community. Social problems courses and dialogues may indirectly foster student involvement in school governance and curriculum and emphasize the value of participatory democracy.

Individual Freedom Versus Social Justice

A central aim of student power is to provide students with greater control over their own school programs and activities. All our schools experimented in this direction and found themselves struggling to resolve the dilemma between "doing your own thing" and "working for the good of the collective unit." A genuine individualism of interests was found often; but a cultural pluralism, which requires collectivities of individual interests, was usually lacking. These issues are especially poignant in all new social systems attempting to integrate and serve both individualistic and collective priorities. Individualism is important as a cultural priority among many middle class youth—the main consumers of some of these alternatives. When survival of the collective unit appeared to be at stake, all rallied around and depressed individual priorities; in time of affluence and sustenance for the school, students again pressed their highly individual priorities. These high needs for individual autonomy made collective organization by students difficult and caused them to project multiple, diffuse, and often conflicting goals upon their school programs. Students

wanted freedom and also community: programs tailored to suit widely
varying individual needs but also unified as coherent, clearly untraditional
alternatives.

The dilemma between individual and collective values stresses further
the problem of creating or maintaining a pluralistic or antiracist school.
Clearly, pluralism is difficult to create experimentally in the midst of a
monolithic culture. Furthermore, a concerted revision of racist structures
and practices is difficult in an atmosphere of individualism and "doing
your own thing." The latter was a major barrier in our innovative schools.

Student and staff populations were all white at MIS and Sudbury
Valley; and though the other four schools had racially mixed student
bodies and staffs, few of their curricula and organizations ventured far
in a pluralistic or antiracist direction. White control predominated: Some
black students found it difficult to work in the white-oriented Metro
High School; even CH was not sufficiently pluralistic to meet the needs of
black students, who first formed their own tribal unit and then left the
school to form "Black House," a separate black alternative. All the interracial schools lacked sufficient black or other minority staff to create a
a truly multi-ethnic support system. Nor did pluralism exist on a social
class level within these schools; middle class values, in curriculum content
and organization and career guidance, predominated.

The counter-culture, white, middle class orientation of most innovative
schools leads many people (Arthur Pearl, Jonathan Kozol, for example)
to question the ultimate value of such new programs if they perpetuate
racist, elitist schools. If students and teachers continue to give priority
to the goals of personal growth rather than social justice, they cannot hope
to reform their own racist institutions. They may change themselves, but
in all probability they will not change their schools as rapidly or as per-
vasively as they might if their primary goals were other than they are. A
commitment to pluralism and antiracism means that other goals, programs,
policies, and activities must follow from that primary goal statement.
Courses in antiracism, white awareness, ethnic studies, and social change
must be offered in addition to such studies as organic gardening, psychology, batik-dyeing, candlemaking, and so on.

Despite the failure to deal with ethnic or cultural pluralism, more student power than is traditional did permit a more pluralistic set of values
and norms in youth-adult and client-professional relations. Students acting
as teachers, teachers learning from their students, teachers open to legitimate student influence and curriculum determination, and students active

as program and policy makers meant that adult authority was not taken for granted and teacher and student roles were modified. Rather than perceiving themselves as professionals with all the expertise, many teachers in these new programs credited students—their clients—with expertise and the ability to make important decisions for themselves.

This paper has analyzed student power from various perspectives. We have discussed its value in creating more pluralistic, less oppressive, schools. We have examined structural aspects of governance, finding that a clear and comprehensive formal mechanism is most successful, especially when supported by an open, active network of honest and respectful informal relationships. We have detailed the ways in which student participation in the instructional process strengthens their involvement in school governance and argued that student power in governance is not possible without student power over classroom and instructional processes. We have detailed other barriers to student participation: early socialization for dependency and lack of political skill training. And we have mentioned sponsibilities to teach and guide, a premature hands-off policy advocated important barriers which adults present: teachers' abdication of their re- by administrators, and their creation of structures and processes for all school members that are most comfortable for adults, making it easier for them to dominate. Finally, we suggested that planning, training, evaluating, and sharing data are vital aspects of a school program in which students and adults participate in governance.

Readings

Bryant, B. Intergroup conflict and the instructional process in seven secondary schools. Unpublished doctoral dissertation, University of Michigan, 1970.

Chesler, M., & BenDor, J. *Interracial and intergenerational conflict in secondary schools.* Ann Arbor: Educational Change Team, The University of Michigan, 1970.

Chesler, M., & Lohman, J. Changing schools through student advocacy. In R. Schmuck and M. Miles (Eds.), *Organization development in schools.* Palo Alto, Calif.: National Press Books, 1971.

Coleman, J., et al. *Equality of educational opportunity.* Washington, D.C.: United States Office of Education, 1966.

Coser, L. *Continuities in the study of social conflict.* New York: The Free Press, 1967.

Crowfoot, J. Conflict in high schools: Theory and illustrative data. Doctoral dissertation, University of Michigan, 1972.

Danforth Foundation. *The school and the democratic environment.* New York: Columbia University Press, 1970.

Divoky, D. (Ed.) *How old will you be in 1984?* New York: Avon Books, 1969.

Farber, J. *The student as nigger.* New York: Pocket Press, 1970.

Friedenberg, E. Current patterns of a generational conflict. *Journal of Social Issues,* 1969, 25, 21.

Gross, R., & Gross, B. *Radical school reform.* New York: Simon & Schuster, 1969.

Gross, R., & Osterman, P. (Eds.) *High School.* New York: Simon & Schuster, 1971.

Hess, R. Political socialization in the schools. *Harvard Educational Review,* 1968, 38, 528–536.

Horowitz, I. Consensus, conflict and cooperation: A sociological inventory. *Social Forces,* 1962, 41, 177–188.

Kozol, J. *Death at an early age.* Boston: Houghton–Mifflin, 1967.

Kozol, J. *Free schools.* Boston: Houghton–Mifflin, 1972.

Leonard, G. *Education and ecstacy.* New York: Delacorte, 1968.

Meil, O. *The short-changed children of suburbia.* New York: Institute of Human Relations Press, 1967.

New Schools Exchange Newsletter. 301 East Canon Perdido, Santa Barbara, Calif.

Newmann, F., & Oliver, D. Education and community. *Harvard Educational Review,* 1967, 37, 61–106.

Pearl, A. What's wrong with the new informalism in education? *Social Policy.* 1971, 1, 15–23.

Rasberry, S. *Rasberry exercises: How to start your own school—and make a book.* Albion, Calif.: Freestone Publishing Co., 1970.

Resnik, H. *Turning on the system.* New York: Pantheon Books (Random House), 1970.

Rhea, B. Institutional paternalism in high schools. *The Urban Review, 1968,* 3–4, 13–15.

Seligson, T. Free schools vs. public schools. *Evergreen,* 1971, 29–35.

Silberman, C. *Crisis in the classroom.* New York: Random House, 1970.

Stretch, B. The rise of the free schools. *Saturday Review,* June 1970, 76–79+.

Wasserman, M. School mythology and the education of oppression. *Schools,* 1971, 5, 25–36.

Wittes, S. *Contemporary school crisis: A diagnosis.* Ann Arbor: Educational Change Team, The University of Michigan, 1971.

21

Some Conclusions and Questions About Decision-Making in Alternative Secondary Schools
by The Center for New Schools

The "conclusions and questions" in this paper were reached as the result of the concentrated cooperation of 31 people who attended[1] the national "Conference on Decision-making in Alternative Schools," in February, 1972, held at the Woodstock Center, Woodstock, Illinois, sponsored by the Center for New Schools and UNESCO. The conference purpose was to follow up on research the Center for New Schools had been conducting about decision-making in alternative schools. The report from which the questions and conclusions below were extracted was prepared by the Center for New Schools.

The conference participants attempted to address the ingredients in the development of decision-making in alternative schools with a focus on students and staff. The following are some of the conclusions the group reached:

> "... the need for further analysis and experimentation should not obscure the extent to which the conference participants were able to agree on the common threads in their past experience and the common issues that are key to strengthening of alternative school decision-making in the future. The commonalities are summarized below:
>
> 1. You can't build a healthy alternative school merely by opposing everything the old school stands for.
> 2. Even when teachers, students, and parents leave traditional schools, they still bring with them their past experiences, atti-

---

*Prepared by The Center for New Schools, 59 E. Van Buren, Chicago, Ill. 60605 (copyright 1976). Reprinted by permission.
1. See end of Chapter for list of names.

tudes, strengths, and weaknesses. These characteristics often emerge in the new situation rather than some "natural" man or woman.

3. The staff of any alternative school will almost inevitably play a central role in the school because of their experience, constant access to information, professional stake in the school, etc. Ways must be found to reconcile this reality with an effective plan for shared decision-making.

4. Certain functions must be carried out for an alternative to survive and reach its goals, and there are a limited number of approaches that can be used to carry out these functions effectively.

5. Many values and approaches that have been dubbed "natural" by the alternative school movement reflect, in reality, the particular world-view of the American white middle class.

6. There are strong similarities in the specific ways in which various alternative schools have tried to reach their goals and in the problems they have encountered.

7. The alternative school is in danger of becoming the latest national fad in education.

8. Alternative schools that are just starting are repeating many of the same energy-consuming mistakes of existing alternative schools.

9. Direct democracy through all-school or community meetings is inadequate as the primary method of decision-making. Some effective form of representative governance must be found.

10. Students who enter alternative schools typically have limited interest in becoming involved in decision-making, beyond insuring their freedom in areas touching their daily personal lives, such as dress, movement, association, etc.

11. Students strongly distrust anything that resembles traditional governance structures because of their negative past experience with student councils, etc.

12. Students generally see their most appropriate role in decision-making in terms of complaining to the staff and letting them solve the problems. But unless they are involved in the complexities of making and carrying out decisions, it seems unlikely that students will feel the institution has dealt adequately with their problems.

13. Student involvement in decision-making is often limited to a small subgroup of middle class hip students. Other subgroups aren't adequately represented by these students.

14. An important goal of an alternative school should be to help students learn to become effectively involved in decisions about key social issues not tied to their immediate personal comfort.

15. In their desire to be open and non-authoritarian, faculty fail to make full use of their competence in alternative schools.

16. Having escaped the phony expertise of the traditional school,

staff members underestimate the need for new forms of expertise in alternative schools.

17. 200 students seems to be the upper limit in school size before a qualitatively different set of problems emerge in decision-making. Beyond this limit, it is impossible to settle many crucial problems through face-to-face contact.

18. It does not seem workable in practice (in addition to whatever ethical problems it raises) for an alternative to be imposed on students who can't freely choose it.

19. Physical location places key constraints on alternative school decision-making.

20. No alternative operates "outside the system." Schools merely choose the points at which they wish to relate to the larger society. The school will constantly face the issue of conflict between its own agenda and the agenda of the outside individuals and organizations to which it must relate.

21. Staff and students of alternative schools act more often on the idea of "doing your own thing" than on the idea of "building a community." In practice staff and students are often unwilling to change their personal priorities or habits for the good of the community.

22. Constant appeals to the danger of external threats are inadequate to build an alternative community.

23. There is often a limited amount of trust between people in alternative schools. This is related to an extreme reluctance to delegate authority or to allow anyone to play a leadership role.

24. One of the primary means for strengthening alternative school decision-making should be to increase its clarity.

25. Without clarity concerning basic goals, continuing conflicts on specifics are likely to immobilize the school.

26. Schools should clarify what external constraints they operate under. Any student or teacher joining the school should understand that at that point in time, these external constraints are a reality of the school's operation.

27. While maintaining an atmosphere of freedom and sensitivity to individuals, alternative schools must define the understandings and limits that have been set up internally. The resulting responsibilities of students and teachers should be clarified as a condition for becoming part of the school.

28. A clear structure for shared decision-making should be developed that tells the school community who decides what, how, and when. The nature of this structure should be effectively communicated to everyone in the school.

29. Since a key danger in a representative decision-making process is that there will be a gap between the decision-makers and the rest of the community, a major activity of the governance struc-

ture should be to inform people about the decisions that have been made and the ways in which additional people can feed back information to or get directly involved in decision-making.

30. An explicit procedure should be followed within the decision-making meetings that clarifies such issues as the relation of the decision to the school's goals, the external constraints that might be in conflict with the decision, etc.

31. Alternative schools have found that carrying out decisions is even more difficult than making them. Any decision must include the definition of clear responsibilities for carrying it out.

32. Members of the school community should agree to comply with legitimate decisions even when they don't personally agree with them.

33. Clear provisions should be developed for the exclusion of staff and students. A process should be spelled out that provides many opportunities for feedback, self-defense, etc., but culminates with the possibility that a person can be excluded from the school.

34. At present, middle class students see their concerns acted on in schools with diverse student bodies more often than other students. Means for remedying this situation must be found.

35. School initiators should carefully examine their reasons for seeking a diverse student body and their capacity to deal with one. Another possible approach is to create a series of alternative schools each with a unique set of purposes, rather than admitting everyone to a single school with vaguely defined purposes.

36. Even as one of a series of focused schools, an effective alternative school must be more effective in dealing positively with diverse cultural backgrounds, interests, attitudes, abilities, etc.

37. Transitional strategies are necessary to help students move from dependent to independent learning. These strategies must not have the effect of creating a new brand of passive learning within a more humane environment.

38. The pros and cons of the smorgasbord approach to curriculum must be carefully explored and alternatives developed that will work in practice.

39. Decision-making about a direction for alternative school curriculum raises all the problems of clarity, trust, commitment, leadership, benefits to subgroups, etc., raised in other decision-making areas.

40. Teachers need to learn about and develop positive alternative approaches to classroom decision-making techniques of teaching, and techniques of individual and group counseling. It is not enough to be a warm open person who wants to move in a new direction unless one is working to develop such skills.

41. There was disagreement about the value of requiring certain competence levels or certain learning experiences for all students. The pros and cons of this issue should be thoroughly explored.

42. Alternative school staff and students have limited amount of energy, and "burning out" is a major threat to alternative schools. Overall decision-making structures and specific decisions should both be considered in light of the best ways of using limited energy.

The 31 participants were:

Paul Adorno, Teacher-Director, School for Human Services, Philadelphia, Pennsylvania

Daniel Burke, Co-Director, National Consortium on Educational Alternatives, Indiana University, Bloomington, Indiana

Paul Coste, Chief, Secondary Education Section, UNESCO, Paris, France

Anne Emery, Principal, Walbrook High School, Baltimore, Maryland

Deborah Ennis, Student, Shanti School, Hartford, Connecticut

Jerry Fletcher, Researcher, Franklin Pierce Experimental Schools Evaluation Project, Tacoma, Washington

Curman Gaines, Administrative Intern, Career Study Center, St. Paul, Minnesota

Preston Garnett, Teacher, Metro High School, Chicago, Illinois

Renny Golden, Teacher, St. Mary Center for Learning, Chicago, Illinois

Charity James, Writer and Teacher, Newton, Massachusetts

Dick Johnson, Executive Associate, Center for New Schools, Chicago, Illinois

Mike Lawler, Counselor, The Group School, Cambridge, Massachusetts

Cal Moore, Teacher, Community High School, Berkeley, California

Don Moore, Executive Associate, Center for New Schools, Chicago, Illinois

Fritz Mulhauser, Researcher, Franklin Pierce Experimental Schools Evaluation Project, Tacoma, Washington

Sumiko Nakadgawa, Student, Berkeley Community High School, Berkeley, California

Frances Newton, curriculum Supervisor, St. Teresa Academy, East St. Louis, Illinois

Dierdre Perry, Student, Cleveland Urban Learning Community, Cleveland, Ohio

Bill Phillips, Principal, Marshall-University High School, Minneapolis, Minnesota

Jim Robbins, Director, Technical Assistance Group, Quality Schools Network, Office of the Superintendent of Public Instruction, Springfield, Illinois

Bob Schwartz, Special Assistant for Education, Kevin White, Mayor of Boston, Massachusetts

Ethan Seltzer, Student, Marshall-University High School, Minneapolis, Minnesota

Ruth Steele, Administrator, Parkway Program, Philadelphia, Pennsylvania

Andrea Temkin, Former Student, Metro High School, Chicago, Illinois

Eva Travers, Alternative School Project, Philadelphia, Pennsylvania

Gilbert Tyson, Student, Metro High School, Chicago, Illinois
Steve Wilson, Research Associate, Center for New Schools,
    Chicago, Illinois
Tom Wilson, Executive Associate, Center for New Schools,
    Chicago, Illinois
Glorianne Wittes, Director, Center Associates, Ann Arbor, Michigan
Saul Yanofsky, Director of Research and Planning, Pennsylvania
    Advancement School, Philadelphia, Pennsylvania
Darryl Young, Teacher-Director, Farragut Outpost, Chicago, Illinois

22

In a System of Choice, Teachers' Roles Change

by Robert R. Nolan and Helen Carey

The classroom is large, square, and sunny. Benches and shelves round the walls hold a variety of neatly stacked ditto sheets and other materials. At the back of the room is a star chart for arithmetic scores; on another wall a large hand-lettered poster stresses the importance of good manners; and above the blackboard is a motto, "Train up the child in the way that he should go and when he is old he will not depart from it." At the front of the room, the teacher is drilling her twelve-year-olds in choral reading. They stand in two rows: a gesture from her slows down two who are outpacing the rest of the class.

In another classroom, a teacher presides over a scene alive with movement. Some of her eight-year-olds are seated at scattered tables, engaged in individual projects; others have their heads together in earnest consultation; others again are working at various "learning stations" dotted around the room. Several boys and girls are grouped round a plastic wading-pool in one corner, showing visitors the latest acquisition: half a dozen three-inch-long scarlet crayfish. They pick the creatures up, eagerly demonstrating each one's peculiarities— "That one, he's got a hurt claw, see?" The teacher glances over to the group and says impartially "You guys still haven't figured out which are the boys and which are the girls."

Two different schools? Yes—and no. Both classrooms were located at Goss Elementary School, one of the schools in the "voucher project" implemented by California's Alum Rock Union Elementary School District.

The Concept of Vouchers

The concept of vouchers for schooling is not new and has a number of variations (Carr and Haywood 1970; Flygare 1973). Most voucher advocates argue that public schools are inefficient and unresponsive to student needs because they are virtually public monopolies. Parents pay heavy taxes to support schools yet have no real choice in where they send their children. Only the well-to-do can afford private schools. Others must go to the public school in their district and normally to the one school prescribed under district zoning regulations.

If schools were subject to the economic forces of the open market, "good" schools would prosper and increase and "bad" schools would fold. The voucher system provides a mechanism for creating this situation. Each parent would be given a voucher equivalent to the value of the current per pupil cost of education. Parents could enroll their child in the school of their choice, public or private, and the chosen school would receive government money as stipulated on the voucher. If parents wanted to spend more on their child's education than the amount on the voucher, they could contribute additional funds.

In a voucher system, schools would compete for students in order to survive—no students would mean no money. Schools would be forced to be responsive to parent demands and would work toward optimum efficiency and effectiveness. If they did not, they would go out of business. Parents would have greater choice, satisfaction, and control over their children's education. Schools would be accountable with a power shift from bureaucrats to parents. Assuming that different children learn best in different ways, each child could attend the school with the "best" approach for him or her. Education would thus become decentralized with more options.

A number of objections to the voucher concept have been discussed (Selden 1971; Glennan 1971). If parents had complete freedom of choice, schools would become racially segregated and if parents were permitted to add to the amount of money provided by the voucher, economically segregated as well. There are constitutional objections to giving tax dollars to church affiliated schools. Teachers and administrators, instead of devoting their energies to the improvement of education, would have to become salespersons and public relations experts to survive. Fake claims and educational hucksterism would abound. Parents, especially the less educated, might not have the experience to make wise choices among conflicting claims.

The Alum Rock Voucher Project

Late in 1970 the Office of Economic Opportunity asked for school districts to volunteer to test the voucher concept. Of the districts which agreed to feasibility studies, only Alum Rock on the outskirts of San Jose, California, proceeded to implement the voucher concept on an experimental basis.

Why Alum Rock? The district is relatively poor and the decision attracted millions of dollars in federal aid. In addition, Alum Rock had an energetic school board and a new superintendent who saw vouchers as a way to achieve two goals: decentralization and increased parent involvement.

The Alum Rock school population is about 50 percent Spanish-surnamed, 12 percent black, and 1 percent Oriental, numbering about 15,000 students altogether. Neighborhood housing is integrated and individual school populations have never been racially imbalanced. About half the students in the district are from low-income families and the vouchers given to the parents of these students reflect an extra allocation equivalent to a per pupil compensatory funding.

Fourteen of the district's twenty-five schools participated in the project. These fourteen schools offered a total of fifty-five alternative programs or minischools. To prevent the possibility of racial segregation, there were upper limits on the number of students from particular ethnic groups who could enroll in a particular program. No private school was involved in the project, not because participation was definitely ruled out, but because no private school was willing or able to meet the project's financial and student admission regulations.

How Did the Voucher Project Affect Teachers?

When the voucher concept was being debated prior to its adoption at Alum Rock, most discussion concerned financing, desegregation, politics, and constitutional and philosophical questions. Little was said about possible effects on classroom teachers. Now that the Alum Rock Voucher Project has formally ended, we can begin to see how teachers were affected when parents and students were given the choice of a number of educational programs. Based on our interviews and discussions with teachers and administrators and classroom observations, we believe those effects were varied and profound.

  a. *Teachers had to assume many responsibilities formerly handled by administrators.*

Teachers had more autonomy in decisions concerning curriculum, instruction, and materials selection. Scheduling of classes and students, staff organization, relations with parents and community, and the business of ordering materials required increased expenditures of time and energy. In fact the organizational burden was the major focus of teachers' complaints. Teachers requested training in administrative skills and in some cases transferred responsibilities back to administrators.

Concurrently, the role of the school administrator changed. Administrators became less directive and more collaborative. Most spent a great deal of time assisting teachers in overcoming commonly acknowledged problems. At Goss Elementary School, for example, the principal and curriculum director met with each teacher to cooperatively identify two or three areas for improvement. These administrators saw their function as facilitating staff development and used a multifaceted approach which stressed constructive peer criticism.

> b. *Teachers were under pressure to innovate since it was important to provide educational options responsive to parents' wishes.*

Since extra voucher funding was given students from low-income families, programs which attracted these students were "rich." Bicultural and multicultural programs were designed especially for these students.

With the introduction of new programs teachers felt an increased need to know about new materials and methods. Often, however, program innovations had been in the minds of teachers for some time. The voucher project simply provided them the opportunity to implement those ideas.

> c. *Most teachers had greater freedom to teach what and how they wanted.*

The majority of teachers taught in their "first choice" program which usually was the one most compatible with their own style and goals. Thus most teachers taught the way they wanted, unhampered by a sense of disapproval from their colleagues. In addition, most teachers felt "more responsible for the educational outcomes, since it [was] 'their' program they [were] implementing" (Weiler 1974, p. xv).

> d. *While teachers had increased control over curriculum and other matters, they also faced increased job and/or status insecurity.*

If their program attracted too few students, teachers faced transfer to a program not of their choice—or worse, transfer to "permanent substitute" status. Even in programs for which enrollment remained steady, tension existed.

e. Teachers had to devote considerable time to "public relations" and assessment of parental input.

Dissatisfied parents could not only complain but also transfer their children to alternative programs—and the money went with the child.

f. With teachers assuming many new roles and duties, the question of appropriate rules and standards to govern teacher behavior in a system of choice became critical.

For instance, there was the risk that teachers would fall into the trap of making inflated claims for their programs. In encouraging enrollments, what constitutes legitimate publicity and what becomes unethical promotional activity? In a very real sense, programs—and teachers—are in competition with one another. What happens to traditional professional norms? Alum Rock teachers never came to a consensus on these questions.

g. All teachers became part of minischool "teams" whether or not they taught in self-contained classrooms.

Most curriculum and scheduling decisions were made by the staff or "team" of each minischool. Each teacher was subject to powerful influence from fellow team members. Each team developed its own distinctive pattern of behavior and interaction. Many minischool teams became social as well as work groups. However, a relatively high degree of tension and isolation existed between teams of different minischools. The old concept of a single school staff gave way to what was in some cases an uneasy coexistence between minischool teams which had conflicting orientations and implemented very different programs.

h. Teachers usually faced classes composed of selected students.

Most students were in their "first choice" programs. Many classes were more homogeneous in the sense of students possessing common interests and common instructional needs. Teachers experienced lower student absenteeism and greater parental satisfaction.

Overall, were these changes in teachers' roles beneficial? As with many educational innovations, an unqualified answer is impossible. It is clear that there were many trade-offs—greater teacher autonomy brought time-consuming responsibilities, within-program cohesion was often offset by between-program tensions, and parental involvement required greater teacher efforts toward improving communication.

As demonstrated by a variety of alternative schools projects (for example, the Berkeley Experimental Schools project), the voucher system of financing is not necessary to create a districtwide system of educational options. Even with the formal end of the voucher project, Alum Rock has retained the concept of choice. We believe that most, if not all, of the changes in teachers' roles at Alum Rock would occur in any school district offering a comprehensive system of parent-chosen options.

References

Carr, Ray A., and Gerald C. Hayword. "Education by Chit: An Examination of Voucher Proposals." *Education and Urban Society* II: 3 (February 1970): 179–91.

Flygare, Thomas J. "An Abbreviated Voucher Primer." *Inequality In Education* 15 (November 1973) 53–56.

Glennan, Thomas R. "OEO Experiments In Education." *Compact* V:1 (February 1971): 3–5.

Seldon, David. "Vouchers–Solution or Sop?" *Teachers College Record* LXXII:3 (February 1971): 365–71.

Weiler, Daniel. *A Public School Voucher Demonstration: The First Year at Alum Rock.* (R-1495-NIE), RAND, Santa Monica (California), June 1974.

23
Removing the Clouds from Sunshine School
by Kathleen M. Huguenin and Terrence E. Deal

1. Introduction

Alternative high schools by definition depart from traditional patterns. Some researchers see the critical distinction as modified governance and organizational structures (Duke 1975); some point to revisions in goals and evaluation processes (McCauley 1972); others speculate that what makes alternative schools unique are alterations in the instructional process—who is involved as well as why, what, when, and where learning takes place (Deal 1975).

Empirical studies of exactly what makes alternative high schools different are rare. It seems reasonable to suppose, however, that such schools —schools-within-schools, schools-without-walls, continuation schools, or any other type—differ from their traditional counterparts in several respects: different goals, different structures, different approaches to instruction, different relationships with their environments, and even different informal norms.

These patterns are the "blessing" that make alternative schools unique and their existence possible. But often these departures from tradition are also a "curse" that makes the stability of such schools—and even their survival—problematic. Problems of survival, conflict, excessive time demands, morale, and staff "burnout" confront most alternative schools at some point in their development. If not much is known about what makes alternative schools different, even less is known about the relationship between these various changes and problems that seem to recur. Little knowledge presently exists to assist alternative school administrators, teachers, students, and parents in designing new patterns in ways so that problems will not overwhelm the school.

This article—an empirically-based study of one alternative high school (here called Sunshine High School)—suggests a link between the patterns and problems that existed and describes an approach whereby such troublesome patterns were successfully altered. First, a conceptual scheme for differentiating alternative from traditional high schools is presented. Next, survey data are used to highlight the existing organizational patterns at Sunshine. Observations and interview data are then employed in an attempt to link these organizational patterns with the problems as reported by the school's staff. Finally, it is demonstrated how systematically feeding back the results of the study (as part of an organizational problem-solving technique) helped the staff revise their existing organizational patterns and thus reduce their problems.

II. A Framework—Comparing Alternative and Traditional High Schools

Although there is probably no such thing as a "typical" traditional or "typical" alternative high school, at least five areas exist in which both types of schools can be contrasted. These five areas are components that comprise any organization. Alternative and traditional schools can be compared conceptually as two totally different organizational types—each with different goals, instructional programs (technologies), formal structures, informal patterns, and relationships with the community environment.

III. Organiaztional Patterns That Existed at Sunshine School

Sunshine High is a publicly-financed alternative school located in a large California city. The school is three years old and has a staff of seven: a head teacher, five teachers, and a secretary. The school has seventy-five students selected from the district's secondary student population on the basis of their dissatisfaction with traditional high school programs.

Problems among individual staff members prompted the school to seek outside assistance in solving what they described as "intense interpersonal and philosophical differences here at Sunshine." As outside consultants, we encouraged the staff to think of these problems as symptoms of underlying organizational difficulties. As the first step in a planned change effort, we conducted a survey to measure all five aspects of Sunshine High's existing organizational patterns.

FIGURE 1

	"Typical" Traditional School	"Typical" Alternative School
Goals:	Emphasis on transmission of subject matter, the basic skills, and preparing students for college.	Emphasis on personal development, creative expression, and "relevant" experience.
Technology: (instructional program)	Age-graded "batches" of students move sequentially through specified class periods. Content, learning activities, and evaluation are teacher determined. All students learn pretty much the same thing, from the same material, usually in large groups. Learning activities take place on campus between the hours of 8 and 4.	Students move individually and non-sequentially through activities determined to a large extent by student interests. Content, method, and evaluation patterns vary by individual student. Learning takes place in individual and small settings in a variety of contexts and at diverse times.
Formal Structure:	Large enrollment. Roles are differentiated by subject matter (history teachers, English teachers) less so by function (counselors, specialists). Little interdependence among teachers who have their individual self-contained "baronies." Formal authority is vested in a principal and department heads who have considerable formal influence over schoolwide decisions. Schoolwide policies determine many aspects of the school's operation. Formal meetings are infrequent, often ritualistic, and mainly for the purpose of exchanging information. When decisions are made, it is by majority vote. Evaluation of staff is sporadic, usually done by the principal or department head.	Small enrollment. Roles are either undifferentiated or differentiated by interest or function. Considerable interdependence among teachers. Authority is vested in the collective—either staff or staff and students. Formal policies often nonexistent or vague. Formal meetings are frequent, used as a format for making important decisions and solving pressing problems. Decisions are usually made by consensus. Evaluation infrequent, often done by fellow staff or students.
Informal Patterns:	Emphasis on autonomy and competition. Informal cliques are the basis for social and job-related interaction. Informal patterns may undermine formal decisions.	Emphasis on "togetherness" and cooperation (often masked competition). Little distinction between formal and informal. Informal patterns have a profound impact on the overall operation of the school.
Community Environment:	Although the environment controls the overall direction of the school, it is "buffered" from day-to-day decision making. The environment determines the clientele as the school must accept anyone who wishes to attend.	The environment often is more active in the day-to-day decision making of the school (although in some cases alternative choices close themselves off). Parents and community often take part as "resource" people. Learning often takes place in the community: The school exercises more control over the clientele.

315

A questionnaire was administered to each of the staff members. Questions focused on each of the five organizational areas outlined above. Staff responses are summarized below. (For details see Deal and Huguenin 1977.) The results confirm that Sunshine fits the "typical" model of an alternative high school organization.

Goals

The instructional areas assigned greatest emphasis[1] by the staff were reported to be as follows:

Table I
Degree of Emphasis Assigned by Staff to Educational Goals

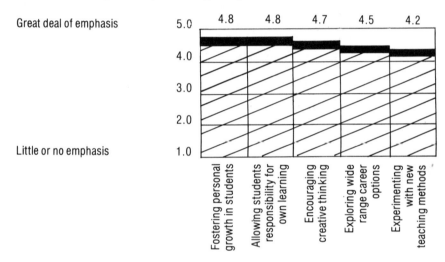

Instructional Technology

Staff members were also asked to respond to questions about classroom activities: grouping patterns, variation in materials, and the amount of student autonomy. First, staff members were asked how students in their classes were organized most frequently. Their response could range (on a four point scale) from "Students Work Independently" (4), to "The

---

1. From a list of fourteen possible areas, these were the areas with a mean of 4.0 or higher.

Whole Class Is Grouped Together" (1). The mean response was 3.4, indicating that teachers were organizing students in a highly differentiated fashion.

Second, a similar question asked staff members to describe the variety of materials used by students. Staff members were given a four point scale varying from "Each Student Uses Different Materials" (4), to "All Students Generally Use the Same Materials" (1). Again, a high degree of individualization was noted; the combined mean was 3.5.

In response to the question concerning how many of the students were regularly given the opportunity to exercise autonomy or to make decisions, a pattern emerged. See Table 2.

Table 2
Extent of Student Choice Across Several Instructional Areas

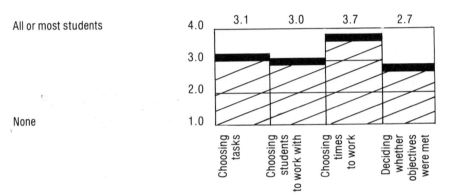

Structure

The questionnaire also contained items focusing on staff roles, relationships, and processes—the formal structure of the school. This area included role differentiation, interdependence, evaluation, authority, policies, and formal meetings.

To assess the degree of role differentiation, staff members were asked (on a five point scale varying from "A Great Deal" (5) to "Not at All" (1)) to what extent a list of nine responsibilities were part of their present assignment. In seven areas three or more staff members claimed "A Great Deal" or "Considerable Responsibility," while in two areas all staff members claimed "Little" or "No Responsibility."

Three questions were used to gauge the level of interdependence among staff members: "How frequently do you share materials with other teachers?", "To what extent do you have to take other members into account in your own teaching?", and "How much do you depend on each of the following members of the staff in performing your job effectively?" All three questions used five point scales with five representing high inter-dependence and one representing low interdependence. Combined means were 2.8, 2.7, and 2.6 for the three areas respectively.

Evaluation patterns were assessed by asking staff members how often and from which sources they learned, directly or indirectly, how well they were doing. Table 3 shows the averages for each evaluation source.

Table 3
Frequency of Evaluation Across Sources

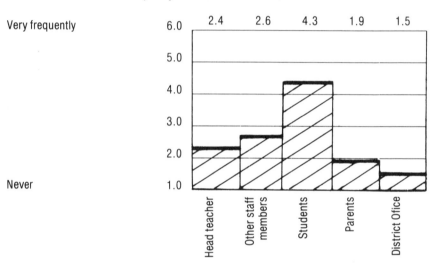

Authority was measured by asking individual staff members how various individuals or groups were involved in making decisions. The average level of involvement for each individual or group is shown in Table 4.

The amount of schoolwide policy was measured by asking staff members to describe school policies in several areas. Three responses were possible: (1) Little or no policy, (2) General guidelines only, and (3) Detailed, explicit policy. The overall mean was 1.8, revealing a relatively low level of formal policy in the school.

Table 4
Overall Involvement in Decision Making Across Groups

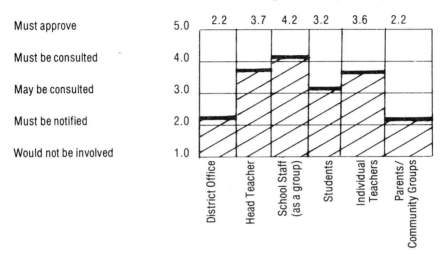

A variety of questions focused on the structure of formal meetings. It was reported that staff meetings were held daily lasting at least two hours. When staff members' responses in this area were compared to responses representative of "ideal" meetings,[2] we found the interpersonal climate of meetings at Sunshine deviated in only two out of nine areas, while the problem solving processes employed in these meetings deviated from the "ideal" in five out of eleven areas.

Informal Patterns

To assess informal patterns at Sunshine, staff members were asked to indicate how frequently the general atmosphere of the school displayed certain characteristics. These characteristics have been used in previous work to indicate a positive interpersonal climate (Schmuck and Runkle 1972). Responses ranged from "Always" (5) to "Almost Never" (1). Ten out of the twelve areas, contrary to the initial staff reports of a "negative" interpersonal climate, had means of 3.0 or higher.

---

2. The "ideal" meeting score was developed by having two organizational development experts independently determine the ideal in each response category.

Environment

Staff members were asked to what extent the school used various kinds of techniques to "connect" the school with parents and the local community. On a five point scale ranging from "Once a Week or More" (5) to "Not at All" (1) the mean response was 2.2.

The results show that Sunshine High's organization fits the typical alternative school pattern in most respects. In summary, its staff members emphasize personal development, student responsibility, creativity, and other less "traditional" goals. Most instruction is relatively individualized, and students have considerable autonomy in what they do, with whom, and when. Structurally the school is small, the staff undifferentiated, and interdependence among staff members moderate; the source of formal evaluation for teachers emanates mainly from the students, authority is centered in the staff as a group, policies are general or nonexistent, formal meetings are frequent, and, we shall see later, the main arena for important decision making. Sunshine's norms emphasize cooperation and togetherness; and the school is essentially buffered from its environment.

IV. Problems of Time, Conflict, and Morale at Sunshine

The survey, on-site observations of Sunshine School, and interviews with staff members further confirmed many of the school's problems: (1) the frequency and the length of formal staff meetings (daily and usually lasting two hours or more), (2) conflict among staff members which surfaced frequently in the formal meetings and to a lesser extent in day-to-day interaction, (3) a high level of dissatisfaction among staff members about various aspects of their jobs—particularly relationships with other staff members, and (4) concern over the increasing negative impact of staff members' "arguments" on Sunshine's instructional program (even students were beginning to notice the interstaff rivalry and conflict). Thus, the problems at Sunshine also seemed typical of many alternative schools.

V. Explaining the Link Between Sunshine's Problems and Existing Organizational Patterns

The analysis of interviews, observations, and questionnaires yielded alternative explanations about the roots of these problems which staff members had previously attributed to personal and philosophical differences and a negative interpersonal climate.

Survey results showed that staff members agreed on the goals of the school. Variations among the staff members' approaches to instruction showed more divergence in instructional means than in instructional goals. Further, the interpersonal climate of the school was relatively healthy. This suggested that the roots of Sunshine's problems were not in the interpersonal or philosophical aspects of the school.

However, the findings revealed some basic flaws in the formal structure. Sunshine High had very few explicit policies, and staff members did not share a uniform perception about the amount of policy in any given area. This meant that each problem or event had to be tackled individually— with different ideas about how the problem should be handled. For example, staff members had to meet and decide the merits of each individual case whenever a student was to be admitted or expelled. Since most such cases were emotion-laden this produced some very sensitive and difficult meetings.

Further, no authority had been granted to the head teacher—or to anyone else—to make decisions in specified areas. Across decision areas, it was found that the authority of the staff as a group was higher than that of the head teacher. Each individual teacher had about as much authority as the head teacher. In fact, even students were reported to have nearly as much authority as the head teacher. The authority structure of Sunshine was essentially flat. No one was allowed to rise above "the pack" and make decisions. In addition, the level of agreement among staff members as to how various individuals or groups were involved in decisions was abysmally low. Each decision thus produced misunderstanding and conflict.

The lack of policies and formal authority placed an overwhelming burden on formal meetings as the sole means for solving problems and making decisions. But meetings operated without an agenda, with consensus as the prevailing decision rule, and without clear understandings about how decisions might be implemented and evaluated. The interpersonal climate at meetings was relatively sound but the formal processes and problem solving sequence were absent. Staff members thus spent an inordinate amount of time in meetings making the same decisions over and over again, while conflict rose without any strategies available for its resolution.

In short, heavy demands were put on the staff of Sunshine School. They were striving toward some difficult organizational goals, operating a fairly sophisticated and complex set of instructional activities, and carrying out the various functions of the school with a relatively high degree of staff interdependence.

In theory, organizational coordination, problem solving, and decision making could have been handled in one of several ways. Policies could have been created for a uniform and predetermined approach to recurrent problems. Individuals could have been granted authority to make decisions or solve problems in a given area, or formal meetings could have been structured to allow participants a chance to define problems and develop strategies for their solution.

However, none of these alternatives were being utilized. Weaknesses in the formal patterns of roles and policies thus placed an unduly heavy burden on formal meetings as the primary means for dealing with an unending series of problems. At the same time, high levels of interdependency increased coordination needs and overlaps in roles and responsibilities increased the probability that staff members would step on each others' toes. No mechanisms were available to minimize "toe-stepping" nor to deal with it when it occurred.

In sum, Sunshine School had arranged its human resources in such a way that the structure was working against staff members rather than enabling them to effectively carry out their tasks. From this perspective, the interpersonal difficulties, philosophical struggles, and conflict were symptoms of the more basic problems in the overall organizational patterns of Sunshine School.

VI. The Intervention: Survey Feedback

The intervention used a version of one Organizational Development (OD) technique—survey feedback. This version of the process has three essential components: (1) a framework conceiving of schools as complex, dynamic organizations is explicitly shared with participants, (2) systematic information about the five areas of the organization is collected and fed back to participants, and (3) the participants are trained in group problem solving and involved in identifying problem areas and generating possible solution.

At Sunshine School the process involved the following steps:

1. We (the two authors) met with the school's staff to outline the basic approach, and to define respective roles and responsibilities. As the problems of Sunshine School were obviously centered within the staff, it was decided to survey just the staff, not the students and parents who, under ideal conditions, would be included.

2. Staff members completed interviews and questionnaires and were observed in operation. The information from the survey was then summarized for presentation to the staff.

3. The core of the survey feedback process was conducted in a two-day

workshop with the staff. The first day was devoted to: (*a*) providing the staff a way of viewing problems organizationally. This overview of organizational theory focused attention on the five organizational subsystems (goals, informal patterns, formal structure, instruction, and the community environment) and their dynamic interrelationships; (*b*) training the staff in group problem solving skills, and techniques; and (*c*) familiarizing the staff with various methods of gathering information, and highlighting how such information can be summarized and interpreted.

The second day was devoted to feeding back the actual survey information about the five areas of Sunshine School's organization. For each area, a strategy session defined specific problems, possible solutions, and implementation plans.

As an illustration of how the process worked, the staff was presented information in Table 5 on their role differentiation.

Table 5

Number of staff members claiming:	Great Deal or Considerable Responsibility	Little or None
(1) Work with individual students in counseling	5	2
(2) Work with individual students in basic skills	5	1
(3) Work with individual students in enrichment activities	7	0
(4) Work on administration and coordination	4	1
(5) Liaison with district office	3	4
(6) Work to involve parents	0	3
(7) Provide community with information about the school	2	1
(8) Involve students in career fields	3	2
(9) Keep school records	3	0*

* While there were 7 respondents to each question, the total is not always 7 in each area due to the middle category not being included in the chart.

In discussing existing roles, the staff pinpointed a problem of overlapping responsibilities in some areas, coupled with the fact that in other areas tasks were not being assumed by anyone. It was easy to see that, if three out of seven staff members perceived a great deal of their responsibility to include acting as a liaison with the district office, while no one saw it as their major responsibility to work with parents, some problems were bound to develop. More importantly, the staff was able to identify this problem and to generate possible solutions—most of which focused on manipulating roles rather than changing individuals to fit the existing context.

In this case, the staff arrived at the decision to keep a specific account of the responsibilities and time requirements of each staff role, and to bring in a consultant, if necessary, to help them realign their roles and responsibilities to the demands of their instructional program.

For the other areas specific strategies were also selected. The staff decided to: readminister a specific part of the survey to determine whether the high level of goal agreement still existed; change staff meetings in several ways, including the provision of time for consideration of pros and cons of agenda items; devote several staff meetings to the development of an agreed upon set of schoolwide policies; and investigate and specify the involvement of individuals and groups across decision-making arenas. These strategies reflect the staff's emerging realization that the basic problems of Sunshine—and their eventual solutions—lay in changing the structural rather than interpersonal aspects of the school.

Following the workshop we periodically observed and interviewed the staff. This allowed us to assess the extent to which any or all of the survey feedback components became a regular feature of Sunshine's operation. Based on observations and interviews, we noted that staff members were defining problems organizationally. Staff members shifted their focus from problem definitions based on personalities to those of role conflicts and formal structural relationships. Staff members were demanding an examination of role definitions rather than each others' resignations!

Staff members were also utilizing many of the specific skills and techniques encountered in the workshop. Staff meetings, particularly, took on a new dimension. A rotating facilitator and a clearly defined agenda were evident. Various techniques for solving problems (matrix, force field analysis, fishbowling) were used repeatedly. Meetings and their duration were set in advance.

At the year's end a condensed version of the original questionnaire was readministered to the same staff members. Results from this second survey further substantiated changes in Sunshine's organization. While the goals, instructional program, and informal climate at Sunshine remained relatively stable, significant change was evident in several facets of the formal structure. Staff roles became more differentiated and more clear; interdependence among the staff increased. Authority patterns leveled even more and sources of evaluation became more diversified; policies became more specific and agreement over their existence increased. Meetings were shortened and their frequency dropped to once a week; the interpersonal climate of these meetings moved even closer to the "ideal." The structure of these meetings showed dramatic improvement. Overall, staff members' satisfaction levels increased while conflict decreased.

Problems at Sunshine by no means evaporated, but were redefined and handled in new ways. We were also able to show that a school like Sunshine can change.

VII. Summary and Conclusions

Sunshine High is a fairly typical "alternative" school because of its new and different organizational patterns and its problems.

In approaching these problems Sunshine—and other such schools—could have taken a variety of courses:

First, and consistent with the predominant "psychologized" view in education, the focus could have been on the Sunshine staff members themselves. Individuals could have been replaced or their individual attitudes, behavior, and so on, changed. At Sunshine School, however, no one was particularly amenable to resignation, transfer, or "retraining," and given the constraints of tenure, time, and cost, such individualistic solutions are probably not realistic for most schools.

Second, the problems at Sunshine High School might have been improved by changing the goals or instructional program. However, these areas represented the very tenets upon which Sunshine was based and therefore the staff was unwilling to make modifications. The attachment to particular goals or instructional techniques is generally true of alternative schools, and are often the very things that make such schools unique and provide the glue that holds the staff together.

At Sunshine, largely due to the survey feedback process, a third alternative was selected to attack the problems. The formal structure—roles, relationships, and processes—became the focus of the problem-solving process and the target of change strategies. In similar alternative schools, the formal aspects of the organization may be the root of many problems and also the most promising source of eventual solutions.

Organization Development, a field which applies theory to improve organization, includes techniques which focus attention on the formal structure of organizations. Survey feedback is one such technique and lends itself especially well to the context of alternative schools. Alternative schools are small and thus able to collect and process systematic information more easily than are larger, more complex, traditional settings. Most alternative schools already rely heavily on collective problem-solving, hence the group process skills which participants become acquainted with as part of the process have a ready-made niche. And, by their very nature, alternative schools are already perceived of as "different." Thus they are often able to shift their organizational patterns more easily than traditional schools where many more things are seen as "given."

The "alternative" label needs to extend beyond just referring to altered instructional methods, curriculum, and teacher-student relationships to include the development of organizational patterns necessary to sustain desired changes. Perhaps then alternative schools such as Sunshine will be able to realize the "blessings" of these new and different educational approaches without being overwhelmed by the "curses" that invariably accompany such change efforts.

References

Deal, Terrence E., and Kathleen M. Huguenin. "Using Survey-Feedback in tive Schools." Stanford Center for Research and Development in Teaching. Stanford, Calif.: Stanford University, 1975.

Deal, Terrence E. and Kathleen M. Huguenin. "Using Survey-Feedback in a Small Alternative High School." Stanford Center for Research and Development in Teaching. Stanford, Calif.: Stanford University, 1977.

Duke, Daniel Linden. "Challenge of Bureaucracy: The Contemporary Alternative School," *The Journal of Educational Thought* X, 1 (April 1976): 34–48.

McCauley, B. L., S. M. Dornbusch, and W. R. Scott. "Evaluation and Authority in Alternative Schools and Public Schools." Stanford Center for Research and Development in Teaching. Stanford, Calif.: Stanford University, 1972.

24

Teacher Education for Alternative Schools
by J. Kelly Tonsmeire

Alternative schools are designed to offer options to parents, children, and teachers that would not be available in a traditional school. Yet, almost all alternative school teachers have been trained traditionally. If alternative schools are to truly offer an alternative, people who teach in these schools must be trained in a different manner. It seems obvious that traditional teacher preparation programs are not the best way to train people to teach in nontraditional learning environments. In this article I will deal with both preservice and inservice education for alternative school teachers.

There are two ways to train alternative school teachers. The first way is by preparing teachers specifically to teach in an alternative learning environment. The second way is by training teachers who have been trained and have worked for some time in a traditional learning environment to function effectively in a nontraditional setting. The University of Massachusetts has developed some exciting programs in the area of teacher preparation for alternative schools. During the 1973–74 academic year I had the opportunity to administer an alternative teacher preparation program there. I was responsible for coordinating the second year of a two-year undergraduate teacher preparation program for future public alternative school teachers. Our program was one of several University of Massachusetts programs that were cited for excellence by the American Association of Colleges for Teacher Education.

In attempting to prepare beginning teachers to cope with different environments and role expectations, we made two basic assumptions. First, teacher training programs for alternative schools should be based on the development of multiple competencies. Since the literature on teacher effectiveness indicates there is no common denominator, no single criterion which determines whether or not a teacher is effective, we decided to turn to the schools for the definition of the competencies an alternative school teacher must possess. Second, since teachers tend to teach the way they were taught, the teacher education program, itself, must model the behaviors and processes which are vital to innovative teaching and decision making. Our program identified and attempted to develop the following five teacher competencies: (1) the ability to interact with students, (2) the ability to teach collaboratively, (3) the ability to accept the idea of innovation and change as part of the school, (4) the ability to design and implement curricula, and (5) the ability to build and work within institutions.

Undergraduate students were eligible for admittance to the program during the first semester of their junior year. The two-year alternative schools teacher preparation program was divided into three phases. Phase one lasted one year and was organized around the Inquiry Group, which was composed of ten students and one staff member. The Inquiry Group collaboratively addressed the basic issues of alternative education. Field experiences, which were individually negotiated, were closely linked to the Inquiry Group. Discussion of and commitment to field experiences increased over the course of the first year. A methods component, which could also be individually negotiated, was closely linked to the Inquiry Group as well. The summer experience was also seen as an important part of the program. Students were expected to enroll in Outward Bound, or a similar program, during summer vacation or winter intersession.

Phase two, which lasted one semester, was organized around student teaching in an alternative school. Intern teachers were placed in areas containing clusters of alternative schools. Clustering permitted us to establish field based support groups, which provided a place for mutual involvement in issues and support for personal actions as well as an arena for curriculum development. During phase three, which occurred during the final semester of the senior year, students participated in a final Inquiry Group that addressed the issues that emerged from the student teaching experience.

Even though I was quite pleased with the teacher preparation experiences we were able to offer our students and the quality of students we were certifying, the realities of the job market for beginning teachers made me realize that inservice training for public alternative school teachers was much more important than preservice education. The ideal delivery system for a quality inservice program for alternative school teachers is a teacher education center sponsored collaboratively by a university and a cluster of alternative schools, either in the same school district or general geographic area. One or two alternative schools could also join with several traditional schools to form a center if there weren't enough alternative schools in their area. Universities need placements for student teachers. They also need to attract a new clientele to make up for declining preservice enrollments. School districts need to start offering meaningful training experiences to their teachers. The teacher education center provides an ideal opportunity for school districts and universities to work together on these common problems.

I am presently directing a center that provides field based inservice experiences free of charge to 200 elementary and secondary teachers and student teaching opportunities for sixty-five preservice teachers each year. Our total yearly budget is $30,000, financed equally by the Charles County Maryland Board of Education and the University of Maryland. The center is governed by teacher representatives and administrators from the two alternative schools and two traditional schools that are served by the center. The inservice program, which includes both courses and workshops, is based on teachers' needs. The teachers, through their representatives, decide how the budget will be spent. Many teachers have come to see the center as theirs and have volunteered to do many things, including setting up a resource room where teachers could make materials such as learning centers for their classrooms and offering a series of teacher-taught workshops for their peers. These things could have never been done if we had to rely totally on our small budget. Through the center staff development has become a reality for many Charles County teachers. A group of teachers, community members, and university faculty from the center also got together and developed a Teacher Corps proposal which will provide additional funding for an even more ambitious inservice program during the next two years.

Alternative school teachers face a large variety of complex problems every day. Continuous professional development that addresses their inservice needs will help them deal more successfully with these problems. The teacher education center provides a way to seriously address these problems in spite of limited resources.

25

From Alternative Schools to Options in Public Education: The Alternative Schools Movement and State Education Agencies
by Gary Natriello

During the late sixties and early seventies when the alternative schools movement was at its height, State Education Agencies generally refrained from responding to the movement in any official way. Those agencies which did take note of the movement treated it half-heartedly as a peripheral phenomenon. Yet today, with the movement for alternative schools past its high point, a few State Education Agencies are formulating policies to promote options in public education. Thus the alternative schools movement seems to have evoked a two-phased response from state agencies. While most agencies are still operating under the first response phase, a few others such as California and New York have moved to the second phase.

This response pattern should be a point of interest not only to political analysts but also to alternative school leaders who must deal with State Education Agencies. Alternative school leaders should realize that they have much to gain from using their state agency as a resource. To do so successfully, they should be aware of the response phase under which the agency is operating and be sensitive to the problems that they are likely to encounter in dealing with agency representatives.

With this in mind I intend to characterize more fully the first response phase, examine the points of contact between alternative schools and State Education Agencies, and consider tactics that alternative school leaders can use for dealing with state agency representatives. Finally, I will present examples of agencies with policies representative of the second response phase in an attempt to understand the general SEA response pattern.

Alternative Schools and the First Response Phase

Among the earliest official State Education Agency responses to the alternative schools movement was the decision made in 1972 by the representatives of the Upper Atlantic Regional Title V Interstate Project to designate alternative schools as an area for inquiry and project focus. Title V was designed to encourage cooperative efforts among State Education Agencies to develop expertise in new areas of state administration and educational governance. The Upper Atlantic Project, based in New Jersey, involved a group of middle-Atlantic states and the territories of Puerto Rico and the Virgin Islands. The selection of alternative schools as a project focus would seem to indicate a direct interest in the movement by the SEAs involved. In fact, this was only partly true.

When I joined the project in New Jersey in 1973 I soon discovered that a number of state representatives to the project interpreted the word "alternative" to mean simply that each state could take some project money and pursue an independent "alternative" activity of its own choosing. This provided much of the motivation for adopting alternative schools as a project focus. As a result, when the project got underway, New York used a portion of the money for an instructional television project and Connecticut obtained money for a bilingual instruction program. Although these state projects represented educational options, they had little to do with the phenomenon that came to be known as the alternative schools movement.

At this point it becomes important to distinguish between alternative schools and options or alternatives in education as they were understood in the early seventies. Alternative schools, whether public or private, at least in ideology if not in practice, represented attempts to provide full educational services apart from those services offered by the traditional public school system. Alternative schools were competing political and educational systems, institutions or quasi-institutions which challenged the traditional institutions of the public school system.

The notion of options or alternatives in education is something quite different. It casts alternatives under the less politically challenging rubrics of "environments" or "programs" and provides an image of alternatives as supplements to the existing educational institutions. While the earlier alternative schools movement is responsible for the adoption by State Education Agencies of second response phase plans and policies for options in education, the movement itself received little serious attention from SEAs.

This point is well illustrated by the Upper Atlantic Regional Interstate Project. Those of us who worked on the Alternative Schools Project at the New Jersey State Department of Education from 1973 to 1975 learned to keep the project files in two brown boxes. In three years of existence the project was regularly moved from office to office and building to building. Its part-time, some-time staff learned to work with few or no resources under a variety of directors. To say that the project had a somewhat less than tenuous position in the minds of SEA officials might be to overemphasize its importance in the state educational bureaucracy.

Nevertheless, in the midst of this first response to alternative schools, there was evidence of the elements of the second phase response to options in public education. As a staff member of the project I soon learned that if I wanted to encourage support for the activities of the project among representatives of the states and territories, I had to speak of alternative schools as only one type of alternative, the most prevalent other type of alternative being the traditional public school. Moreover, I had to speak of those aspects of public or private alternative schools which could be incorporated into the local public school. Only when I spoke in such terms and phrases did SEA representatives respond at all to proposals for project activities.

But this is not a discussion of the Upper Atlantic Regional Project. I mention it only to illustrate the way that SEA representatives have typically treated the alternative schools movement. How then can the SEAs' first response to alternative schools be characterized? In an exploratory policy paper prepared for the Upper Atlantic Regional Project, Natalie Gubb distinguished four positions a State Education Agency might adopt regarding alternative schools. Gubb noted that an agency could:

> (a) encourage and initiate alternatives on its own, (b) facilitate and support the efforts of others to initiate alternatives, (c) maintain a stance of ambivalence, or (d) actively thwart the creation of alternatives.[1]

For the most part, State Education Agencies have not adopted meaningful policy positions on alternative schools. In fact, most State Education Agencies seem to maintain a position, actually a nonposition, of ambivalence. This means that in most states there is no agencywide policy regarding alternative schools.

---

1. Natalie Gubb, *Issue Paper: Alternatives in Education* (Trenton: New Jersey State Department of Education, March, 1975), pp. 12–13.

The reasons for this first response are not hard to understand. When an incumbent political and educational system is confronted with a challenge from a competing political and educational system, any recognition of the challenger by the incumbent, even in the form of criticism, can only aid the challenger in its attempts to gain recognition and support. Unless the challenging system becomes a real threat to the incumbent system, there is no reason for the established system to respond and plenty of reasons for it to avoid responding at all. This is exactly what SEAs did in the face of the alternative schools movement.

Nevertheless, SEAs could not totally ignore alternative schools. Because of their mandated jurisdiction over certain aspects of the education of children in their respective states SEAs were forced to deal with alternative schools. When forced to respond either because of state law or because of requests by alternative school leaders, SEAs did so in a very limited manner, treating alternative schools as they might treat any traditional public school. These interactions between alternative schools and SEAs centered around four points of contact: health and safety, teacher certification, curriculum requirements, and finances. Closer examination of these points of contact will serve both to illustrate the nature of the first response phase and to suggest ways in which alternative school leaders can deal with an SEA operating from such a position.

Points of Contact Between Alternative Schools and SEAs

Health and safety regulations generally pertain to the facilities used by the school. SEAs have typically held alternative schools to the standards set for traditional schools. Even when adherence to normal standards was clearly not necessary, State Education Agencies acting under the first response phase often refused to make allowances. As an example, one alternative school teacher told me of his battles with state officials who insisted that he couldn't use his building as a school because the water fountains weren't the proper height.

Thus those schools which are in the same building as the regular schools (that is, those which supplement it rather than compete with it) have the least trouble in this area. Schools which use a building originally constructed to be a school or public meeting place (for example, church, community center) have few problems. Schools not so situated—often competing alternative schools—will run into difficulties both with local officials who must enforce general health and fire laws and with State Education Agency officials who enforce school health and safety regulations.

While no leader of an alternative school wants to negotiate on the question of safety regulations designed to protect students, there may be occasions when alternative school officials feel unjustly prevailed upon by unnecessary regulations. In such instances the general ambivalence of SEAs operating under the first response phase can be used to advantage by those alternative school leaders willing to press the issue. Tactics for obtaining such advantage will be discussed later.

Teacher certification requirements present few problems when alternative school programs can be staffed by regular teachers from the local district. However, programs with a particular focus may require the use of uncertified specialists. Once again, SEAs have avoided dealing with alternative schools while making provisions for options in public education. A number of states have provisions for noncertified personnel such as artists, musicians, and craftsmen to work with teachers temporarily in the public schools, but few have recognized that right of such persons to work permanently as full-time professionals in alternative schools. Once again this is an area in which alternative school leaders may have to negotiate.

Curriculum requirements are a third area in which alternative schools are likely to come in contact with State Education Agencies. Those who advocate the notion of options in public education usually argue for a broadening or extension of the curriculum and thus encounter no difficulty in meeting minimum state requirements. After all, the idea of options does not imply a negation of existing school programs. However, alternative schools with a special focus may have trouble convincing state agency representatives that certain aspects of their offerings meet state requirements. Persistent efforts will be required.

A fourth point of contact is the area of finances. Although private alternative schools usually rely on private sources of funds and public alternative schools are locally funded, both, particularly public alternatives, are often in a position to seek state assistance in the form of seed money, planning grants, or special program grants. However, in SEAs operating under the first response phase special grants are usually not earmarked for alternative schools, and alternative school leaders must be on the lookout for programs and money for which their schools may qualify. In states operating under the second response phase the advocates of options in education will not have to be so aggressive in seeking funding from SEAs.

Because the problems of alternative school leaders in dealing with State Education Agencies operating under the first response phase are so difficult I would like to reconsider the nature of the SEA in that phase and discuss certain tactics which alternative school leaders might use to deal with their SEA more successfully.

Tactics for Dealing with State Education Agencies

Under the first response phase because there is no agencywide policy regarding alternative schools, different individuals and offices in the State Education Agency may adopt policies and procedures based on their own attitudes. While the lack of an agencywide commitment to alternatives, that is, a commitment from the Chief State School Officer, makes it nearly impossible for individuals and offices at the state level to actively encourage and initiate alternatives, it is still possible to find some individuals in the state agency who are working to facilitate and support alternative schools. At the same time, however, other individuals and offices in the same agency may be working to thwart local efforts to establish alternatives. This was dramatically demonstrated to one of our project representatives when he made a visit to an alternative school to which we had been providing assistance and received a rather cold reception from the school's director. Upon inquiry, our representative found that representatives from another office in our own agency had visited the day before and ordered the school closed because the building failed to meet some safety requirement.

This is not an isolated incident. While visiting alternative schools in five states in 1973–74 to conduct a survey and offer assistance, we rarely encountered alternative school staff members who had not had bad experiences with someone else from the state office. The important lesson for alternative school leaders to remember is that in dealing with their State Education Agency operating under the first response phase they are dealing not only with an offical monolithic organization, but also with a conglomeration of individual personalities, most of whom have no more expertise in schools, alternative or otherwise, than they themselves. Alternative school leaders should plan their strategy for dealing with the state agency operating under the first response phase accordingly. There are a number of tactics which they can use to improve their bargaining position.

First, alternative school leaders should try to obtain the support of their community and their local school board. This can often be accomplished by presenting their case to a local community group such as a community council, a parents association, or a civic group such as the Lions Club, and obtaining their help. However it is gained, evidence of local support will encourage state agency personnel to pay serious attention to requests or problems and make it more difficult for them not to respond in the desired way. To get action from an SEA operating under the first response phase a problem or request must be made to seem more important than all the other business on the desk of the state agency representative. If enough local support is gained, a situation may even be termed a "crisis." This will greatly improve the chances of obtaining a favorable response. It means little to a state bureaucrat to have "handled the request from the River City alternative school," but to be able to say that he "solved the crisis in River City," he may do just about anything.

The second tactic is one that is useful in dealing with any large bureaucracy and the personalities that comprise its staff, but it is particularly helpful when dealing with such an organization in an area in which there is no agencywide policy. In dealing with SEAs operating under the first response phase alternative school leaders would do well to find a member of the state agency staff to act as their contact person and protector. Such an individual should be able to talk with alternative school leaders in a friendly, supportive way and help them deal with the State Education Agency either by expediting matters himself or by telling alternative school leaders how to approach and deal with other agency staff members. There is no sure way to find such a person. Alternative school leaders must simply be on the lookout and hope to find such a person as they deal with the state agency. Although it is helpful if this individual is in the office a school leader must deal with for a particular problem and if he is highly placed, neither of these is necessary and either of them alone is helpful. Once such contact is established, efforts must be made to maintain the relationship. Alternative school leaders should keep in touch by phone, letters, and visits. A particularly effective way of keeping in touch is to periodically invite the SEA representative to visit the school to observe some special program or event.

As a third tactic alternative school leaders should be certain that all agreements and understandings with the SEA are put in writing with a copy sent to the local board of education. Without an agencywide commitment all decisions hinge on the dispositions of individuals. Gentlemen's agreements are fine, but no gentleman will be reluctant to commit himself in writing. Moreover, alternative school leaders should always make sure that any dealing they have with state agency officials is reported to the local superintendent. More than one project has been lost when the ruffled feelings of a local administrator got in the way of his sound educational judgment.

A final tactic for alternative school leaders in their dealings with State Education Agencies would be to cast themselves as proponents of options or alternatives in education. Removing the threat of political and educational competition will cause the State Education Agency to shift to the second response phase and result in more favorable treatment.

The Second Response Phase

As the discussion of the last tactic for dealing with State Education Agencies suggests advocates of alternatives will have a much easier time dealing with an SEA which is operating under the second response phase. Unlike the first phase which was a reaction to the alternative schools movement, the second response phase entails action on the part of an SEA to facilitate and support or actively encourage and initiate alternatives in education. This phase can perhaps be best characterized by examining two SEAs currently operating under policies which facilitate and encourage alternatives to public education.

In late 1973 Ewald B. Nyquist, the Commissioner of Education in New York, issued a policy statement on his agency's position on alternatives in education. In that statement Nyquist noted the need for multiple options in education, the variety of options then available in New York, and the necessity for new state department policies and procedures to relate to such experimentation in a positive manner.[2]

This statement, one of the earliest to speak to the issue of alternatives, dealt not with the competing political and educational systems of the alternative schools movement, but with the complementary programs or environments which made up "options in education." Nyquist makes this distinction quite clear:

> Since 1968, we have witnessed the development of a wide variety of "alternative schools" within the public school system, and a rapid increase in the number of nonpublic "free schools" and other alternatives to both the traditional public and nonpublic schools. Many of the latter alternative schools have survived only a short time—an average of 18 months nationwide—and were identified by some as "alternatives to schools" rather than as viable alternative schools. A few

---

2. Ewald B. Nyquist, *Providing Optional Learning Environments in New York State Schools* (Albany: The State Education Department, October 1973).

alternative programs have developed outside the system that remain as exemplary models of well-designed and well-operated "open schools" or as parallel institutions that complement the public schools. Although the term "alternative school" is still widely used, it has taken on a somewhat negative connotation because of early identification with those types of programs perceived by the general public as alternatives to school. We prefer to think in terms of the need for providing complementary "optional learning environments" or simply "options" rather than in terms of "alternatives" that offer a choice between two incompatible things. Thus in our thinking, the present program with its ever-evolving modifications still presents a legitimate and viable choice for many students. When we use the term "alternatives," it will be in the sense of offering a choice among many programs, each of which may serve the needs of some students.[3]

Nyquist goes on to indicate his department's support of options and presents guidelines for the development and implementation of alternatives. A central feature of the guidelines is the part played by local school officials. Included in the guidelines is an item which reads:

Evidence should be submitted to indicate that the Board of Education in public meeting has approved the experimentation on recommendation of the chief school officer, and that it will provide the necessary support for the proposed duration of the program.[4]

Thus whether or not the public did, in fact, react negatively to the competing political and educational systems represented in the alternative schools movement, the State Education Department of New York certainly did so both by ignoring the movement in its most challenging form and by seeking to incorporate a politically acceptable form of the movement for alternatives into the public school system.

California is another state which has shifted to the second response phase. The *Report of the California Commission for Reform of Intermediate and Secondary Education,* The RISE Report, states that a "new learning environment must provide a wide range of options in terms of approach, materials, locations, and times."[5] The commission noted the scarcity of choice among programs, courses, and approaches in relation to learner and parent needs and desires and called for a personalized instructional process for all learners.

---

3. Ibid., p. 7.
4. Ibid., p. 23.
5. *Report of the California Commission for Reform of Intermediate and Secondary Education* (Sacramento: California State Department of Education, 1975), p. 10.

In adopting the commission's recommendations the State Department of Education committed itself to a policy of encouraging and supporting alternatives in intermediate and secondary education. In the department's implementation plan the individual school site and local school district administration are viewed as essential in providing leadership for reform.[6] This, of course means that all options will be developed within the established educational system and will supplement rather than compete with the traditional offerings.

Conclusions

In this article I have tried to accomplish two tasks: (1) explain the shift in SEA policy regarding alternatives from the first response of ambivalence to the second response of encouragement and support, and (2) offer suggestions for alternative school leaders who must deal with State Education Agencies. The speed with which an SEA moves from the first phase to the second is in part a function of the way in which advocates of alternatives present their case. Thus it has been necessary to discuss practical concerns and political analyses at the same time. Those alternative school leaders who feel comfortable with and adopt the notion of options in education are likely to find their State Education Agency moving to a more favorable position, a move which can only aid alternatives of all types.

6. *Reform of Intermediate and Secondary Education in California: A Summary of the Implementation Plan* (Sacramento: California State Department of Education, March 1976), p. 5.

26
Financing Public Alternative Schools
by John Theroux

Do Alternative Schools Cost More?

A strong selling point which has been used for alternative schools has been that they cost no more than the conventional schooling; that the alternative school(s) simply requires the same per-pupil expenditure as the other schools in the district. Other proponents of alternative schooling have advanced the argument that the schools cost *less* than the per-pupil requirements of the conventional schools. Experience in this realm is mixed; indeed, some alternative schools have cost the same as or less than the traditional schools, but many have also cost more. The factors which contribute to these figures are complex, and this section will begin to outline some considerations which contribute to such calculations.

Why would the alternative schools cost less?

The single largest cost in the school budget is for personnel. It is in this realm of personnel utilization that alternative schools can realize the most substantial savings. Alternative schools have the potential to mobilize volunteer staffing personnel from a variety of sources, including parents, community agencies, the local business community, and teacher training institutions to teach in various capacities in the school to a much greater degree than the traditional schools. If the students themselves are given some legitimate teaching roles in the school, then other personnel resources are mobilized. Most alternative schools have capitalized on such possibilities as significant inputs to their learning environments.

---

*Prepared for National Alternative Schools Program, School of Education, University of Massachusetts, Amherst, Mass. 01002.

Alternative school planners should be aware of at least two dimensions of personnel utilization for their schools. First, it is important that the personnel budget allotment for the school consist either of transferred district staff or funds for replacement staff. Otherwise, the staff for the school will be an additional cost to the district and will undermine the per-pupil costs argument. Planners should be aware of the procedures for making such arrangements.

Secondly, if personnel funds become available, then there should be considerable thought as to how many and what kind of people it should be used for.

The use of the community as an instructional resource is another factor in many alternative schools which contribute to substantial savings. Learning experiences in the community through such groups as social agencies (police department, social service organizations, hospitals, museums, etc.), local businesses, and private groups (parents, churches, etc.) can mobilize a vast range of rich educational settings at minimal cost. Indeed, some alternative schools, such as those designed around the school-without-walls model, depend upon such experiences as the major component of the school program.

Donations of materials, equipment, etc., from the community can significantly add to the resources of the alternative school. Alternative school people are generally proficient scavengers of instructional resources—a parent donates a tape recorder, a church donates an old television, a library donates books—situations such as these often result in significant contributions to the resources of the school. We have found seven sources to be particularly rich:

1. Parents can be important sources of teaching supplies and other resources. Enthusiastic parents will pop up in the alternative school as time goes on. If some system is developed in the school for plugging these individuals into the program, there will be a whole range of benefits, from an exciting, participatory learning and teaching environment to a supportive parental political force, to a strong resource-gathering group. Particularly involved parents may serve as a lobbying force in support of the school on all levels of its existence. To capitalize on this potentially huge source of resources, the staff of the alternative school should be sensitive to such possibilities and be flexible enough to incorporate them into the school.

2. Cooperative arrangements for sharing facilities with other schools in the school district are often possible. Libraries, high-cost

equipment such as video tape units, physical education facilities, special area laboratories, etc., are often not used to their full potential in district schools. Some schools have surplus supplies. Access to such resources can often be negotiated.

3. Local teacher training institutions can be a source of teaching personnel in the form of interns. Although selectivity is very important, many teacher training programs can offer interns to alternative schools as the practicum component of their programs. Also, technical assistance can be negotiated with other components of the colleges.

4. Businesses can be a surprisingly rich source of input. Many businesses are trying to find ways to serve their communities. Some are quite open to donating facilities and personnel for instructional input to the schools, particularly if it is for an innovative effort.

5. Government surplus outlets give tremendous discounts to schools. If you can get some formal documentation from your school district, then you can get some great materials at low prices from government surplus outlets.

6. Charitable and community institutions such as the church, YMCA, police department and other local governmental institutions, etc., can be another source for personnel, supplies, etc. As with all the rest of these sources, the key to marshalling such resources is to mobilize the staff, students, and parents to go out and get them.

7. Most alternative schools make arrangements for more effective sharing of facilities than conventional schools. An example of this type of arrangement is an alternative school which uses the local YMCA as the site for physical education.

In the long run alternative schools may be able to offer the school district some services which would otherwise cost additional resources. If, for example, an alternative school were able to develop a solid, community-oriented program, then after some period of time the school may be able to offer other schools in the district such services at no cost. Long-run tradeoffs such as this should be delineated by alternative school planners.

Why would the alternative school cost more?

Start-up costs for the alternative school can entail additional expenditures. Start-up costs may include funds for release time for staff members who are planning the alternative school plus miscellaneous planning costs, funds for staff training before implementation and after the school is operating (the transition into the alternative school will often entail major readjustments in staff attitudes and behaviors), funds for equipment if no co-operative arrangement between the alternative school and other schools in the district is made, and funds for building rent or renovation if necessary. As is indicated by these comments, some of these costs may be avoidable, but if they are incurred, significant additional funds may be required for the implementation of the school.

If the staff of the alternative school does not consist of transferred, district personnel, then the additional personnel costs would have to be absorbed by the school district. It is often difficult to release staff from the traditional schools to serve in the alternative school, particularly if only a few students from each school volunteer for the alternative school. If this were to be the case, then the funds for hiring additional personnel for the alternative school would constitute an added expense. As has been mentioned before, this expense is the greatest proportion of the school budget.

Transportation costs can be greater for an alternative school than for the conventional schools. Getting the students to and from the community learning experience can entail additional transportation costs for the alternative school. Also, getting the students to the school itself may entail extra expenses if the students come from a variety of districts or localities within the district.

The alternative school may have a student population which is too small for efficient use of central resources. Many alternative schools are in the 50–150 range of student population. This size may imply an inefficient use of equipment and facilities in the alternative school. Also, many of the fixed administrative and other district costs may be duplicated in the school. Although schools normally budget a teacher for every 25 students, an alternative school often adds a director or two to this personnel allotment.

The myths and realities of per-pupil costs.

As the comments in this section have indicated, calculating the exact costs of the alternative school is a complex process for the school district. In many cases the alternative school budget could be operating on a level equal to or below per-pupil expenditures district wide, but many of these costs may be duplicating expenditures in the district. In other cases the operating budget of the alternative school may accurately indicate the per-pupil costs expended for the alternative school students by the district.

This discussion simply indicates that selling the idea of the alternative school from the perspective of equal or less per-pupil cost may or may not be appropriate, depending upon the local circumstances of the planning and implementation of the school. If this simplistic promise or prediction is made, the survival of the school may be in jeopardy as the real costs become evident. The costs and benefits of the alternative school need to be outlined as clearly as possible to everyone involved.

Why Invest in Alternative Schools?

This is the first question which any School Board or administrator will ask when confronted with the possibility of supporting an alternative school. Beyond the basic educational appeal of the idea (which should by *no* means be played down), the alternative school should be a *sound* investment. This means that if the School Board should support the idea, then there should be some real payoffs to it in the form of economic, psychological, or political assets. It is important for the alternative school planner to clearly lay out what these benefits will be when asking for support for the school. This section will outline some of these tradeoffs within four categories: payoffs to the school district, payoffs to the students, payoffs to parents, and payoffs to the community.

Local control and incorporation of educational alternatives can create a basis for effective district change. Change in school districts generally requires consensus in order to be implemented. Combined with the fact that the school district represents an absolute monopoly in the educational affairs of its locality, this fact inevitably leads to the compromise of educational innovation. A commitment to the concept of alternative education provides an opportunity for total institutional reform within a variety of alternatives available in the district. The continuity of educational experimentation which this situation creates can give the conventional schools a comparative perspective on all facets of their operations. In this manner alternative education provides the school district with a framework for constant evolution of educational techniques.

Establishment of alternative schools creates the possibility of marshalling outside funds.

The school district can begin to more effectively serve the needs of students and parents. The growing pluralism in our communities demands educational options to be available for our diverse needs. As these options become available, the educational system can begin to satisfy a greater number of families. With more satisfied "customers," the budgets and referenda of the Board will have a greater chance for support.

If parents feel that they have a real voice in the type of education which the schools provide their children and that the school district is attempting to satisfy their needs, then they will become better integrated into the educational effort. Parental alienation from the education process is easy to understand:

> Imagine a town in which every family is arbitrarily assigned to one local doctor by a ruling of the Board of Health. Imagine that the Health Board assigns families only on the basis of the shortest distance from the home to the doctor's office. Imagine finally that if a family complains that the assigned doctor is not helping one ailing member of the family the Board of Health replies, "Sorry, no exceptions to doctor assignments."
>
> If this sounds like a totalitarian nightmare, stop and think. This is nothing less than a description of the way that Boards of Education assign children to schools and teachers. The fact that it is a time-honored tradition does not change the meaning of the process. In fact, a better case can be made for assigning families to doctors than to schools and teachers.
>
> Richard Kammann
> Bell Telephone Laboratories

If parents could become as involved in their children's educational process as they are involved in their children's health and medical care, then the entire educational process would be invigorated. Alternative education opens up this possibility.

Children have different learning needs, and no single program yet devised can meet all educational needs. If the student is provided with a variety of positive learning options, school will be a more vital place. This is an extremely hopeful possibility to most students. It is reasonable to expect positive changes in behavior and motivation in this new situation.

In many alternative schools, the student's education becomes vitally intertwined with the life of the community. Apprenticeship production of saleable services or products for community use are often found as components of alternative school programs. In each of these cases, the agencies in the community receive real, economic benefits from the alternative school. Definition of the alternative school as a service institution for the community should be laid out with some specific estimates as to costs and benefits by the alternative school planners in order to contribute to the economic picture of the school.

Also, a better understanding between youth and the community should be fostered in breaking down the segregation of elements of society (students in school, businessmen at work, etc.).

Fiscal Planning in Alternative Schools

A vitally important aspect of the financial position of the alternative school is to make its fiscal plans clear and understandable. If the expectations of all those involved in the alternative school effort are created ahead of time, the alternative school will gain credibility and there will be smoother and more fruitful relationships created between the school, district administration, school board, and community. In order to facilitate such relationships, this section outlines a few tips to individuals making fiscal plans for their schools.

Be as exact as possible in your budget. To the extent possible, be explicit as to how you will use the funds which you request. This will not only give your program more credibility and "investibility," but it will also guard against unnecessary expenditures. You may be spending money unnecessarily on resources which could easily be provided from other sources if your plans were made clear. The process of delineating expenditures will also add clarity to your program. This budgeting strategy does not mean that you should make your funds completely inflexible; indeed, a line item of "mad money" with suggestions of different contingencies for its use seems reasonable. It does mean, however, that you should make it clear which funds would be discretionary, what the reasons for the funds are, and what the other funds will be used for.

Make honest and accurate predictions of the financial needs of the school as it progresses through different phases. This activity will entail planning some years (3–4) ahead. Again, the alternative school will benefit from specifying the financial needs for its future stages because the planning will entail defining some clear, long-range goals and directions for the school. This type of planning can orient the alternative school to a broader context of its development which will solidify its foundation. The school district, in turn, will be able to consider the needs of the alternative school in its long-range fiscal planning. Again, this planning should not be so inflexible as to exclude new factors which may arise, but it should provide a useful framework for the school.

Make it clear who is accountable for the funds. It should be clearly defined as to who keeps the school's books, who has authority to make expenditures, and where the funds come from. In one case, an alternative school which did not negotiate an advantageous situation in this regard found itself subjected to a debilitating process of procurement of supplies. The school enrolled 1/15 of the high school population of the district.

It, therefore, had access to 1/15 of the resources of each department of the high school. If the high school art department head decided to buy 15 paint brushes, the alternative school received 1. The department head held authority for making such purchases. Although the alternative school staff had some influence in these decisions, the degree of their influence varied from department head to department head; the flexibility of the alternative school resource requests was limited. Of course, this situation poorly affected the entire program of the alternative school. By making the arrangement of the transfer of funds as clearly defined as possible, these types of situations can be avoided.

Make a clear statement concerning the cost effectiveness of the alternative school. It will be worthwhile to spend some energy making some specific estimates of the cost effectiveness of the school for presentation to the appropriate committees of the Board. Figure out items such as the deferred costs of vandalism, etc., in the school, savings on building costs, etc., which can be expected in the school. Social costs (deferred costs of arrest, confinement, etc., for the percentage of dropouts who will be expected to get into trouble, etc.) are also reasonable to present. Being organized and thoughtful in this area of cost effectiveness will be extremely helpful in all your negotiations.

Have options available for the above. When presenting your fiscal plans, have options available for consideration if your initial plan is for some reason unacceptable. Never compromise to the extent that the basic quality of your program will be in jeopardy, but make sure that you do not pin all of your hopes on one plan.

Create a framework for analyzing the alternative school costs which you can defend on your own terms. Do not be afraid of presenting arguments which don't conform to the standard rationale; make clear, forceful arguments as to the analysis of costs which are logical and which address your situation. If you gain acceptance of your rationale at the beginning, then you will have a sound basis of discussion later when possible problem situations arise.

Alternative Schools Grantsmanship

Most people involved in alternative schools actively seek out grants from sources outside their local school districts. This section attempts to outline some of the advantages and disadvantages to alternative schools in participating in such grantsmanship.

Advantages in grants from outside sources.

The alternative school which receives substantial grants from outside agencies is in a good bargaining position for negotiations with the School Board and district administration. In order for the concept of alternative schooling to be a viable strategy in public education, the integrity or autonomy of the alternative schools must be preserved. In order for the alternative to provide a really *different* educational program, traditional norms will be changed within the alternative. Although the local educational system accepts this concept in supporting the alternatives, complications and serious constraints often arise. If the group proposing the alternative school has substantial financial independence, it is in a better position to negotiate beyond such constraints. In many cases, this effect has been clearly demonstrated—alternative schools with substantial outside support succeed in establishing viable alternatives more than those alternatives conceived and directed solely from the local educational system. It should be mentioned that this dependence on outside funding can and should be a short-termed (1–3 year) phenomenon. After the integrity of the alternative is established its payoffs become evident and the district becomes acclimated to the idea. Thus, the need for fiscal independence diminishes. Even at the beginning of the school, the dependence on outside funding sources should not be complete—there should be a process where the district seriously invests in the idea.

With outside funding, many of the start-up costs of the school can be absorbed without cost to the school district. If many of these costs, which were outlined briefly in a previous section, could be absorbed, then the commitment on the part of the school district to support the development of the alternative school will be reinforced. In many cases, absorbing these costs may be essential for the district to support the school.

The uniqueness of the alternative school program can often attract funds for the enrichment of the educational program of the alternative school and the district as a whole. If the alternative school specializes in a field which is a category for funding of some agency, then the school, and indirectly the district as a whole, may stand a good chance to receive such funds. This, of course, is an attractive prospect for the school district in that it adds to the total resources in its domain.

Accepting outside grants can have the effect of building in evaluation of the alternative school program. In many cases, evaluation is one of the most difficult issues for alternative schools to come to grips with. New assumptions about learning and the products of the educational process result in difficulties in assessment of the accomplishment of proclaimed aims. Oftentimes, the alternative school does not spend enough time or energy in considering this issue. With the stipulation of evaluating the use of outside funds, the school's consideration of evaluation is often facilitated.

Receiving outside monies in support of the alternative school gives it prestige which can be important in the development of alternatives in the district. As the community and the local educational system see that their alternative school(s) receives recognition and funds from outside sources, the acceptance of the validity of diverse educational processes serving different student learning needs is reinforced. These people will inevitably go through an educational process which will change their views about education to a view more consistent with a changing society and school system. This type of process is important for the evolution of the educational system as well as for the survival of the alternative school.

Disadvantages of outside funding.

Grants tend to be an unstable source of income, and the alternative school would do well to avoid dependence upon them. Grants are generally given for a one year period with some sketchy promise for continuation which may or may not be realized. Some funding agencies are notorious for leaving projects "in the lurch." Unless the alternative school has someone who is extremely well-connected and competent in grantsmanship, the income from such agencies is susceptible to yearly fluctuations. This lack of dependability can create a harrowing atmosphere for alternative schoolers who already are occupied with building an entire institution in a short period of time.

Proposal writing and fund-raising can be extremely time and energy consuming. Alternative schools staff tend to be overcommitted, full-and-a-half time workers simply in keeping the alternative school program going and growing. Proposal writing and fund-raising can be activities which take large amounts of time. Many alternative schools simply cannot afford this energy.

The alternative school program may be compromised by accepting funds for activities outside of its priorities. In many cases, the strings attached to grants to alternative schools may not be within the priorities of the school. The money may be so badly needed that the decision makers in the school accept it in spite of its incongruities. This type of departure from the defined purpose of the school program can be dangerous to the effectiveness of the school.

Generally, the attitude toward grants should be to use them on your own terms, and to avoid depending on them. They should be levers to achieve the objective of local support of the alternative school as a permanent, semi-autonomous institution.